Endorseme

"Gary Benton is a master wilc[...] easy to read, and offers so[...]ing to everyone. *Simple Survival* is simply the one survival tool next to your compass that no outdoorsman should be without."

Tom Rose
Editor – Administrator
Modern Sportsman
http://www.ModernSportsman.com

"Survival, by nature, is a subject that demands simplicity. *Simple Survival* is required reading for anyone that has even a passing interest in the outdoors."

Kevin Rider
Editor
Big Game Hunt
http://www.BigGameHunt.net

"Readable, easy to search, and highly useful for all outdoorsman, *Simple Survival* is one of three books I would want with me on a deserted island."

Forrest Lee Horn
Senior Associate
http://ParadigmAssociates.org
Captain, Inf, USA (Retired/Disabled)

"I can firmly resolve that this book is definitely worth adding to your arsenal of knowledge as it could very well mean the difference between life and death."

James L. Bruner
Editor
Water and Woods Magazine
http://waterandwoods.net

"*Simple Survival* is straightforward, delightfully humourous, factual, trustworthy and most importantly, understandable—something that many survival guides available today fail to be. It is a pleasure to read a book with a serious subject and learn so much in a user-friendly way."
Andy Coleman
Owner
United Kingdom
http://www.ironclad-surplus.co.uk

"*Simple Survival* is the freshest survival book to cross my desk in a decade. Gary has written one of the must-have books for anyone interested in the outdoors, and I have no hesitation in recommending it."
John Egan
Owner
Australia
http://www.SurvivalistBooks.com

"Gary Benton combines sound survival advice with a fun and engaging style of writing. His *(Simple) Survival Guide* is illuminating for both novice outdoor enthusiasts and experienced wilderness users."
Lucia Hyde
Editor
Wonderful West Virginia Magazine, www.wonderfulwv.com

"I consider myself very lucky to have had Gary Benton as my egress/ejection and survival instructor when I was in the United States Air Force in the mid 1970's. I personally know of at least four people who survived to fly another day due to his training. The sign of a true survival professional is one who keeps you alive, and this man does it! Gary is no armchair survival expert, but a real hands on individual, and this guide can make a serious difference in a life and death situation."
Mark E. Zlotkowski
Major, USAF, Retired

Simple Survival

A Family Outdoors Guide

Gary L. Benton

LOOSE CANNON ENTERPRISES
Paradise, CA

No part of this book may be reproduced, stored in a retrieval system, or transmitted by any means, electronic, mechanical, photocopying, recording, or otherwise, without the written permission of the author and/or the publisher. Any resemblance to actual persons living or dead, events or locales, is entirely coincidental, unless stated otherwise.

3rd *Revised Edition*
ISBN 978-1-793445148

Interior Photos and Graphics Copyright © 2010 by Gary L. Benton and licensors
Author Photo Copyright © 2009 by Melanie D. Calvert-Benton

Print History:
Original Manuscript Copyright 2005 by Gary L. Benton
Original Book Published by Emerald Ink Publishing, Hot Springs Arkansas
Revised Edition Copyright ©2018 by W. R. Benton, LLC,
All Rights Reserved.

This book was produced and printed in the U.S.A.

www.loose-cannon.com

DEDICATION

To my late mother, Edna Marie Benton, for motivating me as a young man to reach for my highest dreams. I love and miss you mom.

To all members of our Armed Forces, past, present, and future. It's with the deepest respect I salute each of you. I personally know your tasks are always difficult.

Simple Survival Contents

Foreword	11
Desert Survival	12
Arctic Survival	19
General Survival 101	25
Float Trip Survival	30
My Car Has Broken Down and It's Snowing	34
Surviving Alone	38
Rain and Survival	42
Ten Rules to Survive By	46
Terrorism	51

Water
All Wet	58
Where's the Water	61
Winter Water, How to Make Your Own	64

Shelters
Emergency Shelters	67
Simple Survival Shelters	69

Food
Having A Bug As A Dinner Guest	74
Outdoor Camp Cooking	77
Small Game Dressing	82
Nutrition and Survival	84
Plants, And Edibility Test	90
Snares and Survival	93
Survival Cooking	97
Dressing and Preparing Large Game	101
Packing Foods for Camping	106

Fire
A Hot Time Tonight	109

Emergency Fire Making	113
Man and Fire	117

First Aid
Foot Care	122
Frostbite	126
Hygiene	130
Hypothermia	134
Tick Borne Diseases	140
Shock and General First Aid	144
Heat Related Illnesses	149
A Hot Time	152
Survival Psychology	155
Will to Survive	160

Signaling
Survival Signals	164

Clothing
Winter Family Wear	168
Clothing, What to Wear	171
Making Your Survival Clothing	176

Snakes
Snakes, How to Avoid Them or Find Them	179

Weapons
How to Make Survival Weapons	184

Tools of Survival
Using an Ax	188
Ax Me	191
Know your Knife	194
Select a Good Pocketknife	199
Make a Survival Kit	203
Make a Survival Vest	207

Rescue and Recovery Operations
Rescue and You   211

Camouflage
How to Apply Camouflage and How to Move   215

Children and the Outdoors
Camping is Fun with Kids!   219
Camping with a Child is not like with an Adult   225
Camping with Children is a Time to Share   228
Survival with Kids   232
Hiking with Children   238
My Child is Lost in the Woods!   241

Maps and Navigation
How to Use a Map   244

Tips
Backpacking   250
Boat Safety   254
Experience Counts   259
Survival the Military Way   263
Solar Cooking   269
Dogs and Trips   273
Close Encounters of the Wild Kind   276
Making Safe Jerky   283
Surviving a Natural Disaster   289
Long Term Storing of Foods and Water   299
Water and Ocean Survival   305
Hooked on Fishing (Removing Fish Hooks)   311

Foreword

Wilderness survival is a very dangerous situation and, as such, your decisions in the wild could mean the difference between life and death. That is why in most of the articles I have the contents of various types of survival kits listed. To venture out of doors without a survival kit, in my opinion, is extremely dangerous. And, each trip may require a different survival kit, depending on where you venture takes place and the weather. If the listing of survival kits bores you, then ignore them. This book is for the novice, not the experienced survival person who may have attended a few schools.

Additionally, the information in this book is written with no assurance that it will keep everyone alive in all survival situations. No two survival situations are ever the same and as such, any action taken by a person in a survival situation will have associated risks. *The author, publisher, and printer assume no responsibility of any sort for actions taken, or injuries sustained, as a result of information provided in this book if used either correctly or incorrectly. Use this book at your own risk.*

This survival book is for your enjoyment and perhaps to get you to thinking about survival. I have over fifty years of wilderness outdoors experience and I have camped in various states and countries, as well as under some extreme weather conditions. I grew up mostly in the country, near the Mark Twain National Forest, in the Missouri Ozark Mountains. We hunted and trapped to eat, not for trophies or bragging rights. Often, we'd come home from school on a Friday night, grab a can of pork and beans and then head out camping. As we camped, we hunted during the day. As a United Stats Air Force Life Support Technician, I taught parachuting and survival classes to countless air crew members, from 1971 to 1883, with assignments to combat zones. Thanks to the military, I slept in the jungles in the Philippines Islands, the far arctic north of Alaska (minus 20 during the day and we spent two nights in the field), the mountains of Washington State, and the desert of Arizona, I feel my knowledge base is extensive.

Simple Survival is for those who wish to improve or learn emergency survival skills. I do not support radical survivalist movements or subversive groups in any way.

Gary L. Benton
Pearl, Mississippi
October 12, 2018

DESERT SURVIVAL IS NEVER EASY

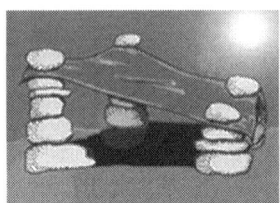

Many areas of the world are arid and seem to be completely lacking in water. I wrote the word "seem" on purpose. In fact, these areas do receive water, but not regularly. Some deserts can go for long periods, perhaps years, without water and then experience a heavy rain. For a survivor though, the desert environment is a harsh and often victorious enemy. It is unforgiving of mistakes and often your first mistake will be your last.

Desert Survival is never easy. Just being in a desert is uncomfortable, and it becomes almost unbearable when you combine the physical and psychological factors of survival. But, with the world being smaller now than it was even fifty years ago, there is always a chance you could end up in a desert environment. Or, perhaps you live in or near the American southwest. What makes desert survival so different than, say, mountain, general, or even arctic survival? There are a number of factors, but let's consider the lack of water and the extreme heat as the two big ones. As you read more, you will discover some of the dangers associated with survival in the desert.

If forced to survive in a desert environment, your first step is to seek shelter immediately. The heat of a desert, at times as high as 120 degrees F, can kill you in just a few hours. Look for an outcrop of rock, the shady side of a gully or streambed, or any shade that you can find. Initially you are looking for an emergency shelter for a few hours perhaps, not a long term shelter. A better shelter can be constructed once the sun goes down. Just remember, you must get out of the sun and into the shade.

Keep your whole body covered if you can. Keep your sleeves rolled down and your hat on. Never remove boots, socks, or any piece of clothing in the direct sunlight. Additionally, you should cover the back of your neck to protect it from the sun. Experienced individuals often remove a t-shirt and use it as a scarf. Or, I have seen them push one end of the shirt up under a cap, and allow the other end to hang over the neck. Regardless of the technique you use, you should keep your neck covered at all times. It reduces water loss through sweating and it also prevents sunburn, often a painful situation for a desert survivor. Dress as much like an Arab as you can; they are masters of the desert.

Once you become concerned about your location, or believe yourself to be lost, STOP. If you are not one hundred percent of your exact location, DO NOT continue walking. And, make sure even if you do know where you are headed it is a very short distance. The desert heat can kill you in very little time. Let's consider some basic water facts about travel in the desert. Most survival manuals will state in the 120F heat of a desert, if you rest and do nothing, you might live for two days. If you go meandering out into the desert, you most likely won't cover five miles. However, if you know where you are, wait until nighttime; you could cover up to 25 miles. So, STOP. Go no further and seek shade immediately!

After you have a shade and you have decided to stop, what next? **THINK!** Did you file a trip plan (always recommended by this author) with a friend, wife, or your boss? Who knows where you are, how long you intend to be there, and the exact time and date you intend to return? Someone should always know these details prior to your trip. It will speed up your rescue a great deal. Be sure to phone in with any changes to your plans. Nothing is more frustrating to rescue teams than looking for someone who is not where they are supposed to be.

While you are in the shade thinking, you should also **inventory** the equipment you have on hand. I strongly recommend that you carry at least a minimum survival kit on you at all times in the field. If you have a *proper minimum survival kit*, you will have:

- A quality penknife or jack knife.
- Condoms for water storage, un-lubricated.
- Water proof matches
- Flint and steel or a metal match
- Water purification tables

- A long strip of aluminum foil folded up to cook with.
- Fishing kit, i.e., hooks, sinkers, and some line. Nothing fancy.
- Commercial back packing first aid kit (with instructions). I carry a very small one.
- One small pack of gum and one of hard candy (energy)
- A small signal mirror
- About 25 feet of cord
- A space blanket

In the desert you should become nocturnal; once the sun goes down your "day" will start. So, as you think, consider the type of shelter design you want to use, look the area over for possible sources of water, and find out how much water you have on hand. Do all of this from the shade of your temporary shelter.

In the desert, always think before you act. Do nothing that is not absolutely life threatening in the daytime. You want to keep your sweating down to the minimum.

Once the sun goes down, you should get busy. Your first priority is to construct a shelter. If you have a space blanket, a casualty blanket or a poncho, you can make a simple lean-to type of shelter, using the 25 feet of cord in your survival kit. I also carry a casualty blanket (a super quality "NASA" designed space blanket) and a poncho with me at all times in my survival gear. This extra equipment gives me two materials for shelter construction and one for sleeping (counting the space blanket in the minimum survival kit), if needed.

Simply secure one end of the material to the ground (called the secured end), using stakes or heavy stones, and angle the other end of the material up (called the angled end). Do not make the angle too steep, or you won't get the needed sun protection you need. I suggest you make the angled end no higher than 4 feet off the ground. At the angled end tie it to bushes, stakes, or rocks. Then, place five or six pieces of brush on the material, and then cover the whole thing with material once more...it will be shelter material, brush, and shelter material. I use a casualty blanket for the first layer of material and my space blanket as the top layer of material. I place the space blanket on the shelter with the florescent orange side up, to aid for an emergency signal.

Most survival professionals agree to the need for this type of "sandwich" shelter. It forms a dead air space between you and the sun.

It insulates and keeps the shelter cooler than a single layered shelter. Remember to only construct this shelter in the cool of the evening, NOT during the day. Now that you have a way of keeping the water you have in your system, let's look at how to procure additional water needed for your survival.

First, ration your water. If you drink more than you actually need, you will pass it out in the form of urine. And, when you urinate, check the color of your urine. Dark colored urine indicates you need to increase your water intake. Many survival professionals recommend that have a least one-quart of water for every two lost. But remember, less fluid will NOT result in less sweat! In extreme heat, you may not even feel yourself sweat because the sweat evaporates very quickly. Always be on the lookout for additional sources of usable water.

So, you need water, right? Not sure where to find it? Well, here a few suggestions. Not all of them work all the time. But, all are worth the attempt. First, keep in mind that water flows downhill. That means that water may be at low points in your area.

One place to look for water, using the above information, is on the outside bend, lowest point, of a dry streambed. DO NOT dig for water during the day; you will lose liquid from your body you might not be able to replace. Do not do anything that causes you to sweat that is not necessary. Keep that water inside of you!

Another possible water source can be added by making a **solar still** or using **condensation bags**. However, both methods require plastic sheets of material.

To construct a solar still, dig a hole approximately 3 feet across and about 2 feet deep. Make a smaller hole, or slump in the middle of the hole. In this slump you need to put a container, pan, can, or pot to collect the water. Once the hole has been dug, cover the hole with a plastic sheet. Be sure to secure the edges of the sheet with sand and rocks. Next, place a rock in the center of the sheet, so it sags down.

How it works is simple. The temperature in the hole, both the soil and air, rises due to the sun. This increase in heat causes vapors, which condensates on the inside of the plastic sheet and runs down. It then drops into the container in the sump hole.

Condensation Bags are easy to construct. Leaves and small branches may be cut and placed into clear plastic bags. **How it works**: The heat from the sun causes the liquids in the foliage to be extracted, much like the solar still, and collect in the bag. However, this method may produce bitter water and the taste test should be used to determine if it is safe to drink. If the water has a bitter taste, do not use it for drinking. **WARNING**: This method of water procurement may produce water with toxins and thus not be safe to drink.

Another method of procuring water is by using a **transpiration bag**. In this method a large plastic bag is placed over a living limb of a tree or large bush. (I suggest it be high enough to be off of the ground). Insert the limb or bush just like you would a hand into a mitten. Then, tie the open end of the bag around the tree or bush. At the closed end of the bag, tie a rock so the bag is weighted and forms a collection point for the water. **How it Works**: Like the solar still and the condensation bag, it uses heat and evaporation.

Cactus as a source of water is often, in my opinion, over rated. We have all seen the cowboy movie where the hero, lost in the desert, kicks over a barrow cactus and is saved. It just doesn't happen that way.

In our American southwest there are many different kinds of cactus, from the **barrow cactus** to the prickly pear. All can be used for gaining additional moisture, but it can take a great deal of work to open a full sized barrow cactus, not to mention the fight you will have with the spiny thorns that protect it. If you decide to take on a cactus, do it in the cool of the evening. (Chunks of freshly cut cactus can be added to the sloping sides of your solar still to increase the water level collected). Using caution, remove the top of the barrow cactus. Once the top is off, you will find a white a white substance that reminds me of "water melon meat" inside (this is a liquid filled inner tissue). Using your survival knife, cut out hand-size chunks and squeeze the moisture from it.

The prickly pear is easier to collect and prepare. I use a long sharp stick and a good knife. I stab the round prickly pear with the stick, and then cut it off with my knife. Then, returning to the fire, I simply burn the thorns off of the cactus. Make sure you sear the cactus well to remove even the smallest thorns.

Once the thorns are removed, I peel the green or purple colored outer substance off, and eat the inside. Prickly pear "meat" is so tasty, that in Arizona and New Mexico you can find jellies and candies made from it. It is the moisture filled inner tissue you want to chew, not the rough outer "bark."

Use caution with all cacti. The thorns will usually cause infections if you are unlucky enough to be "grabbed" by one. I use sharp sticks, knifes, and fires to handle cactus safely. Any injury from a cactus plant should be treated immediately to reduce the risk of infection.

Now, we have discussed the immediate requirements to survive, what about additional information? Well, you should also be aware of a few other things about the desert.

Food is not usually much of a problem. If you don't have enough water, **don't eat**. The USAF taught us if we did not have more than ½ a liter of water a day **NOT TO EAT**. When your body processes food into waste, fluids from your body are used. So, if you do not have enough water in you, you can speed up dehydration by eating. Besides, most healthy North Americans can go for a long time without eating. Water is your primary concern in the desert. If your urine color is not dark, food intake may be considered.

Insects can be a problem at times. If your water source is adequate, you can always fix up a nice meal of bugs. See the article on my site on preparing insects as food sources. In any case, avoid scorpions, spiders, and other "may hurt you" bugs. This includes centipedes, or brightly colored insects.

Spiders are there with you as well. While the large spider most often seen in movies (the tarantula) is scary and it can bite, the bite is usually just disabling and very rarely fatal. And yes, the tarantula lives in the desert of the American southwest. Be sure to always shake out your removed clothing and your boots prior to putting them on. You may be surprised what will set up home in your gear. Avoid any spider you see in the desert.

Snakes may be dangerous to you, but they can also provide a filling meal. For the sake of simplicity, we will consider only the American rattlesnake. As a safety consideration, always keep your clothing on and your boots (I would never even consider going into a desert with sneakers or shoes on). Additionally, use caution when you move around at night. Rattlesnakes do not always warn with a rattle prior to striking. Most snakebites occur to the legs, below the knees, or to a person's hands. The rattlesnake may be found in rocky areas, or in holes or shadows. Do not put your hands where you cannot see. If you see a snake, and know you can kill it, it does make an excellent source of food. Some states in the southwest have an annual rattlesnake roundup. These snakes are caught, killed, then cooked and eaten. I have had eaten rattlesnake and it tastes just like...snake, believe me, not chicken.

Lizards are found in the desert as well. The Gila Monster is seen at times in the American southwest. It is a fat, short, lizard with a rounded head and a bright yellowish colored body. It will run away from you if it can, so avoid cornering it. The bite is very poisonous and should be treated the same as a snakebite.

Surviving in a desert environment is never easy. Even for the best prepared and most knowledgeable there is no assurance of survival. The heat, dehydration, and hazards of desert survival often win in the end, even when against the most determined and prepared victim.

If you want to survive in the desert, you *must* maintain your body's fluids, do nothing that is not absolutely necessary, and find ways to procure water. The key to living is to maintain your water level. Nonetheless, with the information provided in this article and with a strong, determined will to survive, you too will have the tools that could make the difference between your being another victim of the desert, or a survivor.

I Survived Three Days in the Arctic! And, So Can You!

Those of us who enjoy big game hunting very rarely consider the real dangers associated with the sport. We frequently hunt in the extreme cold and snowy country of the far north. As a result, we often find ourselves miles from anyone or any place as we search for game. While the day may start out nicely, it only takes a short period of time for the weather to turn bad, and we will be forced to seek shelter quickly. But do you really know how to construct a shelter in arctic like conditions? Could you survive until the weather clears, or help arrives? I can survive, thanks to the United States Air Force Arctic Survival Course.

"Alright, gentlemen and ladies, listen up! The weather right now is minus twenty degrees, and it *will* go down with the sun." The grizzled old sergeant said as he moved around our training site with his gloved hands on his hips.

I was physically and mentally overwhelmed, not to mention cold. Less than an hour ago I was snug and warm in a military survival classroom preparing for this venture. I had expected it to be cold, but not this cold. I actually felt the start of panic at the thought of three days in this weather with very little more than my mind. I was able to fight it to the back of my mind by telling myself that I had just received days of intense arctic survival training. I was better prepared than most folks would be in a real survival situation, because I was actually in a semi-safety training site. At least the instructors had radios to call for help if need be.

The sergeant disrupted my daydreaming once more. "I want each of you to start constructing a shelter, get an insulated sleeping area made, and get a fire started. I want all of this done by the time I return. Remember the buddy system. Keep your eyes out for the safety and health of the one you have been paired up with. What this means is that each of you do your own work, but stay within sight of each other. If you are injured during this training to the point you cannot continue, you will be returned to camp for medical treatment and then, once the doc says you're healthy again, you will start the program all over again at day one. Are there any questions?"

No one had any questions, but as I looked into the eyes of my fellow students, I could sense fear, uncertainty, and confusion. Oh, we knew what to do, as well as how to do it. But there is a certain psychological feeling of doom or dread as you face the reality of survival at minus twenty or lower. I knew I had to shake that feeling off, because it is a killer, so I started making my fire.

Since we were not so far north as to be out of the tree line, I walked to a nearby tree and started looking for "squaw wood" or the dead twigs under or on the tree. These are not very large, often about the diameter of a pencil. I soon had a couple of hands full and placed them on the ground near where I would make my fire.

What I wanted next was Mother Nature's own fire starter, pine pitch. I walked to a group of large pines and found globs of the light orange sap that burned like gasoline when ignited. It is sticky, like gum, and is easy to remove, but at times leaves an oily feeling (residue) on hands. (While not actually needed, it was there and would make the fire starting that much easier). I placed the pine pitch on the "squaw wood" and returned to the trees once more.

Gathering up armload after armload of dry wood (as dry as I could find), I stacked it near my fire pit. I quickly had enough for at least one night of continuous burning in a small fire. I did not want a large fire because I would not need it. I intended to spend a great deal of time in my shelter, out of the wind. While there was no wind now, there might be later that night. I knew from training that the shelter would be warm, and I did not intend to lose any more body heat than I had to.

I placed four of the larger pieces of wood I had gathered in a line, sides touching sides. Essentially, I had just made a platform for my fire. I knew that as the fire burned, the logs of my platform would burn as well. Thus, over time the fire would sink lower and lower into the snow, until it did me little good. At that point, I would have to start all over again and make a new fire pit. If I could, I would have covered the logs with sand, dirt or stones to keep the wood from burning. But, I was unsure how deep the snow was or how hard the ground would be. I did not want to work up a sweat, or use up energy, digging for ground level. Additionally, I would have used green logs, only I didn't have an ax to cut them with. I had to make do with what I had on hand.

Simple Survival

As I said earlier, I intended to spend as much time as possible out of the cold and in my shelter, so the problem of the fire sinking like the Titanic was a small concern. I mainly wanted it to warm my hands as I constructed my shelter and made my sleeping platform.

After making my fire platform, I placed two pieces of pitch in the middle. I then made a very small teepee from the twigs I had gathered, taking care that I allowed room between the pieces of wood for airflow. This teepee was constructed right over most of the pine pitch. Next, I needed a fire source.

There are many different kinds of fire sources available and I usually carry at least three on me at all times (matches in a water proof container, lighter, as well as flint and steel) when I hunt. On this day, however, I had to start a fire with flint and steel. Not an easy task in the numbing cold of the arctic. I did have an advantage because the instructors allowed us to prepare individual survival kits, which they inspected closely for unauthorized food items, to bring along. This was to get us used to the idea of *always* having a survival kit of some sort, as well as learning what should go in it.

I had used an old survival trick of putting dried lint from a clothes drier in my survival kit wrapped in a plastic sandwich bag. I gently placed the lint up against and part way into my tee-pee of sticks and twigs. Once again I took airflow into consideration. Since the lint was dry and not compressed, it only took one tiny burning piece of flint from my trembling hands to start the fire.

As the flames slowly grew in size, I gently added more and more wood until I had a nice fire burning. Now my attention turned to constructing my shelter. Having been warned to avoid sweating in arctic weather as it leads to chilling and possibly hypothermia, I removed my parka and started to work.

My first step was to dig down into the snow and clear a trench about three feet wide, three feet deep and seven feet long. This was a little longer and wider than I am, to allow me to store my meager field gear in the shelter with me. I was looking for emergency protection from the environment, not a suite. The actual size used in construction is an individual preference, but I wanted a small and compact shelter with only my immediate needs in mind.

As soon as I had the trench made, I lined the floor of my shelter with pine boughs from the nearby pine trees. Other sources of insulation can be used if pine is not available where you are (If you survive an aircraft crash, the insulation from the walls or the material from the seats on an aircraft provide excellent protection from a cold sleeping surface). I placed the boughs a little over a foot thick. I would have piled them higher, but I had to be able to crawl into the thing once I had a roof on it. I have discovered, in my opinion, that you can never have too much floor insulation in a survival shelter.

Next, I put my gear in the shelter up against the far wall, away from the entrance. I walked to the nearby trees and started gathering up logs and limbs to cover my trench. I had been cautioned to avoid rotted wood for the roof. As I gathered the logs, I stacked them near my trench until I had a large supply to work with. Once I started working on the roof, I didn't want to have to keep walking into the woods to find more material.

Starting at the end opposite my entrance, I laid the logs and limbs over the open trench until I had it all covered with the exception of a small opening. This opening would be my entrance. You will have to estimate the size of your entrance based on your body size, but keep it as small as possible.

I walked around my shelter and made sure the logs overlapped the sides of my trench by about a foot on each side. I did this to give the roof strength and additional support. After the logs were in place, I returned to the pines and brought back enough pine boughs to cover the top of my shelter. These pine boughs would provide the insulation my shelter needed. This insulation would prevent body heat from escaping and help keep the shelter protected from the wind and elements.

Once the boughs were placed on top, I covered them with a small part of my parachute. While it is unlikely most people in a survival situation will have a parachute, a poncho, sheet of plastic, space blanket, or any material could serve the same purpose. If you do not have any material to cover the boughs with, then proceed without it. I anchored the edges of my "chute" material with wooden stakes and started covering it with snow.

As I worked covering my shelter, I began to sweat in the freezing cold and removed a layer of clothing. I wanted to avoid sweating because of the danger of the sweat freezing. When I felt myself becoming too warm, I would stop for a few minutes. Also, as soon as I had the shelter about half covered with snow, I stopped and boiled me a cup of "pine needle" tea. Yep, it is exactly what it sounds like. Not my favorite drink, but it did the trick and refreshed me as I took a much-deserved breather.

The rest of my shelter was quickly covered with snow. All in all, it was not a difficult task, but one that required some planning and hard work. I had to ensure it was long enough and wide enough to hold me, and all of my equipment. Additionally, I wanted it high enough to be able to move around in, but not high enough to stand up in. The smaller I kept it, the easier it would be for me to heat. But, I still had two more tasks to complete before it was ready for an occupant.

I crawled inside my shelter and poked a hole approximately three inches in diameter in the top. I did this to allow for ventilation. Since I planned to burn a candle in the shelter, and wanted some fresh air, I would constantly, over the next few days, be checking to make sure the hole stayed open. Without the ventilation and with the candle burning, carbon monoxide poisoning was a real threat. Always keep your shelter well ventilated.

My very last step was to make a door for my shelter. I took a large piece of parachute material (you could use a poncho, tarp, space blanket, etc.) and spread it out on the snow near the entrance to my shelter. I piled snow on the material until I had enough snow, or so I thought, to block the hole I used for an entrance. I pulled the ends and sides of the parachute material together and tied them in place using some cord. I now had a door, roughly the shape of a circle. I could use the ends of the parachute material as a crude door handle to pull the "door" closed once I was inside my shelter.

By the time the old sergeant had returned, I had completed my assignment. My fire was burning well, my sleeping area was lined with pine boughs, and my shelter was complete. I was actually proud of myself. The earlier fears of survival I had fought in my mind were now gone. (Remember, an active mind is less prone to the psychological dangers associated with wilderness survival). Actually, I had expected a small compliment when the sergeant returned, but he just took a long critical look, turned to me and said, "Not bad. Not good either. We will see tonight if it is good enough."

Well, it was good enough and then some. I spent the next three days living in my snow trench shelter. While not exactly the most comfortable place to live in, it did serve its purpose; it kept me alive in sub-zero weather. I learned how cramped, lonely, and boring it can be when a howling blizzard is pounding on the outside and I was confined to my shelter. I actually felt how warm and comfortable a small candle can make such a dismal place feel.

Most of all, it honestly amazed me at the end of the three days of training to open my shelter door and emerge as an arctic survival school graduate. Before, I never would have thought it possible; would *you* have?

CAN YOU SURVIVE?

In the mid 1960's, three of my young cousins left home and walked to a nearby river to do a little fishing. They didn't come home until three nights later. While they were fishing a storm moved in on them, and they decided quickly to go home. As the wind blew, the clouds darkened, and the rain started to fall, they made a serious mistake. They chose a shortcut one of the boys said he knew. They spent the next three days in the woods, lost. Now, you may think it happened to them because they were just kids. But, I know the oldest was fifteen and knew those woods like his back yard. Yet, when the rain hit and day became as dark as night, they got turned around. They slept buried in leaves, ate insects, and drank creek water. Keep in mind, they were in the southern United States and the weather was agreeable; well, at least when compared to some weather in the north. Nonetheless, they had *the will to survive* and did so. Could you do the same where you are? I believe I could do it and be somewhat comfortable at the same time. How do I know? I know because I have survived before.

I know most of you have never seriously given the idea of being lost in the woods a second thought. But those of us who hunt, fish, or hike in the North Country should always be prepared to survive. This is some of the prettiest and most dangerous country in the world, but it can be unforgiving to the careless. Getting lost can happen to even the best and most experienced of us. Imagine being out and having bad weather hitting. Instead of stopping for a while, you continue on. Soon the weather turns worse and you become disoriented. I use the term disoriented because no true outdoors person is ever lost. With the weather and you being disoriented, what do you do next?

Your first step is to stop. Find temporary shelter if you can, sit on a log, or just stand there. Stop. Look around you. Do you honestly know where you are? Beyond any doubt? You must be totally honest with yourself at this point; believe it or not, your life could depend on it. If the weather is wet and cool, notice I did not say cold, you might even have the beginning symptoms of hypothermia and not be aware of it. (If you are not aware of what hypothermia is, you should not be in the woods. It is the lowering of the body's core temperature and can kill). If the weather is cold, your life may depend on your next step. Stop, take a look around, and decide then what needs to be done. If you are honestly lost, relax. All is not hopeless nor may you even be in serious danger. But plan as if your life depends on it, because it may. As long as you keep your wits about you and have planned in advance, you should be all right.

Take a look around and find a place for a shelter. An ideal shelter would be a cave, but those can be few and far between. If a cave is not available you may have to construct a shelter. Now, in a survival situation, a shelter is not hot and cold running water, a heat lamp, or a set of bunk beds. Many nights I have slept under a shelter made with a tarp or rain poncho. They are easy to construct, are somewhat water resistant, and keep you safe. The key in constructing your shelter is its location. Avoid making it under dead tree limbs, in dry streambeds, or too close to running water. High winds, rain, or other weather conditions could make them very dangerous. Two trees, eight feet of cord or line, a poncho, and you are set for the night. Merely tie the cord to the trees, drape the poncho over the line, and secure the bottom of the poncho so it does not blow around. I usually tie the end of a piece of line to the poncho grommets and the other end to sharpened wooden stakes I hammer into the ground. A kind of poor man's tent, but it does work.

In cold snowy weather, you should insulate your shelter. Place pine boughs on top of the tarp or poncho (as constructed above) and then add about six to twelve inches of snow on top. This snow will act as insulation and actually keep you warm. Have the opening to the shelter facing your fire. Do not have a fire inside the shelter. Keep the shelter well ventilated to avoid carbon monoxide poisoning. (I have used a shelter of this type in Alaska when the temperature was minus twenty degree Fahrenheit for three days.) Of primary concern is to conserve your energy and to keep out of the wind. Wind chill can be a real killer.

Next step, usually for purely psychological reasons, is a fire. Keep it small and keep your firewood dry. Wet or green wood is difficult to keep burning. I usually keep a small bit of kindling in my shelter as well, so it stays dry. That makes it easier to start a fire in the mornings. Also, keep your fire small. You will use less wood and a small fire is much easier to cook on, if you have food. A good fire will also assist rescuers in finding you, especially at night. A small fire in front of your shelter and you out of the wind will really make you feel much better.

Once you have a shelter and fire the battle is half won. Stop once more and relax a minute and **take inventory of the equipment you have on hand**. Look at what you have, how it is to be used, where it is to be used, and who is to use it. I mean, fishing equipment will not do you much good as fishing equipment if you are land locked. However, the line and the tackle are priceless. You can make snares with the line or use the pole to catch snakes for dinner, if need be. Look at abnormal uses for all of your gear as well. Let your imagination take over. I once saw an Alaskan Native start a fire by using his boot laces and a piece of wood. I have even seen women's sanitary napkins used as dressings when a person sustained a serious cut. Keep the mind active. Your desire to survive and your mind are your best tools. Keep them both finely tuned.

After inventory is completed, start on the most serious task you have; **procuring drinking water**. Not all water found in the woods is good for drinking. If you camp, hunt, fish, or hike, always have some fresh water on you. I carry a small baby bottle filled with water, and it fits into my cargo pocket of my pants. But for long term drinking, carry water purification tablets or boil your water. It is funny, when you think of survival most people think of the lack of food, not lack of water. Most of us, especially me, can do without food for a long time with few ill effects. No, I am not suggesting it is healthy, just that water is more of an immediate need. If you have adequate shelter, fire, and water, you can survive for a surprisingly long time. Food, for most of us anyway, is a habit. We eat too much. Besides, the odds are you will be found within forty-eight hours if others know where you went. So, get comfortable and relax.

When you are surviving, you will get dirty. This cannot be completely prevented. Nonetheless, attempt to *stay as clean as you can*. Dirty clothing loses its insulating properties and will not keep you as warm as clean clothing. Beside, good sanitary conditions will assist your body in fighting infections from small cuts and scratches you will receive. Keep your clothing and yourself as clean as you can under the conditions. Keeping your clothing dry is important as well. Try to wear wool, Gore-Tex®, Thinsolite®, or other commercial products that are known to keep you warm even when wet. There are lots on the market so get the best you can afford. Wool is one of my choices.

Once you have a shelter up, fire going, and dinner on the grill, **stay there**. It is much easier for folks to find you than you to find them. I

NEVER go out without someone knowing where I am, when I left, and when I expect to return. You can tell a family member, girlfriend or a buddy. It is safer to do this and will assist the authorities if they have to launch a search and rescue effort for you. Have you ever wandered all over a mall looking for someone? Difficult to find them, huh? But if you take a seat on a bench they will walk by you sooner or later. Two trains of thought here; 1) let them come to you, 2) you use less energy. This energy thingy is very important when you don't know where your next meal is coming from. Conserve energy, let them find you. Besides, you have already established all the comforts of home, right? Why leave it then?

One aspect of all of this I have saved to the last is **being prepared**. Once you are forced to spend the night in the woods is not when you should discover you don't have matches. Or, that you don't know basic first aid or how to use some of your survival gear. Prepare. Be a scout and remember the scout motto, always be prepared. I never go out without my survival kit with me. No, it is not very big and it does not weigh much, but it could prove to be a life saver. I actually carry most of it in a small plastic box about three inches wide and about five inches long. I have it in my right pants cargo pocket at all times.

Also, I carry three other things on my person. I carry a good quality space blanket, dry socks, and about twenty feet of cotton cord. I have found I can survive with the above items. And, all of this stuff weighs almost nothing. I carry it all in one cargo pocket and still have lots of room left. It is my insurance policy.

One other area I need to discuss is **how you dress** when you are in the woods. I usually wear military cargo pocket styled pants and shirts. These can be picked up in surplus stores at a good price. I also have good boots, warm socks, and always have a belt. I wear a wide brimmed hat to shade my eyes from the elements. Of course you know I also have a poncho, but not much else is really needed. If you want to get a fanny pack and wear jeans, all of the equipment I have listed will easily fit into the container. Once you are in a survival situation is not the time to decide you need the gear. You have it with you, or do without.

With today's electronics and gadgets it is very difficult to really become lost. GPS (Global Positioning Satellite) systems, cellular phones, and other devices make it safer. But many people, me included, prefer not to carry those things out of doors. I go out to avoid noise and technology, not to carry it. Keep in mind, all it takes is a touch of bad weather, a serious mishap, or a wrong turn, and you may find yourself in a survival situation.

Simple Survival

In the far north, you are isolated and in some very remote country. Often, what you have with you will be all you have to use for survival. Remember, your mind is your best tool. Your determination to survive is your best motivation. With a survival kit, your mind, and determination, you too can survive until rescued.

Float Trip Survival

The sky had turned black, and the thunder crashed just a few minutes before a light rain started. Lightning streaked its long bright fingers across the dark afternoon sky as we pulled onto a gravel bar in the center of the river. We had to find shelter, and quickly; the weather was turning terrible. I didn't want to spend the night on the gravel bar in the middle of a river, in case the river level happened to rise due to the rain. If that happened, we would be trapped or washed away.

I didn't like the overall situation that much either, with three inexperienced (wilderness camping) adults and four children along. Glancing quickly at both shorelines, I saw a spot that might offer us a little cover from the wind in some oaks.

I turned and looked at my small group, gave a weak smile, and said, "Let's head to the right side of the river, then down about sixty yards. We are going camping. See that small group of oaks?" I pointed at the site with my right arm and my index finger extended.

"Let's make for it and set up a campsite until morning."

Our small quiet group of four canoes quickly covered the short distance to the bank of the river right in front of the oaks. By then, I knew the children were frightened, because they had stopped talking. As we stepped from the canoes, most of us were soaking wet, tired, and very concerned. I knew we had to do something quickly, or I would have some very upset and miserable floaters on my hands.

Once on shore and after we had pulled the canoes up far enough on the sandy bank that they could not be washed away by a wild rising river, we tied them to trees. Since I had a great deal of military training in survival, I was, according to the other adults, now in charge, but this was in no way close to a survival situation. I suspect they had more than just a little fear and wanted someone with experience handling the situation. We immediately had to get organized and we had to do it quickly because of the wetness and our unexpected stop on the edge of the river. While it was not actually a survival situation, it could very quickly turn into one if we were not careful. Actually, my biggest concern was avoiding hypothermia, the lowering of the body's core temperature.

None of us were dressed for an overnight stay in the woods; because the weather had been so nice earlier, we were all wearing swimwear and tee-shirts. One aspect of planning I had insisted on before our trip now made our situation easier; we had some survival gear with us. I had placed a small fanny pack in each canoe, nothing elaborate, but with enough gear to keep us comfortable and alive for a night or two. I had each survival kit brought from the canoes and started to organize.

Inside each canoe survival kit I had placed a small tarp (8ft by 10ft), four plastic trash bags (the big orange ones), one casualty blanket (silver on one side and green on the other), one space blanket (very thin metallic material), and four high-energy bars.

Also, I carried some other things in my kit; a good quality space blanket, a magnesium match (for starting fires), a lighter, and about fifty feet of nylon parachute (called 550) cord. I have found I can survive with the above items, and all of this stuff weighs almost nothing. When I hunt, I carry it all in one cargo pocket of my pants and still have lots of room left. It is my life assurance policy. Thanks to the sandwiches we carried to nibble on while we floated, some snacks, and the soft drinks we had, hunger was not a problem.

We quickly used the tarps and nylon cord to construct four crude lean-tos (I made sure the shelters were not under any dead tree limbs). And, soon after that, we had a small fire burning. The wood we used was the dry and dead tree branches found on the lower limbs of big trees, because we knew it would still be dry. Also, we tore holes in the trash bags for our arms and head and had four rough looking ponchos for the adults to wear as we worked. I relaxed a great deal once the shelters were up and the fires burning. I knew then all was safe. Even the trees we camped near were no taller than others in the area, so I suspected they were not likely to attract any lightening strikes.

Before the rain got heavier, I quickly had the adults pack all of our supplies up to the shelters. Any of our gear that was not in waterproof containers, I placed under the tarps with the kids to keep dry. The small ice chests I placed beside our shelters, knowing they contained soft drinks and food.

By now the kids were complaining of being chilled, so we tore a hole in the top of four plastic trash bags (do not cut the plastic, it will tear much longer than intended). We had the kids insert their heads in the holes, pull the excess bag down their sides, push the ends under their legs, and sit on them (Never do this with a young child or an infant, it could cause suffocation). We then wrapped them sitting up, two to a casualty blanket. I gave each child a couple of small pieces of candy to suck on as well. These simple tricks helped them retain body heat that otherwise would have been lost. And, once the weather improved I would heat up some warm drinks for all of us using my heavy-duty aluminum foil to make crude cups.

While the rain stopped about an hour after dark, we could not continue the float trip safely in the darkness. We knew we were stuck where we were for the night. One of the adults phoned her husband (on a cell phone), who was to pick us up that evening, and told him we were okay, but had to stop due to the weather.

She quickly explained to him that we were not in any danger and then arranged for him to pick us up the next morning. But let me assure you, that night was rough and difficult for all of the kids, as well as most of the adults.

The night was long and the mid-summer evening was chilly. While we had the space blankets and casualty blankets to wrap up in, the space blankets are noisy to sleep in and cracked and popped as we moved (I felt like I was sleeping in a box of my favorite breakfast cereal). I, nonetheless, rather enjoyed the night, and stayed up later than anyone else. I spent hours sitting on a log while looking at the stars, while sipping on a cup of coffee warmed up from a thermos. I knew the kids would talk of this adventure for years, and how they had braved a rough storm on an untamed river, while wearing trash bags and sleeping under a tarp.

I also did some serious thinking. The survival kits for each canoe, as well as my personal survival kit, gave us all we needed to spend the night with more than just a small degree of comfort. Granted, it was not the most comfortable camping I had ever done, but it could have been much worse. Without this equipment we would have been forced to stay wet, sleep in the cold, and do without a fire, or a shelter. While I doubt anyone would have died, the survival kits had given us the basic tools to spend the night protected from the elements of Mother Nature. I was still not sure if any of the people with me would get sick from all of this, but we did have some degree of comfort with us (later there was not a cold or sneeze from the situation).

So, the next time you are outdoors, for any reason, make sure you take a survival kit. While it may not actually save your life, it can make a rough and unexpected night in the woods that much more comfortable. Be prepared for the unexpected, and you too will stay safe this summer.

HELP, MY CAR HAS BROKEN DOWN AND IT'S SNOWING!

How to survive a winter night in your car

As the young woman drove along the isolated rural roadway she started getting concerned about the weather. Her children, ages four and six, were playing, laughing, and yelling in the back seat of the car. The weather, which had been so good when she had gone to visit her mother  earlier in the day, had started turning nasty a couple of hours ago. She left her mother's country home when the snow had started to fall heavily. As she concentrated on driving on the slippery roadway, she noticed the snowflakes were larger now and the wind had really picked up. Occasionally she would have to remind the children to be quieter, so she could concentrate on the road for hazards.

Abruptly, one of the children gave a loud scream and the young woman turned to see what had happened. No sooner had she turned her head, than the rear of the car started to move to the right. Quickly turning back to watch the road, she saw a large ditch in front of the car and out of pure instinct the woman slammed on the breaks. The car, now out of control, spun in circles until it impacted the ditch, continued to turn a half a circle more, and then stopped with the front of the car nose down in the ditch.

The woman must have sat there for many long minutes before she realized what had happened. She could smell the leaking radiator fluid and heard both children crying in the rear of the car. Turning her head, she noticed both children seemed safe and there were no obvious injuries. The woman noticed a copper taste in her mouth and understood she had bit her lip when the car struck the ditch. "The cold! How can I keep my babies alive in this cold? No one drives this road at night!" She silently screamed her thoughts in complete panic.

Does this story sound far-fetched? Well, it isn't, not at all. Each year motorists are stranded in cold weather on our nation's highways and back roads. Some have small children with them and some don't. Most, except for the most remote and unusual situations will survive. Regardless of who is in the vehicle or where you drive, there are some simple rules that all drivers should follow during the winter months. Know the weather forecast and keep up with it at all times. I once got caught in a blizzard while driving in Alaska, and I will never forget that experience.

- Tell someone *when* you are leaving, *where* you are going, *who* is going with you, *when* you expect to return, and *what* you expect to do. For instance, I am leaving in the morning with little Jimmy and we will be back on Wednesday. We will stop at the amusement park on Wednesday morning.

- If the weather suddenly turns severe find a place to stop or do not start your trip. Make sure as soon as possible you notify those who expect you to be at a given point at a given time. If you don't, they may contact the police and a search and rescue mission could be started...for you.

- If you must go out in bad weather, dress properly for it. Many people do not wear boots, coats, or gloves, thinking they will be warm in the car. Then, once the car is stalled, serious problems result. Always dress for the worse weather you will encounter.

- Stay on the main roads if you have a choice. The main road contains higher traffic, the police will cruise this roadway during bad weather, and the snow removal teams will clean the main roads first.

During the winter months carry a survival kit (contents listed below so you can cut them out) in the trunk of your car. Keep wool blankets or sleeping bags in the car as well. Some folks have even added a small lightweight tent. Always, at all times, carry a commercial first aid kit in your car.

If your car stops or becomes stuck, do not run the engine to keep warm. Each year people die from carbon monoxide poisoning doing just that. It is safe to run your engine to keep warm only as long as your muffler is not covered with snow (blocked) and you keep two windows open to allow fresh air in. I suggest you never use the engine to keep warm because it is just too dangerous to do so (snow may block the muffler and you won't know).

Tie an orange strip or triangle of material to your antenna. I carry one that is used on bicycles and it would work just fine. Some car survival kits have these small orange flags. My cousin has one made from an orange garbage bag.

If you leave the car to seek shelter, do not go too far. Rescuers will look in the area of your vehicle for you, and falling snow could easily cover your tracks.

Shelters out of the car should be in a wooded or rocky area, if possible, because trees will assist in blocking the wind. Use a tarp, blanket, or whatever material you have on hand to make a simple lean-to shelter. Do not clean falling snow off of the shelter, since it will help insulate it (unless it starts to bow in from the weight). Do not make your shelter under dead tree limbs, because they could fall during high winds.

If you can, use the natural surroundings for shelter construction. You can usually find a "pit" free of snow under large cedar or pine trees after a heavy snowfall. Or, you can place logs or limbs up against a fallen log or rocks to back a natural shelter.

Make sure your fire is made in a safe area, with no low limbs that could catch fire. If there is a lot of snow, you may have to lay a platform of green logs to make your fire on (fires made on deep snow will burn, melt the snow, and then put themselves out). The logs will eventually burn through, so be prepared for that event. Also, keep your fire small. You can use rocks or stacked logs to reflect the heat from your fire, by making sure the reflector is 180 degrees from the entrance of your shelter with the fire in the middle.

Once you are organized, do not leave. Stay where you are until help arrives. If you leave the spot, rescuers may have to spend additional time (which could prove fatal for you) looking for you, the weather may get worse, or you may suffer from hypothermia.

One aspect of winter survival most people never consider is dehydration. In cold climates we tend to drink less than normal. If your urine is dark in color, increase your water intake. Do not eat snow or suck on ice, as they will lower your body temperature. Instead, melt them in a container first if possible.

Hypothermia is the lowering of the body's core temperature, and it can be fatal. Once you have a shelter constructed and a fire going, stay where you are and keep warm, as well as dry.

While surviving in the winter can be very difficult, it can be done. Just because your vehicle breaks down, or you become stuck, is in some ways no different than encountering a survival situation while hiking.

Simple Survival

Survival is survival, though there are obviously different challenges in each situation. The key to your survival is to think before you act, stay where you are once you're organized, prepare by having the right equipment with you, and gain the knowledge you need to survive before you need it.

As I suggested above, some survival items I always have in my car in addition to my basic survival kit are a two liter bottle of water, a poncho, and a signal mirror. I suggest you consider carrying them as well. Each driver can add additional items and eventually develop a large kit, but remember you do not want to fill up your trunk. In addition, try to select items that serve more than one purpose.

Also, if you are inexperienced with survival, purchase a small survival manual to take along with you. Make sure your car survival kit at least has the following items packed in it:

- A quality penknife or jack knife
- Condoms for water storage, un-lubricated, water bottle, or large zip locked freezer bags.
- Waterproof matches and a lighter
- Flint and steel or a metal match
- Water purification tablets
- A long strip of heavy-duty aluminum foil folded up to cook with.
- Fishing kit, i.e. hooks, sinkers, and some line. Nothing fancy.
- Commercial back packing first aid kit (with instructions). I have a vehicle first aid kit (I have also placed a small hotel size bar of soap inside my kit).
- One small pack of gum and one pack of hard candy (energy)
- Casualty blanket, sometimes called a thermal blanket
- Wool blankets or sleeping bags
- Instant powder broth, beef or chicken, four servings total
- Survival whistle, small, made of plastic and with a lanyard
- A flashlight
- Approximately 50 feet of nylon cord

Could You Survive Alone if Injured?

T he man was in deep pain and knew his right leg was broken. While the bone had not pierced the skin, the foot was bent at an unnatural angle. He removed his sheath knife and cut his pants up past his knee, because he knew the leg would start to swell soon. He leaned back on the dark green moss and thought of how dumb he had been that day. First, he had elected to go out hunting alone, even though he knew it was unsafe. And his second mistake was made when he attempted to step between two logs. His weight had shifted to his right as he twisted and then fell. He had actually heard his leg break. He had a survival kit with him, though it was small, and he knew his wife would notify the police when he did not return at his usual time. But, he was still facing a cold and painful night alone deep in the back woods.

Many of us who hunt often do not consider the potential dangers we face. While it is much safer now than it was years ago, there are still a number of things that can reach out and hurt you. What can we do if we find ourselves in a situation like the man did in the beginning of this article? Well, I suggest we can do many things, and some should be done before we leave for the woods. We should be prepared, first, to be in the woods.

Before you leave on a hunting trip, always tell someone where you are going and when you will return. If you are late for any reason, always contact them and let them know. Additionally, I never hunt alone. I just don't think it makes good safety sense to hunt by myself, because too many things can happen in the woods. I know some of you may do it all the time. I mean, after all, you know the area like the back of your hand, right? I can assure you, I know the area I hunt very well, and I still always hunt with a friend.

First, regardless if you hunt alone or with a buddy, *always* carry a survival kit. You can buy a commercial one or make one yourself. When I hunt, I wear a survival vest, made from an old fishing vest. It has more than enough pockets and space for me to carry all the items I would need to survive for at least 48 hours. But make sure any kit you have along is a small minimum survival kit and not too heavy. Most commercial minimum survival kits will fit in a pocket. Also, if you are inexperienced with survival procedures, purchase a very small survival manual to take along with you.

Now, let's see how our man in the beginning of this article spends his lonely night in the field.

The man groaned with pain as he pulled his survival kit out of the cargo pocket on his left leg. He also removed his canteen from his belt and placed it on the ground beside his survival kit. Making sure his pant leg was off of the injured area of his swollen leg, he washed and cleaned the scrape he had sustained when he fell. Opening his first aid kit, he then cleaned the wound with an alcohol pad, and took two 500 mg pain relievers (per the instructions). After he took the medication, he carefully wrapped his leg injury with strips torn from his tee shirt to keep the scrape clean. Using the same tee shirt, he placed two pieces of wood (one on each side of his broken leg) and made a crude splint. He almost passed out from the pain before he had finished these small tasks.

He realized he was lucky in some ways. He was lying among some dead logs, and within a few minutes he had a very small fire going. While the night would be chilly, he had plenty of small pieces of wood to keep a teacup size fire going all night. With his leg broken, he knew making a shelter was out of question, but his survival kit had a space blanket in it and it could be wrapped around him to retain his body heat. He just had to keep the space blanket away from the fire. He also had his canteen, which was more than ¾ full, so water was not a problem. All in all, he realized, it could have been much worse.

The night was difficult due mostly to his pain. His leg had shot sharp waves of pain up his body each time he moved, and he had moved often. His biggest problem most of the night, was keeping faith that someone would come looking for him. All night he had fought back short periods of deep depression, sudden anxiety, and profound fear. But, deep inside, he knew he could and would survive until rescued. He had once attended a short survival class where the instructor talked about survival and psychology. He slowly remembered the instructor's words,

"**Panic is a real killer**. When you actually realize you are going to have to survive, keep your head about yourself. Stop. Find a place that offers you temporary shelter and think things out. Do not go stomping around in the woods looking for your way out. Just stop." The man realized the part about stopping had been decided for him. He had no option but to stay where he was. What else had the instructor said?

"Consider the, who, what, when, and where of your situation. Who knows where you are? Did you do as I recommend and tell someone about your trip? This should always be done, even if you know the area very well. Tell any person (a boss, friend, wife, husband, etc.) the what, when and where of your trip. They should know what type of trip it is (fishing, hunting, hiking, or travel), when you left and when you will return (i.e., I will leave on Tuesday morning and will return seven days later on Tuesday evening by eight), and where your trip is to be (to the National Forest or to Majestic Lake). Make sure, if you change your trip in any way, to call or contact the person you informed. Many rescues are started each year because of a change in plans and no notification. If you have handled the who, what, when and where of your trip, rescue should be fast."

The man groaned in pain once more as he thought of some other points the instructor had made. "**Always organize yourself.** Unless you are suicidal, this step is a must. Take an inventory of what you have on hand. This step serves two purposes. First, it calms you down. The time it takes to inventory your gear will assist in de-escalating your initial panic. Second, most of us carry a lot of "junk," as well as needed items with us, and this is a time to see exactly what you have. All items on you can be used toward survival. Keep all of it for future use."

The injured man popped two of the hard pieces of candy from his survival kit into his mouth as he remembered, "**Keep busy.**" An active mind is less likely to dwell on the situation as hopeless. Notice I wrote hopeless and not helpless. In a helpless situation, there is no help. While you very well may feel helpless, perhaps due to an injury, you can always help yourself to some degree. But, in a hopeless situation there is no hope. I think you always have hope, as long as you are breathing. *And, don't start feeling sorry for yourself.* It is normal for you to experience some panic or fear. You can expect all kinds of emotions to come out. Resist the negative thoughts and concentrate on the little successes you may experience, while letting the failures slide off. See, the more little successes you have the better you will start to feel. Start with something small, like a fire and a shelter.

A little later the injured man checked his watch and took another pain reliever per the instructions in his first aid kit. He also thought more about the survival class as he added some more wood to his fire. "**Find**

a shelter and start a fire." Do this even if you don't need either. Why? Well, once again for two reasons. The first is to keep you busy as I stated above. The second is they may be needed later when you are too exhausted or weak to make them. Additionally, there is a deep primal need for safety that is satisfied when you have shelter and fire. Ever notice how comforting a campfire is at night? The fire may not even be needed, so the comfort is usually just psychological. Additionally, a fire does not have to be large to attract the attention of those that may be searching for you, too. Anyway, always get a fire going, construct some type of shelter, and wait for them to come to you.

Well, he had a fire going and his shelter was wrapped tightly around him. He felt fairly warm and knew his own actions had helped him fight off a very uncomfortable night. He also realized that the information the instructor had provided had been true. Even with his leg broken, he had been able to treat his injury, start a fire, and find shelter. So, there is something that can be done in all situations after all.

He knew he had not slept but a couple of minutes all night when dawn broke over the nearby trees. It was only a few hours later when he was found by a search team, who had heard him blowing his survival whistle, and rushed him to a hospital. Later that day, in the comfort of his own home, he felt his exhausted face break into a smile as he told his wife how he had survived on his own, deep in the woods, with a broken leg. He also told her he owed his survival to his survival kit, a survival class he had once attended, and the fact he had told her where he was hunting that day.

Survival is never easy. The field can be unforgiving to those of us who are ill prepared, or lack the basic knowledge needed to enter and leave safely. If you spend time in the outdoors, always tell someone about your trip, when you will return, who is with you, and where you are going. It *could* save your life one day.

Rain and Survival, a Difficult Task

The lightening streaked out with long white angry fingers as it reached out in the dark early evening sky. A loud crash of thunder sounded in the forest a few seconds after the lightning flashed. The rain was falling harder now as the man looked desperately for some type of shelter. He was lost, and had been that way since the night before. Somehow, during the hunt that afternoon, he had become separated from his hunting buddy in an area he did not know. And, of course, he had not been carrying a map, compass, or survival gear with him. Now, after hours of chilling temperatures, it had started to storm.

While the man may not have had a survival kit or other needed items with him, he was far from helpless. He had been a Boy Scout in his younger days and also carried years of outdoor knowledge with him. As he mulled over his situation, he looked for shelter, and remembered what he knew about being lost. His first step was to stop and find shelter, according to the Scouts, and that he fully intended to do as soon as he found suitable shelter from the rain. It was then that he noticed a short squat pine tree mixed in with some much taller oak trees. He evaluated the oak limbs that were nearby and decided they were still alive and not likely to fall during the high winds of the storm.

Getting on his hands and knees he crawled up under the lower limbs of the pine and pulled out his razor sharp hunting knife. He noticed the area under his pine tree was completely dry and had not yet been affected by the storm. Quickly he trimmed a few of the bottom branches off and in a few moments he had room to sit. Under the tree he knew he would stay dry, unless the storm started pounding rain exceptionally hard. He could see his breath and realized the temperature had dropped dramatically in the last hour. He needed a fire.

He knew from the Boy Scouts that he would have been in good condition if he had carried a small plumber's candle. But he might as well wish for a million dollars, because he would not get either. He considered the dangers of having a fire under the pine and knew any fire he had would have to be extremely small, or he could set the tree on fire. Quickly using his knife once more, he dug two holes in the dirt, both about eight inches long and perhaps four inches wide. He made sure the holes were approximately eight inches deep. The digging of the holes warmed him up as he worked, and for the first time in more than twenty-four hours he was not cold or wet. Once his two fire pits were completed, he ventured back out into the angry talons of the storm.

Rain pelted his body as he located and removed pine sap, a light orange colored lump found on evergreen trees. Using his knife, he pried the sap loose and put it in his coat pocket so he would not lose it. Then, checking under other trees he removed as much "squaw wood" (small pieces of dry and dead wood) as he could carry. He soon returned to his shelter with his arms full of the wood. Of course it was wet now from the trek to the shelter, but not overly so and would dry soon enough.

As soon as he was back under the protective limbs of his tree, he pulled his knife and removed a few pieces of bark from the trunk of his shelter. He was careful not to completely circle the tree or he could kill it. He merely took two pieces of the dry bark that were about four inches long and an inch wide. Once more, using his knife he shaved the dried bark into very small and narrow pieces of tender. Now he had to think; how could he start the fire without matches? He had tender, kindling, and fuel, but what he needed was an ignition source.

He pulled everything he had from his pockets and stacked it beside him, next to the tree trunk. He found a half of a pack of gum, his car keys, wallet, an ink pen, and one pack of paper matches. He must have stuck them unknowingly into his pocket the morning before the hunt after fixing breakfast at camp. With his hands shaking with excitement, as well as not just a little fear, he opened the cover to the book of matches. There were three of them left and one was obviously very wet. He had two chances to get a fire going. He knew that his fire preparation had to be done properly, or he would be without a fire.

In the bottom of one fire pit, he would start one first, then use the flames from it to start the second one. He figured two very small fires would keep him warm and not be so dangerous as a single bigger one under the tree. He opened his wallet and removed some papers he did not need and shredded one of them up very fine. He then took the second one and tore slightly larger pieces. At that point, he placed a lump of the pine sap in the fire pit, placed a few pieces of the shredder paper and the shaved bark on top of it. He pulled a cartridge from his belt and very carefully removed the bullet with his knife. He used caution as he removed the lump of lead to insure the primer on the bottom of the brass shell was not struck. He sprinkled the gunpowder from the cartridge on his pine sap in the fire pit.

He pulled the first match from the book of matches and struck its head on the striker pad; it immediately burst into flame. His hand trembled as he placed the flame to the gunpowder. With a quick flash the dry powder ignited and the man, surprised by the flare up, dropped the still burning match. But he realized with anxiety filled eyes that he no longer needed the match, his fire was burning!

For the next few minutes, as his fire grew slowly in size, he would add slightly larger pieces of wood to the blaze. Once the first fire pit was burning well, he started the second one. The second fire pit was anti-climatic, when compared to the first, because his immediate need for fire had been satisfied. Of course, it did not hurt at all to know his chances for survival had gone up considerably with the first fire. He knew the moment the first fire pit ignited, he would survive.

The remainder of his night was very cold and uncomfortable. He did not sleep, as far as he knew, any longer than a few minutes at a time. The rain had quit sometime after midnight and it had grown much colder. Dawn was breaking as he added another small piece of wood to his fire. His clothing, still damp from the day before, seemed to cling to his skin. He was concerned about hypothermia and subconsciously moved closer to his two small fires. Holding his shaking hands over the small flames, he watched with aching eyes, as the fire danced and darted in the cold morning air. It was then he heard the voice calling his name.

Within ten minutes of yelling back at the voice, he was sitting before a large fire wrapped in a blanket, sipping on a hot cup of coffee, and nibbling on a chocolate bar. While his body temperature was low, he was not hypothermic yet. He gave a crooked smile as he looked over at his friend and knew his situation was over. He leaned back against a large log in front of the fire and decided he had learned a great deal from his wet night in the field. Never again would he venture out without a survival kit, poncho, and without at least a couple of high-energy bars. He had survived, this time, but would he be so lucky the next time?

Simple Survival

Survival in the woods is a serious matter of life and death. It is never easy, but can be much harder without the proper knowledge, equipment, and determination to survive. I suggest that all of you consider at least packing a survival kit and first aid kit anytime you go out. It could be the only life insurance policy you have.

Simple Survival Tips: Wooden matches can be dipped in wax to make them waterproof. Melt the wax on the kitchen stove and dip each match.

Ten Rules You Can Survive By!

Most of us who spend a lot of time in the woods, but rarely think about survival, are having too much fun. We spend days or perhaps even weeks living in the woods, hunting, fishing, hiking, or just camping out and do it all without a care in the world. I realize that is why most of us spend time with Mother Nature; however, as beautiful as the outdoors is, it can be a very harsh place for those who are not prepared. She can be deadly to the foolhardy. So to assist me when I am in the wilds I have developed the *Ten Rules to Survive By:*

Always be prepared to survive, always! No matter if you are just taking an afternoon hike on a designated trail in a National Forest, and you do not intend to get off of the beaten trail, make sure to take a survival kit. Additionally, carry clothing for changes in the weather; for instance, ponchos, hats and light jacket, even on days it looks like you won't need them. The weather can change a lot in just a few hours and in the mountains this change can occur in just a few minutes. Ensure any clothing, boots (I never wear sneakers in the woods), or gloves you carry fit properly and are in good condition. If you are an inexperienced outdoors person, take a small survival book (I like the British SAS survival manual for its size and information) along with a good first aid book. Both of these could save your life in an emergency.

Your kit should, *at a minimum* have the following items packed in it, or you should carry them on yourself,

- A quality penknife or jack knife
- A canteen, water bottle, or plastic freezer bags
- Water proof matches
- Flint and steel or a metal match
- Water purification tablets
- A long strip of heavy-duty aluminum foil folded up to cook with

- Fishing kit, i.e., hooks, sinkers, and some line. Nothing fancy.
- Commercial back packing first aid kit (with instructions). I carry a small first aid kit (I have placed a small hotel size bar of soap inside my kit).
- One small pack of gum and one pack of hard candy (for energy)
- Casualty blanket, sometimes called a thermal blanket
- Instant powder broth, beef or chicken, four servings total
- Survival whistle, small, made of plastic and with a lanyard
- Any prescription medications you might need or other components you feel you have to have along.

Always tell someone where you are going. Each year search and rescues are initiated for people lost in the woods and the effort is often made very difficult because the rescue team has no starting point. When you go outdoors, always tell someone the who, what, when, and where of your trip. An example might be telling your boss (who) that you and your wife are going camping (what) over the weekend (when) in Big Piney Mountains (where). I suggest you give even more details, such as the date and time you intend to leave as well as when you expect to return. I would also suggest telling more about where you are camping; the exact spot if you know the name of it would help.

If you become lost in the woods, or have to survive for any number of reasons, your first concern (unless the weather is really nasty) is finding safe drinking water. My reason for putting water so high on this list is due to the fact that the human body can only survive for around three days without water (depending on the ambient air temperature, of course). You can carry large zip-lock freezer bags, water bottles, or even rubber gloves to use as emergency containers if needed. I always carry a quart canteen on my web belt. Another aspect of water to consider is just how safe is the water you will be drinking? Even if the water source is crystal clear and fast moving, always treat drinking water with water purification tablets or boil it. If you use a commercial "water straw" or other filtering system, make sure it is rated to do the job you require of it.

Regardless of the weather, construct a shelter. Weather conditions can change quickly, as I said earlier, and you don't want to be caught out in a blizzard, rainstorm, or hailstorm, attempting to survive without a shelter. *And construct your shelter before the bad weather hits!* Another reason to construct a shelter is for psychological reasons. Mankind has a deep need for having a shelter on hand. Just seeing a shelter is often a great psychological relief and while it is not a home, it will assist in making the time you spend in an emergency situation that much more comfortable. I always carry a casualty blanket, and it can be used to make a shelter very quickly. Simply tie a line (from your survival kit) between two trees, about two feet off the ground, place the blanket over the line (centered), and stake the hanging ends of the blanket down using sharpened sticks. It will actually look like a pup tent. While not the best shelter for really cold weather, it will keep you dry in wet weather.

Unless the weather is extremely cold, I usually procure water and construct a shelter before I worry about this step, **making a fire**. While a fire is needed, its importance is often much over rated. Of course in cold weather you need a fire to keep warm and to avoid hypothermia, but in most cases we have a fire for purely psychological reasons. Remember to keep your fire burning in a fire pit and surround the pit with stones (in the winter this may not be possible, but you can make your fire on a platform of green logs). Keep your fire small and not too close to your shelter. Also, use only dry dead wood, because green or wet wood will smoke, burn slowly, and give off little heat. In wet weather you usually find dry wood (squaw wood) on the ground under the lower branches of big trees. Keep in mind it may be up near the base (trunk) of the tree. And, keep your fire safe by having water, snow, dirt, or sand available to use in case the fire gets out of hand.

If you experience an injury, regardless of how slight it might be, take care of it immediately. That means washing it with soap and water, disinfecting it with alcohol or other medication from your first aid kit (always carry a first aid kit with you in the field), and then covering the injury to keep it clean. You can cover most injuries with a simple band-aid; in other cases you may need to rip up some of your clean clothing. Keep the injury clean, too. Each day I suggest you remove the bandage, wash the injured area, disinfect it once more, and then re-cover it. Even the smallest cuts can quickly become infected if not properly cared for in the woods, so take care of all injuries immediately. And, always stay as clean as possible when you are in the field. Good hygiene will help keep you healthy.

Stay as dry as possible. It's my opinion that nothing causes more discomfort to a person in a survival situation like being wet, unless it is being both wet and cold. Gather all possible foods, procure all water, and gather plenty of wood before the bad weather hits, if possible. I realize in some situations you will not be able to do that. But, at the same time, use good common sense; if you don't need something immediately to survive, don't go out in the rain in an attempt to locate it. Stay under your shelter and wait for a break in the weather. Unlike at home, you can't throw your wet clothing in a dryer and wait twenty minutes for them to dry. It can take a very long time for your clothing to dry by a campfire and in the mean time you may be shivering in the cold, or perhaps even experience hypothermia (the lowering of the body's core temperature). Additionally, dry clothing will keep you warmer and feeling much better. A suggestion here; wool, Thinsolite ®, and Gore-Tex ® will all keep you dry and warm even when wet. Of the three types of material, wool is less expensive to purchase and does an excellent job even when soaking wet.

As soon as your immediate survival needs are met, start construction of some sort of signals. Keep in mind, the idea behind a signal is to draw attention to your position. You can do this by using contrasts in color, shapes, or sunlight. For instance, a large "X" could be made by piling snow up in an open field (make the signal at least eighteen feet long and three wide if possible). The "walls" of this signal will cast a shadow (if the sun is out) and should be visible to aircrew members flying nearby, so the higher the signal is, the bigger the shadow. On cloudy or hazy days, make three small fires and place them so they resemble a triangle (with a fire at each corner). Keep one fire burning all the time and the other two ready to light immediately. When you hear an aircraft flying near, add pine boughs or grasses to make the fires flare up (be careful not to let your fire get out of hand at this point or of being burned). Keep the pre-cut boughs close to the fire, but not so close they could catch fire accidentally. The sudden flare of the fires, from the added pine boughs, as well as the color of the smoke will attract attention. Keep your signal mirror, whistle, or other emergency signaling equipment from your survival kit **on you at all times**.

One aspect of survival most folks never consider is hygiene. Unlike a normal camping situation, if you get ill from poor hygiene in a survival situation you are not running off to the doctor or emergency room for treatment. And, survival hygiene is much more than just keeping clean; it also takes some thought.

In the field during normal conditions, I shave and wash daily because I feel better. This may not be possible in a survival situation, but it is important to stay clean to avoid infections from small cuts. Also, designate a toilet area and make sure everyone with you uses it. Locate your "bathroom" away from your immediate survival site (I suggest a hundred feet) and not near any source of water. Additionally, don't locate your toilet uphill from your camp. Wastewater, urine and dirty wash water (if you are lucky enough to have enough water to wash with) will run down hill. When the temperatures are mild, make sure everyone uses loosened soil to cover human waste; it will keep the flies and other insects down (not to mention the smell).

Clean all foods and treat all drinking water prior to using. Dirty food and "bad" water can lay you low in no time at all. Just like home, wash your hands (if you have enough water to do so) prior to preparing meals, keep any utensils you use clean (even if it is only a pocket knife), and keep your survival site clean of bones, scraps of food, and waste. Poor hygiene will not only lay you low, it could keep you low for a very long time.

Finally, consider your mental health. Humans are creatures of groups and as such, we tend to suffer from anxiety when separated from others. In a survival situation, separation is why we are where we are. A mishap has occurred that has placed you outside our society. You must fight back against unhealthy thoughts as you attempt to survive. Remember, people are looking for you and if you just stay safe, they will eventually find you. Keep reminding yourself that they will find you! It is normal for you to experience periodic feelings of helplessness, deep concern, anxiety, or even a deep fear. The key is for you to stay as busy as possible and not to dwell on those feelings. Stay active and remind yourself at times on the progress you are making toward your own survival. Concentrate on successes and not failures. You can expect some failures; so don't keep harping on them over and over again, because it will just wear you down mentally.

Survival is difficult at the best of times. The ceaseless struggle of trying to stay alive, the constant battle with our own minds, and even keeping the will to survive can be very difficult tasks. I suggest while these steps in themselves will not keep you alive, they will give you a better understanding of what can needs to be done in a survival situation. However, I do believe if you follow my ten steps to survival, you too will survive!

SURVIVING TERRORISM

With the threat of a terrorist act happening in America being very real today, it is wise to prepare. No, I am not suggesting we all get paranoid, but simply prepare. See, in survival, the big key is being prepared. If you have your equipment ready and your mind prepared, your chances of surviving are greatly increased. Not to mention the fact that you are usually much more comfortable if prepared.

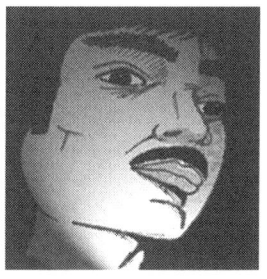

When acts of terror occur, they usually happen when we expect them the least. This surprise comes from the fact that as Americans we have lived pretty safe lives in the past, and also because terrorists plan it that way for maximum effect. The less people suspect an act of violence, the more damaging the results. This is especially true of the psychological affects. Remember the terrible feelings all of us experienced when we first heard of the attack on the Twin Towers? Most of us felt deep shock, confusion, anger, and a very profound fear. Those feelings are exactly the type of psychological responses a terrorist hopes to achieve with an attack.

I recommend that all of us, to various degrees, organize our homes in the event of future attacks. I believe most professionals who deal with terrorists, well tell us that it is only a matter of time before we are subjected to more attacks. An attack could affect our water supply, our fresh foods, and even the air we breathe. As the cowardly attack on New York demonstrated, terrorists have a very vivid imagination. An attack could consist of any conceivable weapon at any location. So, just what can we do to prepare our homes and loved ones if something should happen?

Start getting ready now, not tomorrow. Remember what I said above, an attack will most likely happen when you least suspect it. Take a look around your house. If you live like most people, you have many things you can use for emergencies on hand right now. But do you have special clothing, canned foods, first aid items, battery or self powered radio, or other things that could be placed in storage for emergency use? Don't get paranoid and put everything you own in the closet for emergency use, just those items you seriously don't use much. Limit it to items you may need later. Also, remember most of the things I am listing here you already have in use in your household.

What types of things should you consider storing? I have broken it down to some very simple items. Keep in mind, each household has different supply requirements and the purpose of this article is to get you thinking about an emergency. One of the things you need to consider is the needs' of yourself and your family. If you have a handicapped member, or a person with special needs (i.e. medication or special care), you may have to evaluate your situation much closer than most people. But for most of us we need the same things we need to survive in the bush.

Food is always on the top of most people's desires during survival. I know most of it is psychological, but regardless, the desire is very deep in all of us. Food leads us to feeling content and that all is well around us. I prefer to keep Meals Ready to Eat, MRE's, on hand. I ate them by the hundreds in the military and they are actually quite good. I keep the complete meals on hand, because I eat them a little at a time to get the maximum enjoyment out of one pouch (the meal lasts longer that way).

Other options are air-dried foods; they last a long time and are cost effective. I recommend them for those who wish to feed more than two people and for those who want a large quantity of a single food item they may prefer.

Freeze dried foods are pretty good, too, in my humble opinion. The only drawback to them is the water needed in preparation. If your water source is limited freeze-dried foods are not a wise choice. Never eat dehydrated foods without lots of water on hand; your body will take water from your system to process waste. You can find all different kinds of menu items offered commercially.

One last area I want to suggest you evaluate is a B-4 unit (Basic 4 food groups, wheat, dairy, sugar, & salt, necessary for meal preparation), which has various food items in large #10 cans. Also, you can buy canned goods in bulk at any supermarket and keep the cans boxed for easy storage. I usually buy veggies, canned meats and fruits in cans. As long as I don't have to pack them very far and can stack them to the roof, I go for the bulk foods.

Regardless of the type of foods you prefer, remember to maintain a healthy diet. Make sure you get as close to the daily minimums as you can (keep vitamins stored, too). Actually, if you can afford to do so and have the storage space, go beyond the daily minimums. If you can store the foodstuffs, why go hungry? Plus, remember, in a survival situation we tend to burn more calories just attempting to stay alive.

Once our food problem is behind us, we can start considering what I feel is our primary concern, water. The first step here is to procure several large water storage containers. Depending on the number of people you are responsible for you will need to evaluate your water needs carefully. Most survival professionals will recommend a bare minimum of a gallon a day. You will need much more if you plan on cooking and washing in it, or if the temperature goes way up. Make sure your water containers are designed to store water in and are not discarded chemical containers. Mark each container in large letters, WATER ONLY, and store only water in these containers.

Another tool you will need to have on hand is a water filtration system. A chemical attack on your primary water source may prevent you from being able to use it, so you may have to use water from ponds, lakes, or streams. There are many different types of filters available and at various costs. The key here is, once again, the number of people who will need good clean drinking water. Remember, filtering systems will not protect you from nuclear fallout or some types of chemical agents. If you believe you have sustained an attack in one of those two categories, use pre-stored or packaged (canned, bottled or in bags) water.

Prepackaged water is sold in different quantities. I have seen water sold in pouches, plastic two liter bottles, and in cans. The size of the container may vary, but most survival pouches or cans are around ten to twelve ounces. I recommend everyone have some prepackaged water placed in storage as a precaution. It is relatively inexpensive and it could become your only source of clean, safe water. Once again, you need to evaluate the number of people and their water needs.

Finally, my old favorite, water purification tablets. I keep a bottle in my survival vest, in my tackle box, in my truck, and in the house. They are easy to use; just drop two tablets in the water container, usually a canteen, but check on the label to see how much water the tablets treat. An old vet trick here, add a little flavored drink powder to your treated water to mask the chemical smell and taste.

Let's see, we have food and we have water...I think our next concern is clothing. If an attack happens with no warning, you may have to react very quickly. You may have set aside a portion of your basement, garage, or other area for emergency storage, so you need to store special clothing items there. You may not have the time to look for jackets, rain gear, or special boots. Keep what you need stored and never use it for day-to-day use. Keep in mind, all the equipment there is for emergencies only. Aren't your day-to-day clothes good enough? Nope, not at all.

I feel that survival gear should be tough and comfortable. That is why during most of my outdoor trips I wear military surplus or heavy jeans. I have discovered that cheap imitations of military gear fall short in the long run. I wear some of my old Battle Dress Uniforms (BDU's) and they are perfect. Remember, BDU's have been proven tough, even in combat. I don't plan to fight wars any more, but that makes them strong enough for most survival situations. Jeans are good too, but usually are too tight and restrictive, compared to BDU's . Also, with jeans you don't get all the pockets to put survival items in. Another added incentive for me to buy BDU's is the low cost when compared to jeans.

Other clothing requirements will depend on where you live. If you need rain gear often, then have it available. If your area gets little rain, then decide on what you do need. Consider socks, underwear (perhaps long and insulated), parkas, gloves, good quality boots, and the list goes on. In all situations have a cap, a wide brimmed hat, and at the very least, a nylon windbreaker. Even the desert can get cold at night.

The biggest key to survival clothing is making sure what you store is tough and comfortable. If needed, and in a pinch, you can use sheets, blankets and rope to make some additional items of clothing. Nope, I agree, you won't win any best-dressed awards from Hollywood wearing it, but you can survive with it. If needed, you can always do like our forefathers had to do; if you don't have it on hand, make it. Keep your imagination moving and active!

What about cooking? Yep, we are back to food once more. You have the stored foods, but how can you prepare them? Well, hopefully your electric or gas stove will still work. Determine in advance if you have a separate tank of propane for your gas stove. You should know that by the bills from the company that periodically fills the tank. If you have a tank, the odds are it will still work. However, depending on the target of a terrorist attack, you may be without electrical power or a source of gas for cooking. If this is all that happens then you don't have much of a real problem, except one of comfort (and perhaps the loss of some refrigerated foods). That is, as long as you are prepared with the items I discuss. Make sure before using ANY gas appliance you check for gas leaks. If you smell gas or suspect a leak, do NOT use any open flames. Do not use a charcoal grill or other open flames in the house or in a closed space; ventilation is required to avoid carbon monoxide poisoning.

The MRE's we discussed above can be eaten uncooked and so can many of the other emergency food items. While not very palatable or appetizing, they are safe to eat. I, however, always had a problem eating MRE's cold. They seemed to give me indigestion and heartburn. Each individual is different, but they can be eaten uncooked with no serious side affects.

I recommend that you use the perishable food from the fridge first. Save your canned or stored foods for later use if need be. Use the meats, veggies, and other stuff way before you hit your survival items. Also, if you have ice, place foods in a container before they thaw completely out. They will stay high quality longer if they are stored in a good quality ice chest before they are thawed out.

In your inventory sheet for your survival items be sure and list what you think are the bare necessities. Consider plastic or normal ceramic plates (not paper), eating utensils, pots, pans, drinking glasses, cups, and any other special items you may want. I suggest these items because in today's society many people live off of paper plates and the microwave. Remember to include a can opener, or you will have to discover an alternate method of opening and most are messy. Many of the items you may need can be taken from your normal day-to-day utensils, so you will not have to purchase them. This will also keep your cost down. Nonetheless, list what you have on hand.

If you are without a stove, you may have to cook outside, if it is safe to do so. I would never cook indoors with an open flame due to the dangers of carbon monoxide poisoning. I just don't feel it is worth the risk. I will write other articles on outdoor cooking, as well as fire starting, and you will find them in future updates of the Survival, Search and Rescue Web Site. Make sure you use good fire safety sense and control your fire.

Okay, let's look at sanitation and waste methods. All of us will need to use the toilet at times, but you may use it less often in survival situations. For some medical reason the production of human waste is slowed down when the diet is reduced and stress is increased. I could get into why, but all you need to know is that it is normal for most of us. Nonetheless, you have to prepare for human waste disposal. If your water is working, all is great. If your water source is not there, you may have a slight problem.

I suggest you store a portable toilet with your survival items. No, it is not really needed, but many men, women and children, just do not like alternate methods. You can buy a toilet commercially, or go back in history and make a honey bucket. A honey bucket is a large bucket used to collect human waste. It can be a mop bucket, or an empty coffee can. Regardless of which choice you make, sooner or later, someone will be forced to empty the thing.

Make sure human waste is not discarded along rivers, streams, lakes, or other potential sources of drinking water. Select a spot that is a good distance from your living area. In the old days in Europe, before gunpowder was popular, the flight of an arrow was considered a good distance for toilets. And that was only popular and followed by a select few.

You can buy biodegradable toilet tissue, sanitizing chemicals, and other accessories as you feel the need. Remember, if need be a magazine or newspaper can do the same job as tissue. Yes, I am as concerned about nature as the next person, perhaps more so, but we are talking about survival here. If you centralize your dumping spot, it will be easier to clean up your waste once the emergency is over.

One last item and I will get off of my soapbox. A list of additional miscellaneous items I think would be helpful.

- A portable radio with extra batteries or a Solar or wind-up powered one.
- Condoms for water storage, un-lubricated.
- Good quality blankets and sleeping bags (make sure they are adequate for your temperature zone).
- Any prescription medications your family may need. Make sure you check the expiration dates. Talk to your doctor about special needs you may have.
- A good professional type first aid kit, with booklet or manual. You may be the only medical help available in an emergency.

- A good survival manual or book (I recommend one from our service branches or the British SAS). Videos are great, too, but they are of no use if you are without power.

- Several boxes of waterproof matches and a lighter.

- A small waterproof match container that can be carried in a pocket. This could come in handy if you have to leave the survival area looking for food or water. Or a magnesium fire starter, along with some type of tender (cotton lint from the dryer).

- Any items you or your family may need in an emergency (medication or diet concerns).

The lists of items I have suggested in this article are just that, suggestions. In no way am I suggesting this list is complete for any and all emergency survival situations. I want you to think about what you need. While each individual is different and unique, so is each family. Keep in mind; you may have to improvise to survive.

In today's uncertain world, we are susceptible to terrorist acts from a single person or large groups. We face the risks of the types of attacks history has never seen before. Our choice is simple; we can live in fear and cringe each time the power goes off, or we can be prepared. We can prepare by storing what we will need and preparing our minds on how we will survive. Once the emergency hits, while others are attempting to buy what they need in crowded stores, if they can find one open, we will be comforted in knowing we have what it takes to survive. Be a survivor.

All Wet

During the early American migration across the United States, a primary concern of these early travelers was finding good drinking water.  Most of us never consider the countless people who died from the want of water. Many more of us don't even realize how many more died or became seriously ill from drinking bad water. Water; many of us take it for granted every day. We use it by the gallons and we waste it by the gallons. Why? Because it is always there when we want it.

In today's society, our water supply (North America) is as about as pure as it can be. Sure, in some areas we can smell or taste the chemicals that are used to treat it. I will not get into how safe your individual water is, or your local water treatment procedures, other than to say it is usually safe enough for us to drink. But how safe is your water when you camp or if you have to survive for any period of time?

Let's look at a couple of things to keep in mind about water. First, all water is not equal. This is true in all areas of North America. Some water, while looking pure, may be filled with what I call "micro-critters." Now, I will not get into the various things that can be found in water; it bores me and would you. (But they are ugly under a microscope). Besides, I don't remember most of the names and know I could not even begin to spell them (I would have stayed in the third grade if not for spell check). Nonetheless, untreated water may be filled with micro-critters. Second, use some common sense here and treat all water, unless you bring it from home or bought it in a store. Treat it all as if it is not safe to drink.

Well, I suspect some of you are thinking about using fresh rain water, right? No need to treat it because it is fresh and clean? Think about that for a bit. With acid rain and pollution, do you really think that is a very good idea? Or maybe the tarp or cloth you use to collect it in is dirty or contaminated by a substance. Sure, it may be pure and then again it may not be. I avoid rainwater because it is just too hard for me to bottle. Regardless, if you are forced to use any water of unknown quality, treat it.

Simple Survival

If you have to use water that nature provides, use water that is fast moving. This should not be a problem for those of us living in the far north. Make sure your water of choice is as clear looking as you can find. While having clear looking water is no assurance it is safe to drink, it is easier to drink water that looks like the water we usually drink. Avoid water from swamps, ponds, or stagnate spots (like puddles or hollow tree stumps). Also, avoid water sources near your designated toilets. I always get my water downstream at least one hundred feet from our camp site (even water not intended for drinking). While this is still no guarantee the water is safe, I know what a group of youngsters can do to and in the water in front of my camp site.

Store all good drinking water in marked containers that are sold for that purpose only. Make sure *all your fellow campers* know what water is for drinking only. Do not use containers that have previously held dangerous chemicals, alcohol, gasoline or other possible toxic substances. It would be easy to have good drinking water contaminated by residue in the container. And you might not even realize what is happening to you until you get ill. Remember, use only commercially designated water containers.

There are many different ways to treat water. There are commercial filters that keep the "critters" out (some are almost as small as a drinking straw), you can boil it for XX number of minutes for each thousand feet you are above sea level, use chlorine, or commercial water purification tablets. By now some of you know me and already have an idea of which one I would use...yep, the tablets. Seems the filters cost too much, I can never remember how long to boil it or how high I am above sea level, and I don't like to juggle measurements of chemicals. So, I use the tablets for my drinking water. It is very simple. Just follow the directions on the bottle label the tablets come in. It works for me.

Now, little secret you Vets know. If you treat your water it will taste like it has been treated, especially in a metal canteen. Additionally, it will have bit of a chemical smell to it. Many Veterans know that you can mask this taste and slight smell by adding just a little powdered drink to it. I like the cherry drink, so I add the powder to my canteen. Of course, I do not treat the primary container, just my individual canteen. That keeps the main container clean for everyone's usage and lets us treat our canteens with our individual powders.

In an emergency, if the water you have to drink is slightly muddy or murky you may have to filter it before you can drink it. This can be water from a river or other source. I hate "hard water" (a little muddy looking), so I carry a small piece of cloth with me to work as a filter. This "thick" water may have to be filtered a number of times before it looks good enough for you to even consider drinking. If that still doesn't seem to work, you can construct a filter using many different layers of sand, small pebbles and cloth. This type of filter will usually help the water look better, but it is still not safe to drink. Or, after you filter it you can just let it set for a while. The sediments will eventually settle to the bottom of your container. Keep in mind that once it looks good, it will still need to be treated. *And, one note on the use of emergency water; if you are not in an emergency, don't use it.* Additionally, if you use emergency water, attempt to bring a sample back home with you and give it to your doctor. Bad water is nothing to play with.

Water, we use it every day and we waste it every day as well. When we camp, our water supply suddenly becomes much more important, regardless if we realize it or not. Bad water can cause illnesses as minor as diarrhea or others that are much more severe. In some cases bad water can even be life threatening. Remember to drink only safe water from home or bottled water that has been purchased. If you must use what nature supplies or if you are unsure of its purity either do not use it, or treat it. I always think of the old survival adage about water and food, "If in doubt, throw it out." It is just not worth the risk. Y'all stay safe and have a fun summer.

Where's the Water?

While we may have many needs during survival, most of what we want is simply desired items. We want more or better food, a bigger or better shelter, and the list goes on. Usually, what we have will keep us alive until rescued, but not always. Our actual needs vary and depend on the climate we are surviving in. In all cases though, we will need (not necessarily in this order) food, shelter and water, at a minimum. Water; do you know how to find it in the wild?

Do you know you can live three weeks or more without food while drinking only water? Do you know that in the heat of the desert you can die from the lack of water in as little as a few hours? Water; it is the basis of our being. It is important for most of us to drink two to three quarts of good clean water a day. Also, it is important in survival situations for us to retain what body fluids we already have.

Immediately, once you know you will have to survive, find a shady spot to rest and think. Consider your survival options in the shade and not in the sun, even if the day is not very hot. Do not sit on the hot rocks or the hot ground. Avoid talking anymore than you have to, and breath through your nose; you will lose less water that way. Stay out of direct sunlight and either cut back or stop eating. Foods speed up the dehydration process. The body takes moisture from itself to process waste. And, keep in mind not to drink coffee, tea, or alcohol at all. All three speed up dehydration. Check your urine for color each time you go. If the urine turns brown in color you are dehydrating. These hints will assist you in retaining what fluids your body has stored.

Well, you know you need water, but where do you find it? If you are lucky you may be near a stream, river, lake or a spring. Then, water is not much of a problem. You should also consider snow, rainwater, hail or sleet as possible water sources. Additionally, you can use trapped water if necessary from stumps, holes in rocks, ponds, or even mud puddles. This trapped water should be your last choice and used only in an emergency. Some water may have debris floating in it or contain grasses and stems. You can filter it easily.

If you use trapped water or water from a pond, you may have to filter it. Set up a tepee by sticking three limbs in the ground, tie the tops together and make three platforms from material. In the top platform place grasses, the second platform should have sand, and the third platform should contain ground-up charcoal from your fire. Make sure all three platforms have a drooping center and under the bottom platform you need a container to catch the filtered water. *Remember to purify the water by boiling or use chemicals (I always carry water purification tablets) before drinking.*

Do not take water that has "scum" floating on it, or dead vegetation around it. Also, in the desert check any water you find for excessive amounts of salt. Many desert lakes or ponds may contain a high level of salt in the water. If the water "bubbles" or if it has an unnatural color or smell, avoid it if possible. Always try to take your water from fast moving sources and take only clear, clean looking water. *Purify all water you take from the environment.*

What do you do when you don't have any water? You have looked and can't find any rivers or streams. How do you find water? Do you know where to look for water? Try searching low areas around you. Water will sometimes pool in low areas. Also, on the side of a hill look for eroded places where the water has run down during a heavy rain. Follow the drainage downhill and maybe to a source of water.

Also, you can often find water by digging at the lowest point on the outside bend of a dried up streambed or riverbed. Do your digging in the cool of the evening and not during the heat of the day. You may lose what body fluids you have digging and there is no assurance water will be found. Use your head to stay cool.

Also, go to a high spot around you and take a look around. Do you see a line of trees by themselves? This row of trees may seem out of place or all alone. Do you see a spot of lush grass? Both of those may indicate sources of water, perhaps a small puddle (grasses) or a river (trees). If not, don't panic yet. Look around yourself very cautiously, with a critical eye.

Do you see animal tracks? They may indicate the direction of a water source, especially if more than one trail leads in the same direction. All animals have to drink, though it may be infrequent when compared to humans, so consider the tracks. Or, you can watch birds early or late in the day. The movement of birds (flight direction) may indicate the direction of a water source. Finally, if you can, watch for a swarm of insects, especially bees. They may be located near water. I have even heard of columns of ants leading to water. Most animals and insects will be around water at different times. Keep your eyes and ears open for any sign of movement.

Now, if you are in snow country, do not eat the snow. It will lower your body temperature, speed up dehydration, and may even cause injury to your lips (cracked or chaffed skin) if done over a long enough period of time. Always melt ice and snow before you consume it. Usually, the best way to melt the snow or ice is to place it in a container near the fire. While ice can easily be melted, snow can actually scorch. I know from experience that scorched snow has a terrible taste and smell. If you have a choice, take ice over snow.

Finally, a few things you should *not* do. Do not drink urine. It is a waste product of a body and is just that, waste (think about that for a second...when a body passes urine, it is no longer need or useful). Drinking urine can even make you sick. Also, avoid drinking unpurified water if at all possible. Even clear and clean looking water may contain water borne diseases such as dysentery, cholera, or typhoid (this is why it is important to keep your immunizations up to date). All water should be boiled or treated with chemicals to make it safe to drink.

You will be better off if you sip a little water frequently than if you drink a large amount at one time. Check your urine color to make sure you are staying hydrated, and watch for the dark urine. Remember to stay in the shade, and do as little moving as possible, so you can conserve what fluids your body has already. Think smart, and move only when you have to.

Finding drinking water is not that difficult in most of North America, although it can prove to be a problem in the southwestern part of the United States and in some other isolated areas. However, water is usually all around you. Keep in mind what you have learned in this article and you too can find water when you need it.

Winter Water,
How to Make Your Own

The snow was falling faster now, as I made my way back to camp. The temperature had dropped quickly also, so I was becoming chilled. Snowflakes the sizes of a quarter were falling lazily in the evening air. Off in the distance I could see the smoke from our campfire, so I knew one of the men that had accompanied me on the hunting trip had returned early. I just hoped that he had the coffee pot on, or even had enough sense to melt some snow or ice for water. The small stream that ran by the camp had frozen over the day before.

When camping in the winter, water can be at a premium, while at the same time it looks like with all the ice and snow, water would not be a problem. I agree, it is not a serious problem, if you know what to do and how to do it properly.

If you have a choice between using ice or snow, always choose ice first. Ice will give you more water than snow of equal size. Also, ice is usually cleaner and may not require filtering before you use it. The big problem with snow is that small twigs, rocks, and other foreign objects may be in it. Ice is usually from a stream, tree limb, or other water source and not on the ground.

Okay, now you have either ice or snow, how is the best way to melt it? I carry an old white (I do not recommend a different color because the dye may bleed) pillowcase with a very small hole in one corner of the sewed end. Make sure it is at the very tip. I then hang the pillowcase near but not over the fire. The heat from the fire will melt the ice or snow, and as long as you have a container under the pillowcase, it will catch the dripping liquid.

If you have to melt snow or ice in a container over a bed of coals, avoid scorching. If the container becomes too hot, the resulting water will taste burned. I usually move just a few red coals over and place my melting container on top of the coals. I constantly move the snow or ice to keep it from burning. Also, snow will have to be pushed down into the container occasionally.

When using snow that needs cleaning, I will filter the water through two layers of cloth to make sure it is clean of bits and pieces from the ground. As I stated earlier, ice may not need filtering at all. Even though you have filtered the snow or ice, it is still not safe to drink as is. All water not from a known clean source should be purified with purification tablets, or by boiling. Keep in mind that even clean looking streams, lakes and rivers, may not be a safe source of healthy drinking water. Always purify any water from unknown safe sources.

Also, do not melt snow or ice in your mouth to quench your thirst. While often seen in movies, this is just basically dumb. Using your mouth will not only lead to chapped lips, but will also lower your body temperature. The heat used to melt the ice or snow will come from your core temperature, thus lowering it in the process. Another old trick that you may have heard of is to fill a container with snow or ice, place it in your shirt and allow your body heat to melt it. Well, speaking from experience here, it works...but you will get a terrible chill. There are easier ways to melt ice or snow. Both of these procedures could seriously affect you, if you are close to experiencing hypothermia (the lowering of the body's core temperature).

In a survival situation, you should keep in mind that you might have to do whatever it takes to procure good drinking water. You may even be forced to use the high-risk procedures that I have not recommended, i.e., melting snow in your mouth or using body heat to melt snow. I suggest that a person who is prepared will not have to resort to risky techniques to survive except in the most unusual situations.

Additionally, most folks never consider dehydration a problem in the arctic or in cold regions, but it can be a serious problem. Since it is cold, most folks just naturally take in less water, or only drink coffee. Limiting your water intake will dehydrate you very quickly and coffee will do the same. The body uses water from its tissues and organs to process coffee into waste (urine). Avoid alcohol for the same reason (unlike in the movies, never give alcohol to a victim of the cold). You can tell if you are becoming dehydrated by the color of your urine (dark brown urine is a sure sign of dehydration).

Another area to consider when using ice or snow is making sure it is not near your toilet area. Never use ice or snow downhill from where you designated bathroom is. Urine, dirty wash water, and other waste may melt through the snow, especially if you heat water to wash with, and run under the top layer of snow. Additionally, when the temperature warms a bit, it will all slide down hill on you anyway.

Water in cold areas is a small problem if you use good common sense. Remember not use your body to melt snow, filter water if needed, and always add purification tablets or boil any water you get from ice or snow. Make sure you know the source of your ice and use only "clean" snow. Avoid burning your water source by stirring it and to keep your fire low. By using these simple rules, your winter camping experience can be a real joy, instead of a nightmare.

EMERGENCY SURVIVAL SHELTERS

The weather had changed quickly. The once clear sky was now filled with dark moving clouds, and large flakes of snow had started falling over an hour ago. When I had started my hunt earlier that day, the weather had been perfect. I shuddered as I realized I would not have time to find the truck before darkness fell. It looked like I would have to spend the night in the bush. Nonetheless, spending the night was much safer than meandering around in the dark woods with snow falling. As tired as I was, I knew what had to be done.

My first step was to get organized *before* it became dark. While it is possible to establish an emergency campsite in the dark, it is much more difficult. Plus, with bad weather approaching it was important that I find all the dry firewood I could, and quickly.

Looking around, I was able to find a spot in a group of oak trees that was pretty much out of the wind. I made sure there were no dead tree limbs overhead that could fall on me during the night.

I quickly gathered up kindling for the fire, as well as a full nights worth of firewood. I knew the night would be cold, so I added a little more to the pile than I would usually have. I scraped the snow off the ground, dug a small fire pit, and started a fire. I filled my metal canteen cup with water and put it to boil near the fire as I started on other chores.

Snow was falling faster now as I opened my backpack and took out a poncho and a roll of nylon cord, approximately twenty feet. I tied the cord between two tree trunks and then draped the front of the poncho over the cord. Using the grommets on the poncho, I secured the poncho to the line. (You can also use a casualty blanket.) I then used sharpened stakes to pin the other end of the poncho to the ground. I now had a shelter from the snow and what little wind that was blowing.

While survival was not longer an issue, I wanted a little comfort to go along with my evening in Mother Nature's hotel. In just a few minutes I have removed some green cedar boughs from nearby trees and had placed them inside my shelter. To keep the boughs from irritating my skin, and making sleep more difficult, I covered them with my space blanket. The boughs would form a rough mattress for my nights sleep and insulate me from the cold ground.

Since I *always* carry a survival kit containing foods and emergency supplies, I was prepared for the evening. I soon had a cup of coffee and a banquet of dehydrated stew (dehydrated meals are light and inexpensive to carry). I finished my meal with a piece of hard candy, which I knew was not only a treat, but also a way to increase my body heat. I felt much better with the fire burning, a hot meal inside of me, and a shelter behind me. I was content.

As soon as the meal was done, I picked up my cell phone and called my wife. I informed her that I would not be home that night, explained why, and told her exactly where I was, or as near as I figured I was. I further informed her I was safe, had a shelter, and would call her in the morning as soon as I reached the truck. I did this to avoid a search and rescue mission being call to look for me, and to give her peace of mind.

The next morning dawned clear and bright, with snow covering the landscape. In less than an hour I reached my truck, called my wife, and was on my way. Not a bad situation at all, if you are prepared.

SIMPLE SURVIVAL SHELTERS

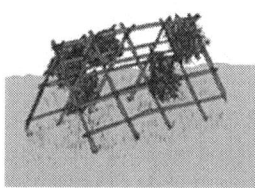

We frequently go out in the extreme cold and snowy country to backpack, hunt, fish, or just to see the beauty. As a result, we often find ourselves miles from anyone or anyplace as we travel. While the day may start out nicely, it only takes a short period of time for the weather to turn bad, and we will be forced to seek shelter quickly. But do you really know how to construct a shelter in arctic like conditions? Could you survive until the weather clears, or help arrives? I do, thanks to a variety of United States Air Force Survival Courses.

There are many different types of cold weather shelters that a person can construct and some take only minutes to prepare. I suggest, even if the amount of snowfall is sufficient, that most people avoid building an igloo. I have found them difficult for most of us to construct. I have found other types of cold weather emergency shelters that work just as well and take less effort to construct.

The first shelter, a "tree pit" shelter is by far the fastest and easiest to construct (I always suggest this shelter in any article I write about winter or arctic survival). As heavy snow falls, it covers the branches of large trees. Under the tree's lowest branches, however, there is usually a "pit" where no snow, or very little, has reached. Usually, all a survivor has to do is clear away what little snow may be there, and perhaps remove a few lower branches and the shelter is almost completed. I suggest building the shelter up by positioning poles around the trunk of your chosen tree (like the frame of a tee-pee) and then covering it with pine boughs. Or, if you have the material, cover these poles with a tarp or poncho, then layer with boughs, and add snow when you are done (I always carry a casualty blanket in my survival kit that works well for this). This will aid in insulating the shelter and help block the wind.

While constructing this shelter, avoid knocking the snow off of the lower branches that you have left intact. The snow on the tree branches will further insulate the shelter. Remember to cover the floor of the shelter with about fourteen inches of pine boughs to insulate it as well. Nothing ruins a good nights sleep like a cold sleeping platform. The drawback with this type of shelter is the lack of a fire pit. A campfire is not recommended due to the hazards associated with the tree limbs. Make sure you make a ventilation hole in the shelter to allow carbon monoxide to escape if you are using a candle or other portable heating device. All shelters should be well ventilated at all times.

Another type of shelter to consider is a simple A frame. This shelter is quickly constructed and is easily made. Once again, if you have a poncho or a tarp, the shelter is done in no time. Another survival item that I usually carry that helps greatly is about twenty-five feet of cord. The type of cord used is up to you, but I prefer nylon parachute cord (550 cord) because it is lightweight and strong enough for most tasks. The cord can simply be run between two trees about two feet off of the ground and secured to the two trees. Then the material can be draped over the line and secured to the ground. Make sure all stubs and sharp points are removed from any limbs you are using to avoid puncturing the material and to avoid head injuries once in the shelter.

If you do not have material to work with, position a long limb between two trees and secure it at each end. Your next step is to construct a rough frame once you have the top pole in position. I suggest you use two poles, crossed at the point where the top is at both the front and rear of your shelter. Then, secure two horizontal poles on each side to make the structure stronger. To make the walls of your shelter, position pine boughs or limbs, standing up along the sides of the frame. Remember to follow the angles of the shelter so the shelter resembles the letter A when viewed from the front. Once the frame is completed, the walls added, you should now cover the shelter with snow. Keep in mind that snow, though it seems very cold, makes a great insulator for shelters.

A fire pit can be made near the shelter, and I recommend you use heat reflectors (boulders or a stack of logs, one on top of the other) to reflect heat back to your shelter. Make this fire pit no closer than 10 feet to your shelter. It is also important to line the floor of your shelter with pine boughs to protect you from the chill of sleeping on a cold ground. Place your gear and enough fire starting materials in the shelter immediately after construction. This provides you with enough wood to get a morning fire going, as well as prevents gear being lost. Falling snow will quickly cover any object left unattended in a very short time.

One shelter I use most of the time is a simple lean-to. This type of shelter is great when you need a shelter quickly, or if there is not enough snow for making a true arctic shelter. I simply tie a cord between two trees, just as I explained in the A frame shelter above. I then drape about a foot of a tarp or poncho over the line, tie a cord to the grommets on the ends of the material and run the cord down to two stakes I have stuck securely into the ground. My next step is to use stakes at the other end of the material to secure in to the ground. Once again, I cover the roof with pine boughs. If snow is available, I add snow to the pine boughs also. Remember, snow is a great insulator!

And, like in all cold weather shelters, be sure to line the shelter with pine boughs to insulate you from the cold ground. Once the floor is lined, you should make a fire pit in front of the shelter. I never build a fire any closer than 10 feet (pine boughs burn very quickly). If you place a heat reflector on the side opposite of the shelter entrance you will be surprised how warm the shelter will be. The advantage to this type of shelter is the speed and ease of which it can be constructed. In a real emergency, speed may make the difference between life and death.

If you have the time to make one, a snow trench shelter is one of the best. I have spent days in one of them, and I know from experience they work very well.

Your first step is to dig down into the snow and clear a trench about three feet wide, three feet deep and seven feet long. This is just a little longer and wider than most people are, to allow you to store your field gear in the shelter. But make sure you make it roomy enough. Keep in mind that you are looking for emergency protection from the environment, not a suite. The actual size used in construction is an individual preference, depending on your body size and amount of gear you have, but I want a small and compact shelter with only my immediate needs in mind.

As soon as you have the trench made, line the floor of the shelter with pine boughs from the nearby pine trees. Other sources of insulation can be used if pine is not available where you are (If you survive an aircraft crash, the insulation from the walls or the material from the seats on an aircraft provide excellent protection from a cold sleeping surface). I suggest you place the boughs a little over a foot thick. I would prefer to pile them higher, but you have to be able to crawl into the thing once you have a roof on it. I have discovered, in my opinion, that you can never have too much floor insulation in a survival shelter.

Next, put your gear in the shelter up against the far wall, away from the entrance. Now you can start gathering up logs and limbs to cover the snow trench. Make sure you avoid rotted wood (the weight of the insulating material and snow may make it collapse) for the roof. Starting at the end opposite the entrance, I lay the logs and limbs over the open trench until it is all covered with the exception of a small opening. This opening would be the shelter's entrance. You will have to estimate the size of your entrance based on your body size, but keep it as small as possible.

Also, make sure the logs overlap the sides of the snow trench by about a foot on each side. This will give the roof strength and additional support. After the logs are in place, cover the top of the shelter with pine boughs. These pine boughs will provide insulation for your shelter. This insulation will prevent body heat from escaping and help keep the shelter protected from the wind and elements.

Once the boughs are placed on top, covered them with any material you may have. If you don't have anything, you can still make the shelter. Just make sure you secure each corner of the material to keep it from moving as you pile snow on it. I recommend you anchor the edges the material with wooden stakes. Once the material has been secured, begin covering it with snow.

As you work on any shelter, avoid overheating. If you get too hot remove a layer of clothing. It is important to avoid sweating because of the danger of the sweat freezing. Also, if you feel yourself becoming too warm, stop for a few minutes and cool down. It is not a bad idea to stop at times and maybe have a hot drink. Just make sure you drink lots of water in cold weather conditions to avoid dehydration. I know it sound insane, but dehydration is a serious cold weather problem. I usually drink hot water frequently, because it assists in keeping my body warm and prevents dehydration.

Once the shelter has been constructed, crawl inside and poked a hole approximately three inches in diameter in the top. This hole is to allow for ventilation. If you plan to burn a candle in the shelter (plus you will need some fresh air) you will have to constantly check to make sure the hole stays open. Without the ventilation and with the candle burning, carbon monoxide poisoning is a real threat. Always keep your shelter well ventilated.

Your last step is to make a door for your shelter. You can use a poncho, tarp, space blanket, etc., and spread it out on the snow near the entrance to your shelter. Then, pile snow on the material until your have enough snow to block the hole used for your entrance. Pull the ends and sides of the material together and tie them in place using some cord or material. You now have a door, roughly the shape of a ball. You can use the ends of the material as a crude door handle to pull the "door" closed once you are inside.

Simple Survival

Survival shelters are easy to make. You can make the lean-to, "A" frame, and tree pit even when there is no snow around. Just complete all of the steps except the part about adding snow. In the desert you can add a dead air space (a good insulator in hot weather) to your shelter by placing another material over the first material you used during the construction of your shelter. Keep the material separated by placing brush between the materials.

The best shelters for general use are the lean-to or the "A" frame designs. They are easy to make and construction takes just a little time. Always consider what you need insulation from, the heat or the cold. In most cases we just need a shelter for comfort (rain or wind) or for psychological reasons. I do, nonetheless, always suggest a shelter for any survival situation. A good shelter will keep you rested, healthy, and if nothing else, happy.

HAVING A BUG AS A DINNER GUEST

As you may suspect, there are many ways of preparing and cooking food procured in the wild. Often, we get lucky and bag a rabbit, or perhaps a squirrel. Yep, I know all about making Apache foot snares (often used for deer) and huge figure four traps, but let's be honest here, the odds are remote that you will feed on venison or bear in a survival situation. Most game procured will be small game, unless you have a gun along. If you have a gun, with lots of game in the area, then this article isn't for you. Most of us will have to settle for less for dinner.

When we enter "nature's supermarket", most of us may be lost in more ways than one. The foods we are used to seeing just aren't there, or at least they don't look the same way we would expect them to look. Keep in mind, many of the foods we now purchase were once, and may still be, wild in the woods. What do you know about vegetables? Do you know that certain vegetables grow underground and some on top of the ground? Nonetheless, many folks have no idea what is edible and what isn't once they leave the house.

I suggest you do some research and find out as much about wilderness food procurement as you can. There are many good books out there and lots of great web sites on wild foods. I also recommend that you buy and carry a good survival manual, either the USAF Aircrew Survival Pamphlet or the SAS Survival Guide. Both publications have information on how to identify poisonous and non-poisonous plants. And since it is very likely that the most common things in the bush will supply a large portion of our "wilderness diet", let's look at wilderness food sources a little closer.

If it isn't winter, you may be able to rustle up a nice meal of insects. They are usually out in abundance and all we have to do is gather them up. What? You don't like the idea of eating bugs? Common sense tells us that insects are usually there, we are hungry, so why not get together for a meal? Now, I have to admit bugs aren't my favorite meal, but they can help keep you alive.

Insects are very rich in fat and protein, of which both are important to the survivor (read my nutrition article in this book to see why). While many insects may be eaten raw, most people prefer them cooked (in some cases, like ants, cooking should be done to remove poisons). I personally think the best way to cook them is to add them to a "survival stew", which is a just a mix of all the various things you were able to find that day. On the larger insects, remove the wings and legs. I suggest you do this so the sharp spines on the legs don't injure your throat, or cause you to choke while swallowing. I don't recommend the beginner bite into an insect. It is sort of like a candy filled with a special middle, but without the great taste. It is important to consider the fact that most of our aversion to the eating of insects is cultural and psychological. In many cultures, insects are eaten regularly.

Insects can be found under rocks, inside of dead logs, obviously on anthills, and in nooks and crannies. Be extra careful when looking for insects, because snakes, scorpions and other biting or stinging critters like to stay in the same places. Wear gloves if you have them and use caution while shopping for dinner. Avoid placing your hands in dark holes or other places you cannot see. Make noise, and keep your eyes scanning from side to side to avoid snakes.

If you happen to see a snake, very carefully kill it with a large rock or long stick. Then carefully cut the head off (the head and fangs are still dangerous even when removed from the body), gut it lengthwise, skin it, and cut it into cubes. At that point I suggest it be added to the stew pot for the day. I usually bury a poisonous snakes head in a hole at least 12" deep. That keeps others from stepping on the head, which still contains the fangs and poison. If you are unsure if the snake is poisonous or not, then treat it at all times as if it is poisonous. And, yes, both poisonous and non-poisonous snakes can be safely eaten.

Now, back to insects. Avoid any insects that are found in animal carcasses, dung, or trash. They may carry diseases or parasites. Also, any insect you see that has a bright body color, or is hairy, try to avoid. Some may be eaten, but many are poisonous. It is easier to remember to just avoid them, than try to identify those that are safe to eat. You should be able to find plenty of worms, ants, grasshoppers, and other bugs to make a good meal.

Lets look at the big three...Worms, Ants and Grasshoppers. Worms may be eaten raw or cooked. I suggest you rinse them off to avoid getting the sand or dirt grit in your teeth. Do not confuse worms with grubs, and there is a difference. Some grubs, especially those found on the underside of leaves, may contain toxins. I would suggest you avoid them. But worms can be dried, crushed, and then added to soups. Or just eaten raw.

Ants, on the other hand, may have a painful bite (formic acid). However, by cooking them for about six or seven minutes the toxins are destroyed. Then, they may be eaten as-is, or added to soups. There is only real problem with this readily available food source; it takes a whole lot of ants to make a meal. However, they do add protein and fat to your diet. Keep in mind; even the huge grizzly bear eats them.

Grasshoppers can be knocked from the air with a shirt, fishing net, or with a piece of cloth. Remember to remove the wings, antennae, and legs before eating them. I suggest they be placed on a flat rock near the fire and cooked. Or, if you have a pot, pan, skillet, or an empty can, roast them in the container. Once cooked, they may be added to soups or stews. Some people prefer to crush them and dry them into a powder before eating them. The method you use is up to you. Of course, some people are capable of sitting around a campfire late at night eating them raw as you might eat potato chips. I have not been able to overcome, completely anyway, my squeamishness of eating raw grasshoppers. But, if I had to eat them to survive, bring on the meal.

Whether you know it or not, you may be eating insects, or parts of insects, every day. You just aren't aware of it. Most food companies have guidelines that detail the allowable percentage of insects in their product. I am not telling you this to gross you out, but stating the facts. Does it make a difference to your body if you know about the insect you ingest or not?

When you consider the nutritional value of insects to a survivor, we would have to be complete fools not to add them to the dining menu. I will be the first to admit, they are not the most appetizing meal, but they do serve a purpose. That purpose is keeping you alive until you are rescued. Bon Appetite.

What's Cookin'?

I shuddered as the thunder cracked loudly, the wind increased in force, and rain began to fall heavily. As lightning flashed a crooked path across the darkened sky, my stomach growled. Bubba and I were sheltered from the storm in our tent. We had been fishing earlier in the day, but bad weather had forced us to hunt a hole. I knew I could go for a long time without food, and a fire right now was out of the question. Oh, I could have had a bag of chips, bread and peanut butter, but I really wanted a real meal. A meal cooked on the open fire. For me, camping and cooking go together like ham and beans, because you can't have one without the other.

When I cook I consider many different aspects. I consider the fire, the type of food to be cooked, the cooking method (boiled, roasted, baked, etc.) and my eating utensils. At times the weather has to be considered, or maybe the time of day. It is more difficult to cook in the dark, or perhaps cooking in a blazing snowstorm or heavy rain is a little more challenging for me. But, all things considered, I do love to cook out of doors.

Depending on the length of my stay I carry different foods for different trips. If the trip is only over night, or for a couple of nights, I use all fresh products. A trip longer than a few days has me considering other vittles. I dislike canned foods because they are so heavy. Now, if you don't have to carry them very far they are fine. But, anyone who has done much back packing knows you sweat for every pound you carry. Unneeded weight is a real killer. If you travel light, you will travel well.

In my opinion, most people attempt to cook with a fire that is too big or they cook directly on the open flame. An open flame will cause most foods to burn. I usually only cook on hot coals and keep my fire small. The reason for this is simple; with a small fire it's easier to control the temperature and it uses less firewood. An open flame may be, at times, good for boiling, but most foods cooked on direct flames burn. It is just too difficult to control the temperature of a flame. Coals, on the other hand, can be added or removed to control the heat. I also use a small grill that has folding legs. I merely place the grill on its legs over a bed of coals. My food is usually done in short order. Save the open flame cooking for marshmallows or a nice, burned black hot dog.

A normal menu for me when I can carry fresh food is just like at home. I usually have steak, chicken, pork and lots of veggies. I always use the fresh stuff up first and save the dried or package stuff for later in the trip. If possible, I take an ice chest to keep the food cool and safe. Pancake mixes, dried soups, or other items not requiring temperature control can be premixed in most cases and stored with your other dry goods. By premixed, I mean all the ingredients in it with the exception of water or milk. Milk, by the way, is best on long trips if it is powdered or the type sold that does not require refrigeration. Due to weight problems of the unrefrigerated milk and the bulkiness of the containers, I carry powdered milk in zip locked bags. Also, most of the foods you eat at home, you can eat while camping. Well, at least for the first day or two.

As I said earlier, there are many different ways to cook foods. Of course the type of food often decides on the method used to prepare it. One meal my kids (when they were much younger) used to love to take camping was what they called "a country man's TV dinner". Let me explain in some detail.

The night before a camping trip I let each person select what they want for dinner the next night. Let's use chicken in this example. I place a chicken leg with thigh attached, some cut-up potato wedges, sliced carrots, and maybe an onion half on a sheet of heavy-duty aluminum. Seasonings are added. I then fold the aluminum over the sides of the meal, then the bottom, and lastly the top. I place the whole works on another piece of aluminum. This time I fold the metal carefully over the first one. I make sure the aluminum is sealed and not torn. All the meals then go into the freezer. All we have to do the next night is place the dinners on a bed of hot coals, turning every few minutes. The aluminum traps the steam and the food cooks very quickly. If the meal is not cooked enough for your taste, just re-wrap it and place in back on the coals. Believe it or not, it makes a very easy and tasty meal. Best of all, *the kids love it!* Oh, before I forget, dessert can be cooked the same way. Wrap an apple, banana, or even pineapple in aluminum and add it to the coals. As far as I am concerned, heavy-duty aluminum is as necessary as water when I camp.

Now, let's discuss how to get the most out of a little meat. Let's say you are camping and your friends show up unexpectedly. Do you still roast that piece of round steak and just give each person a smaller share than you had planned? I suggest you modify your menu. You will get more from the meat if you add it to the stew pot. Add potatoes, carrots, and perhaps some onion and you will have a nice soup. Also, if food is scarce, as in a survival situation, you will retain more vitamins and nutrients if the meat is boiled. If it is roasted the important juices just drip onto the coals.

I have seen old timers bake cakes, pies, and even biscuits in a Dutch oven. I have seen cast iron skillets carried all over the state by backpackers who swear it is the only way to cook. I say go for it, if that is your choice. I carry an aluminum frying pan, a large aluminum pot, an aluminum coffee pot, and part of a roll of aluminum. Yep, aluminum is my metal of choice. I like it because it is light-weight and heats up quickly. Just be very careful with the heat of your coals and it won't be a problem. Additionally, I have each person carry a mess kit.

If you are forced to do so, you can cook and survive with much less equipment. A sharpened stick, chunk of food and a fire is all that is really needed. Nonetheless, most of us prefer a nice meal when we camp. It seems to bring out the best as far as I am concerned. Plus, I find it fun and relaxing to cook when I camp. I suggest you go to a local bookstore and discover the many different types of books out there on camping and cooking. They are filled with original ideas that can add to your camping enjoyment. After all, enjoyment is the main reason we camp.

Here are a few of my favorite items to cook when I camp. Keep in mind all ingredients are suggestions. You will have to experiment to find the right amounts for your taste.

Ham and Beans

Three cups of dried beans
One cup of ham cut into bite size chunks
One ham bone, optional
Pinch of salt and pepper

Cover the beans with water. Allow them to sit over night in a cool dry spot. Place the pot on a bed of coals, adding more coals as need to bring the pot to a boil. I usually add the ham after cooking for about one hour. You can add it whenever you like. The longer the ham cooks the more tender it will become. You can add small pieces of potato, carrots, celery, and onion if you want it to look pretty. Boil until the beans are soft to the touch. Serve with cold cornbread.

Roasted Chicken

One whole chicken
Pinch of salt and pepper
Baking ties (cotton cord)

Place the whole chicken on a spit cut from a tree limb. Make sure the wood you use for a spit is green and strong enough to support the weight of the chicken. Run the spit through the holes in the chicken (neck and rear). Tie the legs and top of the breast to the spit. This will keep the bird rotating and will not allow it to remain stationary as you cook. If the bird is not tied to the spit, the wood will turn, but not the chicken. Cut two strong Y shaped pieces of wood to support the spit. Put the Y's on opposite sides of the fire pit. Rake a bed of coals under the spot the bird will be cooked. Place the spit in the deepest notch of the Y at both ends. Turn the chicken frequently until it is a golden brown color. When the leg bone moves freely in the socket and the dripping juices run clear when pierced with a fork, the bird is done. If not cooked enough for your taste, add it back to the fire.

Pancakes with Bacon Bits

Instant pancake mix, the type that only requires water.
A half a pound of bacon
Water
Plastic zip lock bag, large
Syrup, if desired

Cook the bacon in a pan over the fire and allow it to cool. After the bacon cools, crumble it up and add it to your powdered pancake mix. I carry my pancake mix already in a large zip locked bag, with the amount of water needed written with a permanent marker on the bag. Add the water needed. I then mix the water, pancake mix, and bacon by squeezing the bag. I make sure my pan is clean, and I use a little butter to cook the pancakes. Keep your heat medium and remember to turn the pancakes when the edges start to bubble. It makes a fine breakfast, especially if eggs are added to the menu.

Do You Know How to Dress?

Once you have snared or killed game for the stew pot, do you know how to field dress it? There are different types of game and just about as many different ways to dress it. But since most survivors hardly ever kill a moose or a bear, I will skip the big game part. For our purposes we will stick to birds, rabbits, and squirrels.

Many people are not very excited about the idea of processing their own meals. Seems in our society today we have lost the art of killing, dressing and processing our own foods. While it is convenient for us, it has hurt us in some ways (primitive survival). And I agree with what some of you may be thinking, we don't have a need to do that stuff much anymore. However, once forced in the wilds, we will need that skill if our hunting ability pays off.

Your first step is to insure your animal is dead. I can tell you from experience that most small game, while not able to cause serious injury, can scratch or bite you. Use caution and kill the animal before you pick it up. A quick way to dispatch a snared or trapped animal is with a heavy blow to the head from a club. Or, you can spear it. I prefer to use a club because it kills instantly and the animal does not suffer for long. While I do have to eat, I don't relish the idea of hurting any animal. But as survivors we must eat and part of that diet must be animal proteins and fats. Something must die for us to live.

A rabbit is very easy to dress and takes but a couple of minutes. You can hang the animal by its back legs and grasp the skin on a leg. Make a small cut, from one ankle down and across to the other ankle. You can now pull the skin down, and off, like a glove. Remove the feet and the head. Retain the head for eating. To gut the animal, pinch the upper stomach and make a very small incision. Take the tip of your knife and slowly cut down and then up. That procedure should have opened the stomach cavity. Remove the inner organs, with your hand, using caution not to rupture the bladder (urine). Retain the heart, liver, and kidneys, if they are not spotted. While the thought of it may gross you out, the head and inner organs are very important to your survival diet. You must find a way to cook them that will allow you to eat them. I would suggest you make a stew and just add all of the meats.

A squirrel is a little tougher to skin. It is suggested that you do not hang a squirrel when dressing it. Make a cut about two inches long on the animals back, grasp the two pieces of skin, and pull them away from each other. Then, remove the head and feet. Keep the head for cooking. Gut and retain the inner organs just like you did the rabbit. Remember, *avoid breaking the bladder or you will get urine on the meat.*

Birds can either be plucked or skinned. I suggest they be plucked. This keeps the skin on the meat, which is full of oils and fats. To pluck them you just need to pull all of the feathers out. For small birds it is easy to do, but with a goose or a turkey, it may take you a little time. Gut them immediately, keep the inner organs, and cover them with cloth if you have any. This is to keep flies and insects away from them. I recommend in warm weather that your bird be cooked as soon as possible, and no matter how pretty the picture is of a bird roasting over a fire, make yours into a soup or stew. You should boil it because you will need all of the nutrients in the animal. Roasting will allow those important parts of your diet to drip and burn, while boiling retains them.

The thought of killing, field dressing, and preparing meat is disturbing to some folks and it is easily understood. Nonetheless, in a survival situation, you must learn to prepare your own foods. I have eaten many rabbits, squirrels, raccoons and opossums.

In my travels I have even had monkey, boa (snake), rattlesnake, lizards, and other small animals. You can do the same. Keep the will to survive alive in your head and you too can make it. Learn to live!

Vitamins, Minerals, and Survival

A few years ago, when I first entered the military, I had the chance to read a copy of a survival journal written by a man that was discovered dead. The rescue team had brought out all of his gear, and then turned the journal over to the Air Force. The Air Force had copied the journal and distributed it to various sections to assist in survival training. There were many lessons to be learned from the dead man's situation. The key to his death, or seemed to me anyway, was nutrition.

Most of us know little about nutrition, because many of are not very interested in the subject to start with. Generally, we have nutritious meals (or at least they are available), we take multi-vitamins, and we (as a country) may be a bit over weight. But, what do we, as hunters, fishermen, campers, and backpackers, know about survival nutrition? I suggest we know (and may not even care) much about the subject.

The man with the journal had died in World War II, and was not discovered until sometime in the 1950's. His journal was not printed and distributed until the early 1970's. While less was known about nutrition during the writer's lifetime, there were things known that could have saved his life. However, I think, like most of us, he was neither interested nor very knowledgeable of the subject. In other words, he was typical of many outdoorsmen and women.

The dead man's aircraft had crash-landed on a frozen lake up north (Alaska perhaps). I can't remember exactly where he went down, and it is not very important where it happened, because his situation could be relived in many states or countries. The thing to keep in mind is that his crash site was remote.

As I read his journal, I discovered a man with the guts and determination needed to survive. He was an experienced outdoorsman, with years of hunting behind him. He had also been trained, to a small extent, by the military. His journal showed a man of discipline, as well as a deep "will to survive." Then, you are most likely asking, why did he die?

His journal indicated that while there was no big game in the woods around the lake, it was heavily populated by rabbits. He wrote of eating rabbits regularly, and then as time passed, describing how he was losing weight. Eventually his writing stopped completely. His last entry, if I remember correctly, was of his confusion of starving to death as he ate rabbit after rabbit. I remember one old grizzled survival instructor who commented about the victim, "He starved to death on a full stomach."

The instructor went on to say that the man might have survived, as he had the guts, if he had only known more about nutrition. "A rabbit is a lean critter. Not much fat on 'em, and a man in a survival situation needs fat and oils. See, that man was only eating the lean flesh of the animal. He discarded the other parts that may have kept him alive. If he had eaten the contents of the rabbit's stomach, which contains essentially green leafy grasses (vitamins B, C, E), the rabbits eyes (which contain salt), along with the liver, heart, and kidneys (which contain vitamin A), as well as other vitamins, he might have made it. I suspect he just plain didn't know about it. Or, he didn't like the idea of eating a critter's innards. Keep in mind, in a prolonged survival situation protein alone won't keep you alive"

Over the years I have done a lot of thinking about what the man had written, reliving his fear of death, as well as what the sergeant had said. I have done a little research on nutrition and while I cannot even remotely claim to be an expert, I have found some basic facts we should all keep in mind about vitamins.

First, I suggest all of us carry a small container of good quality multivitamins in our survival kits. They are light and easy to carry. Keep them in the original bottle, because it protects them from sunlight, which can decrease their effectiveness, and it keeps them dry. But, what are the basic essential vitamins for us if we are in a survival situation and do not have vitamins along? Many professionals and "armchair" survival "experts" may disagree, but this is a group of vitamins I think we should be concerned about.

Vitamin A, (retinol). We get this vitamin from milk products, animal fat, carrots, and leafy green vegetables. **Why do we need this vitamin?** It helps keep your vision working well, your immune system up and working, and assists in the functioning of most major organs. **Where do you find it?** From animal fats, contents of the stomach of plant eating animals, wild green plants in the field.

Vitamin B complex, (B1, B2, B3, B5, and B12). All meats, green plants (vegetables), dairy products, grains and cereals (you can get them elsewhere as well, but they are not a source readily available to most survivors, i.e., brewers yeast). **Why do we need this vitamin?** They are needed for the nervous system, maintaining healthy skin, the cell production process, digestive process, respiration, bone marrow production, and to assist our metabolism. **Where do you find it?** Once again, by eating green leafy plants (try dandelions or banana leaf), the flesh of wild animals (including the stomach contents if the environment does not allow you to forage for fresh green veggies), pine nuts, walnuts, and perhaps even wild grains or rice.

Vitamin C, is found in fresh fruits, vegetables. Remember that citrus fruits and tomatoes have high levels of vitamin C. **Why do we need this vitamin?** It helps to build healthy tissues, tendons, and assists in absorbing iron. It is essential for healthy teeth and gums as well as for healing wounds or fractures (which may be experienced by survivors). **Where do you find it?** If you are lucky enough to attempt survival in a jungle, then citrus fruits may not be much of a problem. One source I use in mountains or in general locations is pine needles. The needles on pine boughs can be brewed to make a rough tasting tea. While not that tasty, it does the job of providing vitamin C as well as keeping the drinker warm.

Vitamin D can be found in eggs, dairy products, and fish with fatty flesh (tuna, salmon, sardines, oysters, and others). **Why do we need this vitamin?** It assists in the building of bones and cartilage. Also, it is used to regulate the absorption of phosphorus and calcium in the body. **Where do you find it?** During your searches for food look for bird nests. While the eggs you find will not belong to a chicken, they will serve the same purpose as far as vitamin D is concerned. As far as I know, all eggs are edible and should be eaten if available. Additionally, set fish traps, make a dip net for smaller fish and try your hand at fishing. There may not be much of a problem procuring salmon if you are along streams and rivers they run in. Thousands of salmon move in our nations waterways each year. If you catch too many of them, make a drying rack and save them for future needs.

Vitamin E is in rice and green leafy vegetables. **Why do we need this vitamin?** This is one of the least understood vitamins, but it is known to assist in the prevention of muscular dystrophy. So, it seems this vitamin may be associated with muscular functioning. **Where do you find it?** Look for wild rice. Surprisingly, it is out there. Remember, rice grows in wet locations so check long the banks of small ponds or lakes. You may get lucky and find a source. Keep in mind to constantly search for sources of food and vitamins around your survival site.

Vitamin K is produced by our intestinal tract. It can also be found in egg yolks, leafy green plants, fish liver oils, and other sources. **Why do we need this vitamin?** It assists in the clotting of blood. The last problem a survivor needs is the inability to clot a bleeding injury. **Where do you find it?** Look for eggs as we suggested earlier, search for various green leafy plants, and if need be, build up the courage to eat the contents of an animal's stomach. The contents of the stomach can be added to soups without affecting most people very much, especially if you don't tell them or they don't ask.

Other Considerations are carbohydrates, fats, proteins, and minerals.

Carbohydrates are found in a variety of food sources. They are found in sugars, honey, fruits, roots and tubers (cook these well) as well as in cereals. **Why do we need them?** They are excellent sources of energy and help prevent the nausea often caused by the breakdown of body fats in the body. **Where do you find it?** Look for bees (honey), wild apples, cattail roots, or even wild potatoes. Cattails will most likely be the easiest to find.

Fats are an excellent source of energy and are found in most animals and fish. Additionally, some plants may contain fats, as well as eggs and nuts. While some "survival experts" suggest fats can be found in fungi (mushrooms) I do not recommend eating them. They are not easy to identify by most people and overall, have very little nutrition. They have the disadvantage possibly of being poison if the survivor is unsure of its identity. **Why do we need them?** Fats give us our energy in a concentrated form. A key consideration here is the availability of water. Fats take water to digest, so make sure you have sufficient water when you ingest fats. **Where do you find them?** Animal fats are the easiest way. Keep in mind, wild game has less fat than farm animals. Also, during the winter months or early spring, wild animals may contain less fat. In the fall, after eating well all summer, wild game is usually the fatter.

Proteins are found in meat, eggs, fish, nuts, and grains. While also found in dairy products, you are unlikely to find a cow in a survival situation. **Why do we need them?** They supply amino acids, which are necessary for good health. **Where do you find them?** Attempt to locate wild eggs, fish often, gather nuts and grains if possible, and eat wild meat.

Minerals are needed for good overall health. Some, not all, of the minerals we need are sodium, calcium, potassium, phosphorus, chlorine, magnesium, and sulfur. **Why do we need them?** They all play a role in maintaining good overall health. **Where do you find them?** Salt water may be boiled to produce sodium, or the eyes of the animals you kill will contain salt. Other minerals will be in the foods you eat, and it should not be a problem as long as you eat a variety of foods.

While all of this information may seem overwhelming to you, you are most likely getting most of these vitamins and other things during the course of a day. We are just not aware of what is in most of our meals. Those of us who take a good quality multi-vitamin daily are getting our requirements of both vitamins and minerals.

When in the field, and forced to procure food, make sure any plants you harvest are known by you to be safe to eat. You may find almost any of the vegetables and fruits in the wild that are for purchase at your local market. Remember to wash them, but do not soak them in water (prolong soaking can reduce the vitamin content). I suggest boiling them in soups or stews to retain most of the vitamins that would otherwise be lost. While the idea of eating some of the foods survivors are at times forced to eat may be repulsive to some, what is the option?

It has been less than 100 years since the link between foods and diseases has been identified to some degree. British biochemist Fredrick Hopkins, in 1906, proved in his studies the association between vitamins (though not called that yet) and the human body. He found a "missing link". His research indicated that a body not only needed proteins, carbo-hydrates, minerals, water, and fats to develop, but it also needed what he called "accessory factors." Further research by others has shown these "accessory factors" were in fact what we today call vitamins.

Primitive man had no knowledge of vitamins, but his instincts were fairly good. Often, after the killing of a buffalo or large game, he would eat parts of the liver or other internal organs raw, almost immediately. I have read of explorers who did the same and they described a deep "animal like craving" for the bloody meal. Additionally, Native Americans ate most parts of the game they killed. Were they merely being thrifty with the game they killed or did the act serve some other unknown urge? I think this urge to eat most of killed game was a body's need for life saving essential vitamins and minerals.

If you are ever faced with a true life and death survival situation, remember this article. Keep in mind to constantly be looking for a variety of foods, thus a variety of vitamins and minerals. Eat plenty of green leafy plants (if you can safely identify the plant), gather eggs, nuts, pine needles and other sources of food. Set out fish traps. Consider eating the parts of an animal you would not usually consider a "prime cut." Survival is not for the weak of heart. Those who do whatever is needed still have no assurance of survival. Nonetheless, the will to survive, continuous hard work, and constantly procuring sources of food can increase your chances of survival.

HAVING A WILDERNESS SALAD

Have you ever looked around as you walked in the woods and wondered what you could eat if you were really hungry? Many wild plants are edible, but do you know which ones? If you are like most people, you didn't identify much that you knew for sure you could eat. It is to the advantage of all hunters, fishermen, campers and others to know what is good to eat and how to determine a plants edibility if you are unsure. Any of us who spend any time in the outdoors could one day find ourselves lost, or in a survival situation. Then our knowledge, or lack of knowledge, of plant life could mean the difference between life and death. Many of the elements of a healthy diet are found in plant foods.

While many plants are good to eat, there are ways to identify those that you want to stay away from. Any plant with umbrella shaped flowers on it, beans, peas, bulbs, plants that have a milky sap, or plants that irritate your skin, should be avoided. Additionally, stay away from any fungi, unless you know beyond a doubt it is safe to eat. But, even then, fungi add very little in the way of nutrition to your diet. I suggest you spend your time procuring better, more nutritional, items for your outdoor menu. Fungi are *not worth the risk* you can take eating them.

Well, what do you do when you cannot identify a single safe plant to eat? I suppose that will happen more often than not. If you can avoid them, do not eat unknown plants. However, in a survival situation it is often a matter of eating or going hungry. If you decide to eat a plant you are unsure of, there is no better (and proven) method of determining the edibility of plants than using the US Army's Taste Test (along with my comments).

- Test only one part of the plant at a time. **Comment:** *By eating more than one part you will not be able to determine (if you get ill) what part is safe to eat. The key is to eat only one part.*

- Break the plant down into base constituents: leaves, steams, roots, etc. **Comment:** *Once again, it makes identification of* *safe and unsafe parts of the plant easier. Not all parts of a plant may be safe to eat.*

- Smell the plant for strong or acid odors. **Comment:** *Avoid any plant with a strong or acid odor because the plant is considered unsafe to eat.*

- Do not eat for eight hours before starting the test. **Comment:** *This is so you can be sure, if you get ill, it was the plant that caused it.*

- At first, put a small sample of the plant on the inside of your elbow or on your wrist. Wait 15 minutes and check to see if you had a reaction. **Comment:** *A general rule is if the plant causes a reaction on your skin, it is not safe to eat.*

- During the test period, remember to take nothing orally except pure water and the tested plant. **Comment:** *It you eat or drink anything besides pure water, the test is not valid, and you will have to start over. It may have been another food that caused an ill effect.*

- Select a very small piece of the plant to be tested. **Comment:** *Always use a very small piece of the test plant to start with. If the plant makes you ill, the less you test with the less the suffering may be.*

- Put the selected piece of the plant up against your lip and test for burning or itching. **Comment:** *If the plant causes any burning, itching or numbness to your lips, DO NOT continue the test. Wash your lips to remove any residue from the plant.*

- After three minutes, if there is no reaction, place the selected piece of the plant on your tongue. Hold it there for 15 minutes. DO NOT SWALLOW. **Comment:** *While this step sounds easy, I know from experience, it is difficult to do when you are hungry. But, remember, at this point you do not want to swallow an untested plant yet.*

- If there is no reaction, chew the piece thoroughly and hold it in your mouth for 15 minutes. Once again, DO NOT SWALLOW. **Comment:** *Once again, this is a difficult step for someone when they are hungry. Pay close attention to any burning, itching or numbness while chewing the plant.*

- If there is no irritation at all during this time, swallow the piece of plant. **Comment:** *Be honest about this step. If you have* *experienced any reaction or irritation during the test up to this step, DO NOT swallow the plant.*

- Wait eight hours. If you have any effects from the plant, induce vomiting and drink plenty of water. **Comment:** *It is difficult to wait when you are very hungry. However, this is necessary to insure the plant is safe to eat. If you do become ill, flush the system by drinking plenty of water. You may experience diarrhea or stomach cramps from a bad plant.*

- If you do not experience any ill effects, eat one half of a cup of the same plant prepared the same way. Wait another eight hours; if no ill effects are suffered the plant, as prepared, is safe to eat. **Comment:** *The key here is to always prepare the plant the way you tested it. If you decide to fix it another way, then start the test all over again. Some foods may be safe when eaten cooked but not safe if eaten raw. So, always prepare a plant in a way that you know is safe.*

Survival is never easy. We often are forced to make decisions and take chances that can have terrible results if we are wrong. Just by picking up fungi or an unknown plant and eating it, you could die. Survival is no joke, and it is extremely dangerous to attempt eating plants you are unsure of. However, hunger is often a constant companion to a survival, but it does not have to be. Many unknown plants are safe to eat and now you have a basic idea of which ones. Always use common sense and the US Army's Taste Test. It could very well save your life.

Simple Survival Snares

When it comes to procuring meat in the wild, you will have to work for your next meal. Usually, it takes a lot of work and then you will most likely have to lower your meat standards a bit. You may prefer beef, but in the field, you will be lucky if you dine on squirrel or rabbit. Animals are difficult for the inexperienced hunter to catch. They are very shy of man and often their senses are highly tuned toward survival. However, you can trap most small game, if you know what you are doing.

Now, there are all kinds of traps that can be made in the bush. Some use boulders, huge logs, deep pits, and so on. Those are more work than they are worth. Well, at least they are for the average person who needs meat quickly and is not hoping for a lion, bear or other large game. We will concentrate on small game, mainly because they are easier to trap and they are more abundant. Not to mention, they are less dangerous to catch.

The most common method of catching small game is by using snares. Snares can be made using line, cord, wire, or even vines. I can tell you from experience, it will take a lot of traps to yield one animal, unless you get lucky and discover a place that is full of small game! I recommend you set them out by the dozens and check them first thing each morning. Try to find small game trails, which are small trails through the grass and weeds. Often, rabbits and other small game use the same trails over and over to move to food and water sources. Like man, they are creatures of habit. You may also find trails that lead into briar patches, thorn bushes and other types of brush. Small game uses those types of places as protection, or places to hide. They are good places to put a snare as well.

Snares can be purchased ready-made, with a locking loop. Or, if you prefer, you can make you own from wire, string, cord or vines. I have found wire to work the best and as you may have guessed, vines work less effectively. But, in a survival situation, if you don't have an item with you, then you must use what Mother Nature provides, or do without. I carry about 50 feet of snare wire and about 25 feet of parachute 550 cord. The parachute cord is nylon and has strands of smaller "string-like" cords inside. I simply cut the cord and remove a single strand of the smaller cord and use it to make my snares with. It is small, light, and very strong.

When making a snare there are two very common designs. One type of design simply holds the animal at ground level and may or may not strangle the victim. The second design will flip the animal into the air and hold the carcass off of the ground. Of course as the animal is held off of the ground it is strangled to death. While they are both are easy to make, each design has strengths and weaknesses.

Both designs require the loop in the wire, cord, string, or vine, to tighten and hold the animal. The loop should be free moving. This free movement allows the loop to tighten as the animal struggles or moves forward into the snare. With the flip up design, movement of the wire will trigger the device and fling the animal into the air, which using the animal's body weight tightens the loop. Make sure the loop has free movement.

In both types of snares you should set the loop diameter for the type of animal you hope to catch. I am using the most common small game here, due to the fact that they are most abundant. Additionally, keep in mind that different animals require the loop diameter to be different sizes and to be placed at different heights on the game trail.

Rabbits, the loop should be about four inches in diameter and placed about two inches above the trail.

Squirrels, the loop should be about three inches in diameter and two to three inches above the trail.

Beaver, make the loop about five inches in diameter and place it about one to two inches off of the ground.

For the holding snare, let's say for a rabbit, you make a loop (about four inches in diameter) and place it about two inches above the center of the game trail. Make sure the end of the snare wire, opposite the loop, is secured to a bush, stake, or other stationary object. Make sure what you use to secure the snare cannot be pulled away by the animal. Then, if needed, use brush, logs or other debris to make a funnel toward your snare. In other words, force the animal to the snare and do not allow them to go around it. Since most animals will continue to use a trail they have used daily, this should not be a big issue. But, by using the tunneling effect the game will usually continue down the known trail. The animal's head will then enter the loop and as it continues to move forward the loop will slide and become smaller. Eventually the loop will be so small in size the animal cannot get out. Any struggling will only tighten the loop. Thus, you have dinner.

In the flip up snare, the principle is the same as far as tunneling the animal. The difference is when the animal's head enters the snare it will eventually pull the wire far enough to trigger the flip up part of the trap. At that point the animal will be flipped into the air and strangled. The diameter of the loop and the distance off the ground remain the same in this snare as in the other.

To make a trip snare, you need a flexible limb or bush, the snare wire, a trigger and a method to hold the trigger. I do not recommend this type of snare in extreme cold because the flexible part of the trap often freezes in place and does not function as a spring any longer. If the weather is really cold, use the standard holding snare.

I stated early in this article to check your traps each morning. This is important to remember. Some animals, if snared by the leg, will actually chew the limb off to get out of the trap. While I have no problems snaring my dinner, I do not want to cause pain or suffering to any animal. My goal is to kill the animal so I can survive, not to inflict pain.

When you approach the snare you will usually see right off if it has an animal. If an animal is there, use a club or spear (see my article on primitive weapons) to kill it instantly (Most animals caught in a snare will be dead already, but be prepared) Or, if you are an experienced hunter, you may have a different method. The choice is yours, but keep in mind to kill quickly. Many animals, even small game, will be capable of inflicting pain on the person checking the snare. They may bite, scratch or claw you.

For some of you, snaring an animal may not be a very pleasant task. It may prove to be even more difficult to kill an animal so you can eat. In today's society we are rarely involved in the processing of our meals and it can be a shocker for some folks. I can understand your views, but in an emergency, you will need the fats and protein the animal will provide. Something must die so you may live. Survival is not a game. In a real survival situation your life may very well depend on your ability to snare game, eat insects, or even the eating of certain plants you may not like. It is necessary for your survival. Can you do what it takes to survive?

Simple Survival Cooking

One aspect of survival most people worry about needlessly is food. Most of our concerns are psychological, not biological. For some reason we all have a deeply rooted anxiety over having enough food and eating on a regular basis. While we can go weeks without food, we can die in as little as 24 hours without water (in the heat of the desert). So, I have not convinced you, huh? Well, I am not surprised at all. See, it is the number one question I get about survival, "What do you eat?" The answer is, pretty much anything slower than me. If it is faster than me, I just trap it if I can.

We can trap small game, net birds, gather plants, catch fish, collect shellfish, and the list goes on and on. But do you know how to cook it or preserved it for later use? Most people always think of roasting a piece of meat or fish, but you will get more nutrients and vitamins from it if you boil it. Almost any empty tin or container can be used to boil it. Perhaps, you will have to improvise by using an animal skin or birch bark, and hot rocks. Use your imagination and you will be surprised by the different ways you can do most things. Usually, it will be in ways you have never remotely considered before. But let's discuss how to cook and when to cook certain types of foods.

Most meat (rabbits, squirrels, opossums, rodents, etc.) should be boiled. However, they may be roasted. Make sure the liver of the dead animal has no spots or lumps, is firm to the touch and is an even color. You should keep the head, liver, and kidneys of healthy animals. Boil the head for approximately 100 minutes. After the head has cooled to the touch, remove the eyes and all flesh. You can even collect the blood from any animal you kill and allow it to set covered in a cool spot, until a clear liquid comes to the top. Pour this liquid off and allow the blood below to firm up. Once the blood has "caked", it can be cut into squares and added to soups or stews. Add a few plants and you will have a nice dinner.

Meats can be simply stuck on a stick and place over or near the hot coals to cook. Never cook directly over or in the flames of your fire. The meat will be burned on the outside and be raw on the inside. However, if you have a container, I suggest you usually boil your meats. This allows you to retain the vitamins and nutrients. Or, you can place the meat on a spit and slowly turn it over a bed of coals. Once again, you are limited in cooking meats only by your imagination.

Plants are all around us. Make sure if you do not know which plant is safe to eat, that you use the edibility test (in another article) to insure it is safe. Always eat the plant exactly like you tested it (i.e., if you eat the stem cooked during the test, then always eat the stem and always have it cooked). Another aspect to keep in mind is that toxins in some plants may be killed if the plant is cooked. Roots are excellent roasted in hot coals. Other green plants will make a nice side dish or salad for you. Wild onions add a nice touch to any survival meal and are usually easy to find in most locations. However, you may have to resort to what you would not normally consider food, insects and worms.

Insects and worms are actually very good for your diet. They are high is proteins and may be roasted. A preferred method is to boil them, remove them from the water once cooled, and then crush them into a powder. You can then add this powder to your stews or soups. Most people have an aversion to just picking up an insect and eating it, which is not safe to do anyway, and this "powdering" method will mask the meal's contents a little. I find them easier to eat this way.

Fish and shellfish are excellent sources of food if you are near the ocean. You can wrap them in broad leaves and place them directly on hot coals. Or, you can wrap them in leaves, cover the leaves with mud, and then cook them until the mud dries. Once the mud has hardened, remove your food from the fire, break the mud shell, and open the leaves. Use caution not to get pieces of mud on your food. Fish can be placed on a spit and placed over a bed of hot coals. Remember, all shellfish should be cooked for at least 10 minutes to make it safe to eat. Additionally, immediately eat all seafood caught because it spoils quickly.

Birds are almost everywhere. They also make an excellent source of survival foods. Some, like gulls, may have a strong fish taste. I suggest you skin most birds, because it is quicker and easier. Plucking the feathers takes a great deal of time and may not be worth the energy. Nonetheless, the choice is yours. Carrion should be boiled, but all others may be boiled or broiled. Keep in mind, boiling will retain most of the nutrients you need.

Well, now that you know how to cook foods for immediate use, how do you preserve meats? The fastest and easiest way is to smoke it. Jerky is the term used to describe this method of meat preparation and it is fairly easy to do. While jerky can be made using the sun or the wind, smoking is the best and fastest way.

First, you should build a small fire in a pit. To actually smoke the meat, make a small tepee (three green sticks placed in the ground like a triangle), tie the tops of the sticks together, and make a platform (once again, use green wood) no closer than two feet from where the coals will be.

Remove most or all of the fat from the meat you are preparing. Then, cut the meat cross-grain in slices no wider than ¼ of an inch if possible. Actually, the thinner the meat the quicker it will cure. If you have salt (you have a source if you are near the ocean. You can boil saltwater to produce salt) rub the meat with salt. Salt will speed up the process and make it taste better. Once the meat has been cut, place it on the cooking platform allowing individual pieces to touch slightly, but not overlapping. Do not place the meat in a pile on the platform. There has to be space around the meat for it to cure properly.

To smoke the meat, add green hardwoods, chips or chunks of wood to the coals. These chunks of wood or chips may be soaked in water first if you prefer. This water treatment will give off a lot more smoke and allow the "chunk" to last longer. Leaves from hardwoods may be used as well. Avoid grasses or pine boughs; they will just flare up and burn away. Keep in mind you want smoke, not direct flame. Also, pine or fir will make the meat taste bad. Use hickory or oak for the best flavors.

Once the fire is smoking, is when I add the sides to the tepee. Using cloth, aluminum, or even pine boughs, cover the sides of the structure. Allow a small opening at the top for the smoke to be released. Now comes the hard part, you must wait approximately 18 hours for the meat to be "jerked." Feed the fire as often as needed, but you want smoke and not flames.

However, once the meat is cured in this manner it can last a very long time. Just remember to keep it dry and wrapped up to keep it clean. I usually crumble up a couple pieces of jerky and add it to soups or stews for a very unique flavor! When jerky is added to other soup contents (insects or blood) it may make the meal easier for some to eat. I have also found taking a handful of rice and then adding some jerky to the water makes a great camping soup.

Survival is never easy. It is a constant battle to find enough foods to keep our psychological needs satisfied as well as our physical needs. Remember, you can snare most small game, net birds, catch fish, or find shellfish, then prepare them as I have suggested in this article. Also, try your hand at making jerky so you can preserve your meat for later use. All of the cooking methods I have discussed do work; I know because I have used them. But the taste of some of the foods may not be to your liking. In survival our goal is to live and we must eat what nature provides us to do this.

From the Field to the Kitchen

The young boy raised the long rifle and I watched his arms tremble from the weight, as well as excitement, as he slowly squeezed the trigger. For some reason when the report of his shot echoed through the woods I was surprised at how loud it was.

Well, after about fifteen minutes I suspected that buck was as dead as he would ever get. Brandon and I slowly made our way out of the tree stand we were in and approached the deer. I had told him earlier, "If we knock a deer down, we will both walk up to him from the rear. That way if the animal hears us, he will move or try to stand up. Keep your gun ready when we approach a downed animal and be ready to shoot. Even a wounded deer can hurt a hunter at times."

I spent some time and showed the young man how to field dress a large animal and stressed the importance of him always checking the inner organs for spots or lesions of any kind. I explained that the organs should be a nice uniform color, without any discoloration at all. I picked up the liver and explained this to him as I ran my right index finger around the organ to indicate the even dark red color of the tissue. For a boy not yet sixteen he paid close attention to the entire field dressing process.

Soon the buck was skinned, placed in a fresh game bag, and we were pulling up in the driveway at Brandon's house. His mom was grossed out, as she is every deer season, but his father was as proud as any man could be. While Larry had wanted to go along on the hunt, he had fractured his left leg only the day before and was stuck at home.

Now, my brother Larry loves to deer hunt. He hunts every year and he does it all, bow, black powder, and rifle. I have to admit, overall he is a much better hunter than me and he always has been. He seems to have more patience than I do and I suspect his hunting senses are better tuned than mine as well. With the deer in the back yard, Larry just took over and walked Brandon through the butchering process.

"The first step is to make a long cut completely down both sides of the deer's spine, and use just the tip of the knife blade. This cut is the loin, or back strap, and it is the best part of the deer. Brandon, keep your knife sharp or else go and get a couple more knives. A sharp knife is necessary when butchering any large game (I noticed the knives and other tools, like a hacksaw, had already been cleaned with soap and water by my sister-in-law). Now, you know how to fillet, so run your knife up from the area near the ribs toward the deer's spine. As you cut, make the cuts smooth and keep the blade even. Do this cut on both sides of the spine and remove both pieces of back strap.

Next, raise the front leg and make a nice even cut where it joins the chest. Remember, this leg bone lies flat against the chest and is not in a socket. It is held in place by muscle and tendons. As you cut, lift the leg until you have removed it. Okay, that was easy, now do the other side the same way.

The rear legs are held in place by the hipbone and you have to have a feel for where the joint is. If you place your hand near the hip and raise the leg, you should feel the movement in the hipbone. Make a cut down to the joint and make it smoothly. Remember to cut and not carve or saw the meat, and that's one good reason to always keep your knife sharp. You may have to lift the leg as you do this step, but it's not a big deal if you do.

Now, my grandpa used to cut his deer in half when he butchered. That was before Chronic Waste Disease (CWD) and we won't chance that now. But, if you wanted to, and you knew the deer was disease free, cutting it right down the spine makes handling much easier for you. Also that way you can work on one half of the animal at a time. Oh, and I see you looking at the glaze forming on the meat. The glaze is ok and it actually helps protect the meat from hair, dirt or other debris. It will turn a light gray color by the time we are finished. Now, I want you to trim the flank, or the meat around and over the ribs from the deer now. Place it all in that large pot, so we can wrap it for use later in soups or stews. Ok, move down to the neck and remove as much meat as you can, placing it in the same pot as the flank."

"Do you want to keep the ribs, Brandon?" I asked a few minutes later as he worked on the neck meat, not knowing the answer since it was his first deer.

"No, there doesn't seem to be much meat left on them and not much between those wide bones either."

"Good and wise decision, Brandon. Deer ribs are not like beef or pork ribs, in my opinion, just not enough meat on the ribs of most deer for me. Plus, I hate wrapping them because they are curled and harder to wrap. But, if you had wanted to keep the ribs we would have removed the bullet damaged areas (bruised meat, blood clots, or broken bone) and then cut them as square as we could for ease of wrapping."

"Do you see how the tissue of the meat grows in almost a line up the legs? The direction of that growth is called the grain of the meat. Okay, if you cut with the lines (or grain) on the tissue the meat will be harder to chew, thus it will be tougher to eat. So, we want to make our cuts across that grain or in the case of the rear leg you have there, we will not cut lengthwise, but across the leg. Take your knife and cut a complete circle at the part of the leg where it has tampered down a lot, the remainder of the leg below your cut is called a shank. We can use that as a roast or we can use it to make stews or soups with. It is tougher eating, but still good meat.

I suggest you make a long cut now, from the bone at the top of the meaty portion of the leg down to the circle you cut around the shank. Do that on both sides. Keep your cuts as straight and even as you can. Ok, you're done? Next, lets start cutting the meat into steaks. Make them about an inch or so thick and as you cut down, go all the way to the bone. Do that until both of the two rear legs are prepared. You may have to use your knife to cut the steaks from the thighbone, but if you wanted to, you could simply cut the bone with a hacksaw and make a nice looking steak as well. But today we are not keeping the bone in place, so just cut the steaks loose from the bone.

Now, the two front legs we will cut into three pieces (or two circular cuts) and make pot roasts with them. I have found making roast to be an easy way to prepare the front legs without a band saw, or some other way of cutting steaks from them. Now, pick up the hacksaw and cut through the bone in both spots where you cut. Brandon, take that piece of cloth and wipe the bone dust and chips from the roasts. Keep the meat as clean and free of debris as you can at all times.

Okay, that went well. Now, pick up the loin and lets cut it into pieces that weigh about a pound to two pounds each. Keep in mind, this is the best part of the animal and it is the favorite cut of most venison eaters. Once again, remember, all of our cuts are against the grain, or width wise if you will. Put those in a different container over there, because when we wrap them they will be labeled differently (as loin) than the steaks or roasts. We don't want the meat cuts to get mixed up.

Our final step in cutting, Brandon, is to remove the fat from the flank and trimmings we collected from the neck and rib area. Since we are going to use this meat in soups and stews and it will be cooked until tender, we will not worry so much about whether or not the cut is with or against the grain. Cube the meat into small squares less than an inch thick.

You did a fine job, son. Now, we have to wrap all of this meat up into packages we can store in the freezer. I always double wrap my meat and I have found it will last at least six months in the freezer and still taste as fresh as day one! So, pull out a large piece of butcher paper, place it shiny side up, and lay the meat on there. Now, pull the sides in and overlap them, then the top and bottom, and use tape to hold them in place. Wrap it once more with another sheet of paper making sure the tape from your first wrapping is down on the solid part of second sheet. This double wrap will also assist in keeping freezer burn to a minimal level.

Now, take that permanent marker and mark what cut of meat it is, type of meat, and today's date (Loin, Venison, November 28, 2018). That way we know when we look at the paper we will know what type of meat it is, the cut of meat as well as the date frozen.

The remainder of the day was spent watching Brandon wrap the meat. That night over dinner, I said, "Brandon, what you did today would have cost you over a hundred dollars if a butcher had to do it. And, you know, I don't see why more hunters don't butcher. It's not all that hard is it, son?"

He looked at me and gave me a big crooked smile as he said, "It was my deer from the field to kitchen, plus I did it all! Aren't you proud of me?"

"Yep, Brandon, I am proud of you." And I honestly was.

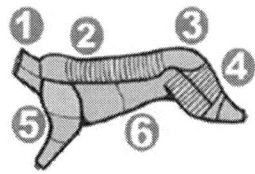

For those of you who wish to know the various cuts of meat, I have included this information.

1. Neck meat, great for stews or soups.

2. Loin or backstrap, the best part of the deer.

3. Rump makes a nifty pot roast, or use in stews or soups, or even as jerky.

4. The rear legs make great round steaks or they can be used to make roasts as well.

5. The forelegs should be cut into three pieces and they make good roasts.

6. Flank, or side meat, and trimmings can be removed and used in burger or sausage making.

7. Shank meat is the lower part of each leg, ground or use as roasts.

PACKING FOODS FOR CAMPING

It was late afternoon when the car pulled up in the campsite next to mine. I was enjoying a cold glass of ice tea, and stood watching them unload their equipment for a long time. I was amazed by how much junk they had brought with them. Now, there are two ways to camp, with gear and with minimum gear. These folks had gear, and then some. It was the next morning before I met my new neighbors.

I had just pulled the coffee pot off the fire and was pouring a cup when I heard a voice ask, "So, have you been here long?" I turned to find a middle-aged man, the same man I had watched unload the equipment from the car the night before, standing at the edge of my site. I invited him over and poured a second cup of coffee.

As I handed him the cup of steaming coffee, I made a comment that I had seen him unloading and wondered, though it was none of business, why he had so much food. I can still remember the look of surprise on his face and his response, "Why, we need a lot food. After all, we are going to be here for three days and we have to eat." I had an inner chuckle at his answer. See, I had been there a week, had another week to go, and I had about half as many containers as he did.

Most folks just don't know how to pack foods for a camping trip. I guess it doesn't matter much if you have a big enough car to bring it with you, but it is still a good idea to cut down on gear and weight. I usually keep my camping foods separated at home, so I can load very quickly when the urge to camp hits me. But, let's look at how we can pack perishables, dried foods, boxed foods, grains and pasta, canned goods, and what tools we need at a minimum.

Perishable items should be kept in an ice chest, or if a nearby stream is cold enough, in the water. I am speaking of fresh milk, veggies, and other such items. I have even stored cheeses in water, as long as they are kept in a waterproof plastic (and rigid) container. The key to using a stream or river is the water temperature must be cold. While I don't store meats or poultry in streams, due to possible pollutants or bacteria, I do keep anything that is sealed well and needs to be kept cool. I usually keep all drinks in the stream if the water is cold. Many mountain streams or spring fed streams are cold enough for storage of perishables. I do not use lukewarm water though.

If you use an ice chest, or cooler, make sure you keep ice in it and the lid stays on. This may be a problem if you have children along, because they are constantly opening the cooler to get soft drinks. Check the lid constantly to keep the inside of the cooler chilled.

I suggest you bring along a large quantity of dried foods when you camp. They are lightweight and do not require any temperature controls. I usually bring home made beef jerky, dried fruits, and I also make my own trail mix. The jerky is made by cutting lean beef cross grain, soaking in a slight salt and water mixture for an hour or more, and then drying it in the oven at the lowest temperature setting. Make sure the meat is not over lapping when you place it on a large cookie sheet. It takes hours for the meat to dry properly. Nonetheless, jerky, if kept in an airtight container, can last for years.

Fruit can be prepared the same way, without the saltwater mixture. My trail mix is made of a dried commercial breakfast cereal, dried fruits, and various nuts. These foods are great for a mid-day meal or for snacks as you fish or hike. Keep in mind to store them in plastic zip lock bags to protect them from the elements and for easy use. Also, I store all of my foods out of direct sunlight.

All boxed foods can be removed from the box and placed in zip locked bags. Make sure the contents of each bag are marked clearly with a permanent laundry marker.

Additionally, any special instructions can be written on the bag as well. You will be surprised how much easier it is to pack and the weight you save, once you have repackaged the boxes. Pasta, grains, dried beans, and any powdered items can be stored the same way. Give it a try, it works well.

Canned goods are to be avoided as much as possible. They are heavy and take up a lot of space. At times, though, you just cannot avoid taking them. If they are along for the camping trip, store them on the bottom, and not too many cans to a container. If the container is too heavy it will be difficult to remove from the vehicle. And, if you are backpacking, you will sweat for every can you pack. I avoid them as much as I can and still serve healthy and appealing meals in the woods.

Milk and some dairy products can be purchased in powdered form in many cases. I suggest you start with the fresh dairy items and keep the powdered stuff for later in your trip. Milk can also be bought in a container that does not require refrigeration. Just ask your grocer where to find these items.

Cooking at a campsite should not be much different than cooking at home. You can eat almost the same meals, drink the same drinks, and even have dessert. I usually bring one large pan, one small pan, a coffee pot, and a large pot. All of these cooking containers are made of lightweight aluminum to reduce weight. Also, I bring a roll of heavy-duty aluminum foil for baking or cooking with. I have found these items to be all I need to prepare a meal as I camp. And, this may surprise you, but the meals are as good as the ones I eat at home. It just takes a little camp cooking experience.

Your primary consideration when camping is keeping your foods at the proper temperatures (too avoid illness), cutting down on weight, and yet be able enjoy a good meal. You can keep almost any foods safe for eating by using common sense, proper storage, and by using what is available around you (snow, cold streams, etc).

Nonetheless, at any time you suspect a food has not been stored at the right temperature, do not consume it. As we said in the military, when in doubt, chuck it out.

Having a Hot Time Tonight

All of us who hunt, fish, backpack or hike, will one day need a fire. Most of the time we just stop, clear an area and start a fire without much thought. While that is all right most of the time, do you know how to really make a fire? Oh, I am not talking about the method you use to ignite the fire, I mean the components needed for a good fire, some of the types of fires, and even heat reflectors. They are pretty simple to make and all serve different needs in the woods.

The first aspect of making a fire, besides the ignition source, is tinder, kindling, and fuel. Let's look at tinder first.

Tinder should be small, shredded, or finely shaven pieces of material. You can use birch bark (it contains a resinous material that will burn hot), dried grass, wood shavings, pine pitch (has a resinous material in it, too), down from birds, charred cotton material, or lint. You want low ignition heat, so keep the material you use fluffed up to allow lots of oxygen flow as you ignite it. You can also coat some parts of your tinder with Vaseline, Chapstick, or insect repellent to make it burn hotter once lighted. Once the tinder has been ignited, you slowly add the kindling.

Kindling is small pieces of material you have decided to use for your fire. I suggest squaw wood, which are the small dead pieces of wood (limbs if you will) found on most trees at the lower levels. This wood is often found on live trees as well. It is usually dry if found on the lower levels of a large tree. The upper limbs keep the rain or snow off of it. But, you can use small twigs and branches found on the ground. Just make sure any woods you select are dead and dry. This is important for your kindling. Also, remember you want small pieces, not large ones. You want kindling in a variety of sizes and thickness. This is so you can gradually increase the size of the wood to increase the size of your fire. If you place a piece of kindling on your tender that is too big, the fire may go out. Slowly increase the wood size. Try to use soft woods for your kindling, if possible. Soft woods burn fast and give off sparks.

This unique trait of softwoods will assist your kindling in burning better and hotter.

Fuel is just about anything you can burn. Animal dung, from plant eaters, can be burned, fuels, oils, animal fats, and even most woods. Wet wood should be placed near the fire to at least partially dry out before being added to the fire. In wet weather, stumps, logs, or limbs may be broken open and the inner pieces of wood removed to add to your fire. This inner wood will be at least partially dry. Keep in mind, soft woods will burn fast, give off sparks, and may be an excellent source to start with. Some soft woods are spruce, pine, cedar, or willow.

Now, some hints to make your fire making easier. Pick up dead wood around your site. There is usually more than enough wood on the ground in most areas. I suggest you avoid chopping wood, especially in a survival situation, because it takes too much energy. You should not do any work in a survival situation that is not absolutely necessary. Save your strength. Also, by carrying a small candle you can start a fire very quickly. Just pile your tinder around it and you simply light the wick. You can hold a small piece of tinder over the candle flame to ignite it, then place the burning tender up against the base of your stacked tender. A fire will usually start, if your tinder is dry and dead, within a few seconds. Then, slowly add larger and larger pieces of fuel to the flames. Use caution here and do not get in a hurry and place fuel that is too large on the fire, as it may go out. You must be patient and allow the fire to grow in size very slowly.

There are many different styles of campfires you can make. Here are just a few.

   • *Teepee fire*, used when you need a concentrated light source, heat, or coals for cooking with.

   • *Pyramid fire*, excellent way of drying wood, needed light, and it produces good coals for cooking on.

   • *Log Cabin fire* is another good source of light and heat. It also is a very good fire to use when making fire signals or when you need to dry damp wood.

   • *Star fire* is easy to use and it conserves your fuel. It is used usually when you want a small fire.

   • *Long fire* is good for cooking. You first dig a trench, no less than 6 inches wide, and then place two large logs (green wood is the best) on both sides of the trench. You can place your cooking utensils on the logs to do your cooking. Remember to cook on hot coals, not open flame.

• *"T" fire* is a good all around fire. You can place your campfire in the top part of the "T" and your cooking coals on the long part of the "T". You should not make the long part of the "T" wider than your cooking pot or pan. This is so it can rest on the soil on both sides of the trench.

• *Key Hole fire* is another excellent cooking fire. Your fire is in the whole part of the fire pit, with the coals in the long trench. Make sure you only cook on coals and not flames in the trench. Your pots or pans will rest on the sides of the trench as you cook.

• *Dakota Hole fire*, this fire is a lot of work. You must first dig a hole, approximately 10 to 12 inches deep and 6 to 14 inches wide (this will be the hole where the fire is made). Then, dig another hole 8 to 10 inches from the main hole. Tunnel them together so they are connected. Your "tunnel" hole should be approximately 6 to 8 inches wide. The tunnel hole will allow airflow into the hole and keep the fire burning. It is a good fire for windy conditions or when you do not want the flames from your fire to be seen.

Just having a fire may not be enough to keep you warm. If you can, build your fire near some large rocks or boulders. The rocks will reflect the heat and help keep you warmer. If a shelter is placed near your fire (no closer than 10 feet), you should construct a heat reflector on the other side of the fire. With a heat reflector you will notice an increase in heat and light while in your shelter. You can also make a reflector from logs. You just stack them on their sides and support them by driving a sharp limb down each side to hold the stacked wood up. Some folks prefer to peel the bark off of the wood used to make a reflector, but that seems to be too much work for me. I am not sure it makes that much difference, compared to the work required to peel the bark.

Also, if the weather is extremely cold, you can make two or three reflectors, at different angles around your fire and sit in the middle. These reflectors will greatly increase the heat generated by your campfire. The key here is to retain (reflect) what heat your fire is producing, not to make a bigger fire! Large fires will consume more fuel, and in windy or snowy conditions that may make finding enough wood dangerous. You may also notice the reflectors assist in keeping the smoke out of your face and going upward.

Fires are often taken for granted. We don't give a second thought to making a fire, piling the wood on, and then forgetting about them. But, in an emergency, a properly planned fire is needed. When you only have a limited amount of matches or fuel to start your fire, you must plan ahead. Have all of your tender, kindling, and fuel ready before you attempt to start a fire. In a survival situation, you must do each task as few times as necessary to conserve energy and resources. Think before you act, and this is especially important when you make a fire. Decide in advance what you will need to start the fire, the type of fire and the fuels you will use. Then make your fire as if your life depends on it, because it may.

Fire and Emergencies

At times we must use emergency methods of starting a fire in order to survive. These methods can be extremely dangerous and should only be done in life and death situations.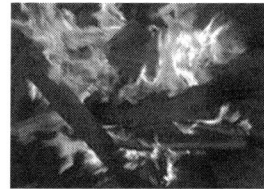

The man looked around and shivered. He was cold. Then wind was strong and seemed to cut through his coat like a knife. He knew that he had to have a fire, or he would soon be dead. He knelt and scraped the making of a fire together. He lit the first match, but the wind blew it out. He only had one more match and knew his very life depended on the ability to start a fire. "What will I do if this match does not start the fire?" the man asked himself. He struck the match and lowered it to the kindling with a trembling hand. As the kindling flared up and then died, he knew the answer to his question; he knew he would die.

While the introduction to this article is make believe, it could happen. And, sadly, it most likely has happened at some point in the past. Most of us are not very good at starting fires, even when we have the best kindling and dry wood. Just imagine how hard it would be with a high wind, heavy rain, or snow to compound the difficulty. I suggest you always carry at least three methods of starting fires, matches, a magnesium match, and flint and steel. I recently added a disposable lighter to my survival it as well. Why so many methods of starting a fire? First, these are by far the easiest ways to light a fire, and second, the alternatives are difficult for most of us.

Some of the alternate methods of fire starting involve friction, the sun, or the use of more primitive methods when compared to matches or lighters. Let's look at friction first.

The most common method of starting a fire through the use of friction is by making a fire bow. It is, however, one of the most difficult methods for most people to use. You need a piece of hardwood, with a socket in it, for the top, a bow (the cord may be a shoe lace, rope, thong, or whatever you have), a spindle (a piece of straight hardwood) and a piece of softwood for the base. As you spin the spindle, a dark (almost black) dust starts to fall on the base. If you move fast enough and with enough pressure, this black dust will ignite into a very small smoking ember. The fire is so small you may just see the smoke. However, if you gently blow on it, flames will appear. This method is difficult because the pressure must be maintained and the spindle must be rotated at an even and continuous rate. I recommend it as a last resort for most people, because it is not as easy as it sounds.

Another method of starting a fire is by using glass. Any convex lens (an outward bulge) may be used. It can come from a camera, a magnifying glass, binocular, telescope, or even a flashlight. All you have to do is hold the lens so that the suns rays are concentrated on your tender. This method is simple and most kids know how to do this. You can buy a cheap magnifying glass and carry it in your survival kit. They cost less than a buck.

Flint and steel is my preferred method of starting a fire. I usually just save the matches for a real emergency. I like the ease of use and the speed of which it works. All you need is flint and steel. Flint can even be found in nature's back yard. I have used sparking stones that were not flint to start a fire, but they do take longer. However, commercial flint and steel kits work as easily as a lighter. You take the striking rod (or a knife blade) and run it down the flint. Small pieces of flint will then fall into your tender and ignite it. The whole system is very simple and very easy to use. Everyone should carry flint and steel. A secret here; if you bring dried lint from your dryer with you, one spark from the flint and steel and you will have a flame. Simple and easy.

Alternate methods of starting a fire are there, but they can be dangerous to attempt. However, in a survival situation, you must consider the need for a fire and then weigh the risks involved. The choice is up to the survivor, and the decision must be made with a full understanding that injury or death could occur. Some flammables, like gasoline or gunpowder are very unstable and are hazardous to use. Nonetheless, there may come a point where a survivor must decide. No one else can decide for you, or take the responsibility if things go wrong.

Gasoline can be mixed with sand and burned, but use extreme caution at all times when using this method. The fuel mixed with the sand is very dangerous to light and should be done by throwing a flame onto the container. Make sure you are not downwind when you ignite a mixture of sand and gasoline. Also, the flames will often flare up when the sand and fuel is stirred with a stick. I have seen this mixture appear to be burned out, but a slight stirring with a stick would bring a low "*whump*" and the flames would once more be visible. Use this method only as a last resort and in life or death situations of extreme cold. I do not suggest it to be used in any other situation.

Oil can be burned as well. While it is more difficult to start burning than gasoline, it is very effective when used in signaling. When it burns it gives off a very dark and dense black smoke, which is visible for miles. It should also be mixed with sand to use more safely. Using oil with a normal campfire is difficult because if it is just poured on the coals it will smoke and not ignite immediately, most of the time. As when you are using gasoline, exercise extreme caution when using oil. Fuels and oils are not to be taken lightly when used in fires. They can injure or even kill you, if used carelessly.

A fire can also be started using a "C" cell flashlight battery and steel wool. I recommend you wear gloves when using this method of fire starting. Take the steel wool and pull it out so it is hanging loosely and is not lumped. Pull the strands apart to allow space for air to flow between the steel wool fibers. Place lint, small shavings of wood, or dried grasses on the wool, at the exact center point. The next step is to place the two ends (opposite ends) of the steel wool on the battery terminals (+ and – posts). Make sure you have nothing but your fire starting material in the middle or center of the steel wool, because it will start to glow. Ignition is easy once the wool glows.

Another method of starting a fire involves the use of your car battery. If you are stranded you may be able, if your car has one, to use the cigarette lighter. Just make sure you use very fine paper (toilet paper works well) to ignite with the lighter. I have discovered the glow does not last very long and thick pieces of paper or wood are very difficult to light. Use the thinnest paper you can find.

Additionally, if you have jumper cables you can arch them to make a spark. This method is very dangerous, because it involves the use of gasoline. Mix a small amount of gasoline, less than a teaspoon, with your tinder. Wait a few seconds for the air and fuel to mix. You should have already removed the vehicle battery and placed it near the tender, as far away as your jumper cables will allow. Connect the cables properly at the battery terminals, making sure the opposite ends of the cable are not touching. Then, very carefully, pick up the two ends of the unattached cable. Holding the clamps of the cables (on the unattached end of the cable) touch them together about four inches above the tender. The fire should start almost immediately. Be prepared for a sudden flare-up of flame as the fuel/air mixture ignites. Once the kindling is burning, add small sticks until the fire is burning well. Then gradually add larger and larger pieces of dry wood. This method of fire starting can be very dangerous and should only be attempted in true life and death situations.

If you have a weapon with you a fire can be started very quickly. We have all seen the movies where a man starts a fire by shooting into his kindling. Well, maybe it can be done that way, but I have never seen it happen. First, it is dangerous to shoot a bullet into your kindling, and second, the muzzle blast from the weapon will most likely scatter your kindling. You can, however, use the powder from the bullet to start a fire. It is dangerous to do, but once again, it can be done when a fire means life or death. The bullet must be removed from the shell, which is dangerous, and the gunpowder sprinkled on your kindling. This gunpowder will flare up and burn from the slightest spark. While this method works, once again, remember it is very dangerous to use.

Now, before you ever attempt any method of fire starting, always have your tinder and fuel nearby. Lint, bird nests, fire sticks, or other materials should be in place before you attempt to start the fire. Pine pitch, a sticky substance growing on the bark of pines or other evergreens, will aid your fire making. Make sure you have enough fuel to feed the fire once it starts; you may not get a second chance. Ensure that all tinder is bone dry and dead wood. Green wood or wet wood will be harder to start. Plus, it gives off more smoke.

The methods explained in this article may be very hazardous for you to attempt. I do not suggest that you go out and try them. I am only offering ways to start a fire without matches or lighters in an extremely serious situation. These methods may be very dangerous and should only be attempted in a life and death case. Serious injury or death can occur when attempting emergency fire making techniques. Neither I, nor the publisher of this article, accept any responsibility for any injuries or death that result from the use of these procedures. The methods discussed here are for use only when the survivor has no choice, except to die.

MAN AND FIRE

The rain had quit and the sun finally poked out from behind a dark cloud. A very heavy rain had just fallen and the air was filled with the smells of freshness. On the deer trail that ran down the side of the hill, water ran rushing through a wildly meandering ditch that had been formed by water pressure and gravity. Water pooled in low spots and droplets could be heard dripping from the nearby trees and rocks. It may have been a time many, many years ago in this part of our great nation. If one listened carefully, slight sounds could be heard as small animals cautiously exited shelters and began to look around. Suddenly, a blue jay made a loud shriek and the animals once more took shelter. It was no longer nature that scared them and sent them to shelter, but man.

The man was short, very thin, and the lower half of his body was muddy. His hair was unkempt, very long, and dirty. It was so dirty and full of debris it was difficult to determine that it was jet black. The man held both of his hands in front of his body and while he moved very quickly, it was obvious he was being extremely cautious. It was as if he was afraid of what he held, or had some deep, almost religious, respect for it. If you looked closely you would notice that both of his hands were holding a large flat rock firmly and level. In the center of the flat rock was a smoldering piece of pine and a small trail of smoke could be seen rising. The man's eyes were excited and large as he neared the mouth of a cave. The man continued his quick but cautious gait into the shelter. His hands were always holding the rock firmly and level. He dared not to rush. Once he had captured the fire, he intended to deliver it to his tribe.

The introduction to this story could have very well happened here in West Virginia thousands of years ago. One of man's (and woman's) most important needs in life is a fire. I suspect in the earliest times, before we learned to make our own fire, a group of cave folks would huddle around a recently lightning struck tree that was still burning, amazed by the warmth, not realizing the psychological comfort it provided. (Imagine the excitement as man learned to cook and enjoy a hot meal for a change). Or, as I opened with this story, someone captured it. I also suspect that early man was a bit scared and bewildered by the magic of the hot flames. Once man captured fire, and learned to keep it burning, he naturally developed the three work shifts we currently have, days, swings, and the mid shift. Keeping the fire fed was a full time responsibility. We still have fire everyday in our lives, but it is presented in a more subtle way.

When it comes to fire, in some ways, I suspect, we have not changed much from the man in my story. Oh, we don't have to find fire now, like the man did in the introduction, we have it with us most of the time. Even when we camp it is simple to make a campfire, right? Anyone can do it. Or can we? How much do you really know about constructing a fire? I know, some of you are experienced campers, and thus a natural when it comes to camping and making fires, but are you? Really? If your life depended on it, could you have one going in a very short time? Do you know how to build your fire safely? Do you consider environment issues when you make camp? I have some suggestions that may assist you, not that you need them, but let this old man babble.

Prepare for your fire, before you need it. I collect lint from the dryer and store it in a zip lock sandwich bag. (Some guys collect cards or match books, I collect lint.) This lint is great for using a metal match or flint and steel. Also, it starts very quickly with a match or lighter. Use common sense here. If you have a job like a fireman or pilot and use a fire-resistant or fireproof type of clothing in your duties, well, the lint from your drying these garments will not work. I prefer cotton lint and I gather it all the time. Also, as I walk in the woods I look for dripping sap on the side of pine trees. There are plenty of pine trees in most states so it is easy to find. This sap is just like kerosene and burns very hot when ignited. You can just pull it off. Do not use a knife, or you may injure the tree. The blotches of sap go into another zip lock bag. Additionally, I recommend you carry commercial fire starters, if you do not collect lint or sap.

Wood gathering, while simple, should be done correctly. Once at my campsite, I gather all the dried dead wood around me that I can find. I make sure I have gathered at least twelve hours or so of firewood. (Ever stumble around in the dark looking for firewood?) Also, I gather the small low branches of dead wood that have fallen from nearby trees. This wood is called squaw wood (this wood, while dead, is often still attached to a live tree, but I never break it off unless it is a matter of life and death). It is usually dry even in damp or wet weather and burns very well. This is because it is protected by all of the upper limbs on the tree. Avoid burning wet wood, grasses, leaves and bark. I have found that wet wood smokes, leaves and grass just flare up, and bark is very difficult to use to start a fire. Yea, I know, shaved bark can be used to start a fire, but why work when it is not needed? Many of you would argue about the types of wood to gather, i.e. hard wood (hickory) or soft wood (pine). I prefer just plain dry dead wood.

Let's discuss some environmental aspects of having a fire in the woods. Never cut down a tree to use it for firewood. There are two trains of thought here. First, the wood is green and will not burn very well, when compared to dead wood. Even in a survival situation, green wood is not a good choice. Green wood, as I said burns poorly and it gives off a lot of smoke. And second, most importantly, it serves no purpose to kill a living tree for something you cannot even use. Avoid damaging any greenery around you. Our natural resources must be maintained and protected for our children.

Preparing the fire pit is my next step. I pull up all grasses and clear away all leaves for at least ten feet around my fire pit. I then use my shovel to make sure there are no roots under the pit. I actually dig down about six inches or so just to make sure. I keep this soil in the pit, but using the shovel I "cut it fine." This keeps the fire from burning under-ground while I am sleeping or after I have left the site. Also, I keep a couple of gallons of water nearby and if my car is close I bring the fire extinguisher. I then circle the pit with hard rocks, not sand stone or rocks from the creek or river. Both may contain water and explode or crack as they heat up. And, when these rocks explode they may cause injury or even death.

I have had a rock explode on me once and it was exciting, to say the least. Nothing worse than placing a pot of ham and beans on three rocks over a bed of coals and then hearing the rocks crack and watch supper turn over. Also, before I decide on a site for a fire pit I check the area above the fire. I do not need to start overhanging limbs on fire. Usually, if I can do so, my fire is completely in the open. (I don't like to sleep under dead limbs either).

Lighting the fire is easy, or is it? I usually place my lint (a ball about half as big as my balled right hand) in the center of the pit and place a couple pieces of pine sap on it. I keep the lint all fluffed up, not compressed, to allow for airflow. A good draft is needed for a good fire. Using my match, I will light the sides of the lint and as the fire starts to burn I add very small twigs. As soon as the fire grows in size, so does the size of my tinder. I slowly add bigger and bigger pieces until the fire is large enough to support a large piece of dry wood.

You and I both know there are preferred ways to add wood to a fire. Some like a tee-pee stacking, some like a box stacking, me, I just place the end of a log in the fire and relax. I just push it in as it burns. I am lazy and prefer the easy way whenever possible. Besides, it works. When camping or in a survival situation, I use as little energy as needed to accomplish the task.

Some safety aspects to consider. It is easy to wander off and leave a campfire unattended, but not very smart. Most of us camp with at least another person, so one of you stays by the fire at all times. Additionally, keep your fire small, so it does not get out of control. There is absolutely no need for a large fire (if possible have a fire extinguisher with you). When you leave, make sure you put your fire out with water, stir the hot coals, and add more water. You should be able to touch your fire pit and not feel any heat. Then, shovel dirt over the pit until it is completely covered. All of us can, and must, prevent forest fires.

Other options to consider. Some folks like to make heat reflectors and other little goodies for a fire, i.e., spits to cook on, hanging rack, and so on. Those are all fine and good, under certain circumstances. But, the purpose of my article is to give you some hints on environmental issues, safety and health, as well as procedures on how to make a fire. While there are many different ways to organize and start a fire, this method has always worked for me. There is nothing more embarrassing than a grown man or woman attempting to light a campfire and not being able to do it with ease. Onlookers will often laugh at the unlucky person, while they know themselves they might not do any better.

Some other things that most of us never think about. When you leave, make sure your campsite is cleaner than when you arrived. Pick up after other folks and if the kids are with you, tell them why you are doing it. Tell them we need to protect West Virginia and to save it for others later in time. It is important we set a good example for the kids; they will mimic our behaviors later. Additionally, always camp in a designated campsite, unless it is an emergency situation. By using designated campsites, you may have access to water, firewood, and even electricity. Not to mention the dangers, and perhaps illegal aspects of camping otherwise.

Finally, a last word of caution here. *Never use charcoal lighter, gasoline or other flammables to start a fire.* I like my hair and eyebrows too much, not to mention my hands and body. Flammables are too dangerous and unpredictable to use starting a fire. I once saw a man start a fire using gasoline, but I am sure he never did that again, once he was out of the hospital. It is dangerous and not too smart.

I know there are many different emergency ways to start a fire and not all include the use of matches, flint and steel, or a metal match. I once started a fire with my truck battery and jumper cables when I was stuck in the mountains one snowy afternoon.

During my military arctic survival training, I watched my survival instructor start a fire using a C size battery and steel wool. He then showed us the old trick of using a magnifying glass and the sun. I watched another instructor do it with bamboo in Southeast Asia. I even watched a Native American survival instructor start a fire with a fire bow and then with a fire trough and a stick. But, you know...while friction is often used to start a fire I never once ever saw anyone make one by **just** rubbing two sticks together like in the movies...not even once. Be honest with me, have you? *So, be prepared and know your fire making.*

STANDING ON YOUR OWN TWO FEET

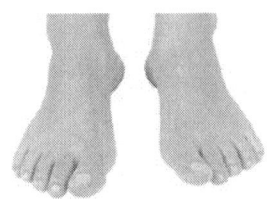

My son and I had only been in the bush for three days, but as I looked down at his feet, I was shocked. The skin was a pale white and it looked like he had been in the bathtub for hours, the skin was that wrinkled. I knew the problem was a result of him not taking care of his feet. He told me he had not changed his socks in days. He thought that since the socks were dry on his feet and he had only carried one extra pair, changing was not needed. He suspected he should have changed them, but he thought he didn't have to worry about his feet. Or, did he? While his problem was not serious; I simply had him dry his feet, apply some foot powder, and place clean dry socks on. He was going to be fine. However, I did warn him that if he had continued ignoring his feet, we would have had serious problems.

Ever since man starting wearing coverings on his feet, we have had problems with our feet. In World War I immersion foot was called 'trench foot'. The injury is the result of the feet being constantly wet (from water or sweat) and it causes tissue death of the feet. Keeping feet dry was a constant problem in World War I, due to the water collecting in the bottom of the trenches. But, trench foot isn't the only foot hazard associated with being outdoors.

Additionally, most of us, if we hunt or hike long enough, will eventually develop blisters on our feet. Usually blisters form due to poorly fitting boots or from new footwear that is not broken in yet. Make sure your new boots are larger than your dress shoes (because the socks you wear with boots are thicker). The boots should be big enough to allow you to wear a good thick pair of socks and still have room for your feet to move without rubbing. It is the rubbing (friction) of the skin on your foot against the boot that causes the blisters to form.

Both immersion foot and blisters can become extremely painful and they do not take a long time to develop, either. Immersion foot can take a lot longer than a blister to occur, but you can have other problems with your feet if they are not kept dry (cracking or dead tissue). Also, as in my case above, keep in mind if your boots cause your feet to sweat when you wear them, or if they fit poorly, you could develop foot problems. Most of us have had minor cases of immersion foot or had a blister after a long hunting trip or a hike (immersion foot takes time to develop, but it is a serious problem). Ok, when it comes to immersion foot, you know what causes it; what does it look like?

Immersion foot is easy to identify and you will suspect a problem with your feet the minute you remove your boots.

- The feet and toes will be white in color
- At times the socks may be discolored from the boot dye
- Bathtub wrinkles on the foot, like you have been in the tub for hours
- In advanced cases, you may have cracked or bleeding feet or toes
- There may be pain at the heel or ball of the foot
- Skin may peel or fall off as you remove your socks or touch the foot

Treatment of immersion foot is very simple. If you suspect immersion foot, dry your feet, keep them warm, and covered. Apply foot powder and put on dry socks as soon as you have completely dried the foot. If the injury is severe (cracked skin, bleeding, or severe pain), I suggest you seek medical treatment as soon as possible. In a survival situation, these steps may be difficult or even impossible to do at times. But, if your feet develop problems, you will have difficulty remaining mobile and that could cause serious survival repercussions.

The best way to prevent immersion foot is to keep your feet dry in the first place. There are boots on the market made of materials that allow your feet to sweat without retaining the moisture (Thinsolite ® and Gore-Tex ® are good examples). However, if you prefer leather or rubber boots, then make sure you check your feet often during the day. At least twice a day, you should stop and check your feet. Remember, your feet just have to sweat, not get soaking wet for an injury to occur.

Also, start the day out with clean dry socks on. I usually change my socks at noon, it they are damp, as I check my feet. If the weather is wet, you may have to change them more often. If necessary, you can dry your socks and boots at night by placing them near the campfire, but avoid getting them too close to the fire, or they will burn. When I change my socks, I also use a good quality foot powder, making sure I cover the "webbed skin" well between the toes. Just keep in mind, before you apply the powder, make sure your feet are completely dry. But what if you find a blister on your foot when applying the foot powder?

Blisters are the result of your feet rubbing against a part of your boot or sock. The outer skin dies and separates from the underlying skin. The space between the two skins fills with a fluid, lymph liquid, and you now have a blister. And, as you know, blisters come in many different sizes and shapes. Well, if you have a blister, do you break it open, or leave it intact?

There are many different trains of thought on how to treat a blister. I will stick with what the military taught me, because I suspect they may know a few things about walking and feet. First, if the blister is small, there is no need to open it. By opening it you may actually increase the risk of developing an infection. Second, large blisters should be drained, but do not remove the "dead layer" of skin over the top of the blister (this layer of skin will assist in covering and protecting the sensitive skin under it). Draining a blister is a very easy process.

The area should be cleaned well with soap and water, or an alcohol pad from your survival kit. You can use a needle or safety pin that has been held over a small flame until the tip turns red. Once the needle or pin has cooled, puncture the dead skin on the edge of the blister a couple of times. Then, gently massage the blister to drain the fluid. Pay close attention to the color of the fluid; it should be clear and not milky or a pus color (discoloration indications infection). After you have drained the blister, *do not remove the top layer of dead skin*. Apply an antibiotic ointment to the blister, cover with a band-aid, and put on clean dry socks. Check the blister each day and if your feet become wet or dirty, check it more often. But, it is easier to prevent a blister than it is to treat one in the field.

- Get properly fitting boots. If the boots are too tight, blisters will form. If the boots are too large, the foot will move inside the boot and will rub against the inside. Your boot should not fit snugly, but rather you should have about a thumbs width of space between your big toe and the boot tip.

- Wear good quality socks and change them often. Even the friction of a sock can cause a blister to form. Wet socks may cause damage to the skin on your feet and increase the risk of getting a blister.

- Always apply a foot powder when you put on clean socks. Foot powder will absorb the dampness on your feet and help keep them dry.

- Make sure your feet are in good shape before you ever use your boots. Keep the toenails trimmed, remove calluses, and smooth any rough spots on the foot.

- Some folks even apply a thin layer of petroleum jelly to their feet to reduce the amount of friction that can occur while hiking.

Each night, especially after a long day of hiking, I will check my feet very closely. I pay close attention to the color of my feet, any unusual smells, and I check for cracks under or between the toes. Any small blisters or cracks found, I treat as minor injuries and cover them with a band-aid after I have cleaned them. I never sleep in the same socks I have worn all day, regardless of the temperature. The socks may feel dry, but they will have condensation from your feet that will keep your feet damp. If you want to sleep in socks, put a clean pair on.

Most of us who hunt or hike take our feet for granted. We often ignore them until they start to ache or hurt, but by then it may be too late. Keep your feet dry, clean, warm, and protected at all times. Remember to use foot powder and do not sleep in your "old" socks, but rather, put on a clean pair. A hiking trip can quickly turn from fun in the sun to a nightmare if we don't take care of our feet. By following these simple suggestions you will always be able to stand on your own two feet.

FROSTBITE!

Combining knowledge with common sense can help you avoid this dangerous condition, and treat it in emergencies.

Winters in the United States can be harsh, but when compared to the far north they are less severe. Occasionally a cold spell will hit and it may last for weeks. We have all seen it happen. One day it is fairly warm, a front moves in, and the temperature drops quickly. Within a few hours there will be snow and temperatures will drop to the below temperatures in the zero range. Nonetheless, most people do not stop their day-today activities; we just slow down a little. Some folks, however, never hesitate when the weather turns sour. This is especially true of skiers, hunters, or ice fishermen.

When severe weather strikes, one of our primary concerns should be frostbite. While usually easy to prevent, it can hamper or permanently injure a victim. Most of us have experienced the beginning of frostbite; the red, painful skin, and perhaps some numbness. If we have suffered the onset of frostbite (also called frost nip), we will vividly remember the pain associated with the warming up. This was deep, aching pain we felt as the affected limb was exposed to warmth. Does this bring back uncomfortable memories? What exactly is frostbite? How do we prevent it? How do we treat it?

Frostbite is the freezing of body tissue during exposure to the cold. Frostbite may accompany hypothermia, so exercise extreme caution if you suspect the onset of either injury. What are the symptoms of Frostbite? There may be a white or waxy appearance to the damaged skin tissue. In the beginning stages of frostbite the skin may still be pliable. In advanced stages the damaged tissue may appear hard, solid to the touch, and there may even be ice crystals under the skin, joints may appear to stiffen, and there can be numbness or loss of sensation to the injured area. Usually, but not always, frostbite affects an extremity or limb, i.e., a finger, toe, nose or ears. I have seen cases on the legs (thigh and calf) from skiing trips. Stay alert for these symptoms on any area of your body.

While frostbite can be a crippling injury, it can usually be prevented with proper dress and common sense. First, let's discuss how to dress for the severe cold. When I lived in Alaska, the first thing I learned was to dress in layers. I would don long underwear, wool pants, and then nylon trousers. This protected me in layers, allowing air to be trapped, which acted as insulation. I then put on nylon socks, wool socks, and finally my boots (made with Thinsolite® or Gore-Tex®). My coat was a three-layered coat, consisting of a fleece under garment, then cotton garment over that, and finally a nylon outer shell.

But I didn't stop there. I wore glove liners and then a heavy pair of mittens (once again, Thinsolite or Gore-Tex). My headgear consisted of a "mad bomber" hat with earflaps. This hat was constructed of leather, usually cow or deer hide, and lined with fur. Also, the most common type of fur used for the lining, and least expensive, is rabbit. The hat should fit loosely and has large flaps that can be secured on top of the hat or lowered to cover the ears. A strap holds the flaps in place once snapped under the chin. With the flaps down, the hat covers most of the head with the exception of the face. This hat really keeps the body heat in.

If the weather turned really severe, I would wrap the lower half of my face, including my nose, in a scarf. All exposed parts of the skin should be protected. Since most body heat escapes through the head, this is an important fact to remember. This layering was how the old timers survived and it still works most of the time. When layering does not work (high winds), or you are improperly dressed due to an emergency, how do you prevent injury from frostbite, and once you suspect you are injured, what steps do you take?

Earlier, I mentioned common sense. Of all the tools you have with you during an emergency, common sense is one of the most important. If you suspect a symptom we discussed, stop. First aid must be given quickly to avoid additional injury to the damaged tissue. Prolonged exposure will only compound the damage and may lead to amputation of the damaged limb or extremity.

Seek medical treatment immediately if possible. If not, then the following steps may be used in emergencies.

Seek shelter immediately. Get out of the wind and into either a natural or man made shelter. An example of a natural shelter might be a group of large rocks that block the wind, a ditch, a cave, or even up under the bottom limbs of a large evergreen tree. I usually have a poncho with me (survival kit item), so if a natural shelter is not handy, I can quickly make a "poncho tent." This quick shelter is made by tying a line (550 parachute cord is the best) between two trees, approximately two feet off the ground, and then draping the poncho over the line. The bottom edge of my shelter can be held in place by large rocks or wooden stakes. You can also make shelters and windbreaks out of a variety of natural items you may find around you, including snow. Your skill at making such expedient shelters will depend on your study and knowledge of this sort of thing, and any prior training and experience you may have.

Get warm. This means more than just having a fire. You should drink plenty of hot fluids, if you can, and if possible generate body heat by eating candy or other foods. In all situations avoid drinking alcohol; you do not need your judgment clouded. Also, remember, two or three small fires will warm you faster than one large one. Make a small fire on each side of you and you will warm evenly. *Do not rub snow on frostbite.* This act, though portrayed frequently in movies, only causes additional damage to the already frozen tissue. The rubbing may increase tissue damage, while the snow may lower the tissue temperature.

Carefully remove boots or gloves. Do not force frozen clothing off of the affected area. If needed, the frozen area (hands or feet) may have to be soaked in warm water to loosen the clothing. Place the injured part in lukewarm water, if possible, using your elbow to test it. The water should feel comfortable, and not hot. It should be around 42 degrees C, or 100 degrees F. Warm the tissue until flushed with a red color from returning blood. Do not rub the warmed tissue. This may cause additional damage as well.

If a fire is not available, or a container for water, you can place the frozen part at the crotch of your arms/legs using body heat to thaw it. Keep in mind, this will lower the body temperature of the person giving first aid, and is done only as a last resort. The process of treating frostbite is very painful. Doctors treating frostbite often use narcotics to lessen the pain during treatment. In the field you will not have that luxury.

Ensure the treated tissue does not become frozen again. If there is a possibility of the area becoming refrozen, do not thaw it. Once frozen, then thawed, the tissue will refreeze much quicker and cause additional tissue damage. Protect the damaged skin by applying a loose dry dressing and do not break any blisters. Avoid bumping or additional injury to the injury.

As soon as possible, seek medical attention. Frostbite is a crippling injury that can lead to the loss of a finger, toe, all or part of a nose, ears, or even a limb. It can happen to skiers, hunters, fishermen, children, or those who have car problems on lonely roads. It is not something to be taken lightly.

But, by knowing the best prevention techniques, symptoms, and emergency treatment, it can be battled. By combining knowledge with common sense, you too, can have an enjoyable winter. Be safe!

Author's note: Various procedures in this article *may be disagreed with* by some readers, especially armchair "Survival Experts." I quickly admit to not being a medical professional, but the above information was gained from years of field experience, USAF Survival Arctic Survival School Training, USAF Mountain Survival School Training, USAF Basic Survival School Training, The American Red Cross and Canadian Red Cross First Aid Booklets, The SAS Survival Manual, and other resources too numerous to list. Besides, I know from experience the steps I recommended work; I have experienced it firsthand.

Hygiene, the Outdoors, and You

My cousin Larry always looks dirty. He is one of those people you could dress in silk and gold and he would still look like a grease monkey after a hard day's work. He looks even more disarrayed while outdoors. See, Larry is not the cleanest guy around, and hygiene is very important when you are in the woods.

To me hygiene is made up of clean water, clean and dry clothing, personal cleanliness, proper food preparation, a clean camp site, clean eating utensils, and good first aid for minor cuts and scrapes. Each of them compliments the other and keeps a camper in good health. Let's take a look at each and see why they are important.

Clean drinking water is an obvious need. Purify all water, use designated water at public campsites, or bring bottled water. Bad water will lay a person low very quickly. Never drink water that you are unsure of. I suggest water purification tablets, which are small and inexpensive to carry. Or there are filtering systems out there if you prefer. The easiest and least expensive way to treat water is by boiling it. Regardless of the method you prefer to use, all water must be treated. Keep in mind that even sparkling clear streams may not have clean water.

All clothing should be kept clean, dry, and in good repair. Carry a small sewing kit to repair rips or tears. Learn to sew your clothing, or reattach a button before you venture outdoors. Clean clothing will retain better insulating qualities in cool or cold weather, and wet clothing, even in warm weather, can cause chapping. Besides, wet or dirty clothing can be uncomfortable to wear. Children, as well as some adults, may find this policy of staying clean completely against why they are in the woods to start with. Nonetheless, it must be done. Wash your clothing regularly when you are on long trips. Use only biodegradable soaps and empty your laundry water far away from any stream or water source. Carry plastic bags to take soiled clothing home if you decide not to wash it at your camping area.

Believe it or not, you will feel better if you shave and bathe while camping. I have used streams and rivers to bathe in and I have taken a "sponge" bath when I could not reach a body of water. Shaving seems to always "lift me up" while camping. It actually feels good to get rid of the whiskers, and I often feel refreshed. The main reason I strive keep clean is to retard the chances of infection from injuries I might sustain. The cleaner you stay, the healthier you remain. I wash my hands often and keep my nails cut short. Underclothing and outer-clothing should be changed daily. While all of this surprises kids when they first start camping, it is a good habit for them to get into.

An area of hygiene we hardly ever consider are dead animals. Never touch a dead animal with your hands. If you must move it, do so with caution, using a shovel or limbs. You can bury it, but make sure you cover the grave with heavy stones to keep other animals from digging it up to feed on it. Some animals may have died from diseases and their bodies could prove to be harmful to humans. Make sure your children, if they are young, know not to play with or touch dead animals.

Food preparation is another area where hygiene is important. If you spend the afternoon putting worms on a hook and return for lunch, do you wash your hands? Come on, all of you guys, be honest here! Not only your cleanliness is an issue, but also the quality of the foods. Have all perishables been kept at a proper temperature? Do you eat the green steak or discard it? Is the meat, especially ground up meats and poultry cooked to the proper serving temperatures? Keep all of the cooking utensils stored within a dry and clean spot. I usually keep mine in a box in the tent or under a tarp. However, it doesn't matter where you store them as long as they stay dry and clean.

How about your campsite? Is it clean? Do you have a designated "trash container"? Or, do you have soda cans, wrappers, and other litter scattered around your camp? Keep in mind, in most states you can be fined for a messy campsite. I separate paper items, cans, bottles, and recyclable items. Each day I burn the paper stuff and food scraps (if you bury them, wild critters will just dig it all up), place the other stuff in large trash bags, or laundry bags, and place it yards away from my camp, usually tied high up on a tree limb. By hanging it in a tree I keep the small hungry critters and insects away from my camp. Raccoons love litter and will make a lot of noise at night as they feed in your camp. Then again, nothing is worse than bees buzzing around the remains of a cola can or spilled sweets. Stay clean and keep the uninvited guest list down.

Clean cooking and eating utensils are an absolute necessity! This means not only cleaning your plates, pots, pans, knives and forks, but rinsing them off well also. Have your cooking utensils been properly washed? Have they been washed at all? If they were washed, has all the soap been rinsed from them? Guess what happens if you ingest soap? Yep, you could get diarrhea. My son (sorry, Dave) once gave the whole group a bad case of the "leaping revenge" because he failed to rinse the dishes after he had washed them. Live and learn, but dirty or poorly rinsed utensils will knock even the strongest person on their knees quickly. Keep your dishes and eating utensils as clean as possible.

Now, speaking of "leaping revenge." At some point or another, all us in the woods will have to use the "bathroom." You can take a portable toilet, use a "honey bucket", or use public restrooms. If no public restrooms are available, use some common sense. Do not designate a toilet area near your water source, uphill from your camp, or near where you store or prepare the food. I usually make my designated toilet at least 100 feet from the camp. Make sure each person, especially children, are reminded to only "go" in the area you have designated as the toilet. Have a shovel, roll of toilet paper, and loose sand or soil near your pit. Now, your pit can be as long as you like, but I suggest it be at least 12 inches wide.

Once you do your thing, add a few shovels of dirt or sand over your waste. This will assist in reducing the smells from your bathroom (when the wind shifts) as well as the number of flies and other insects down.

When you construct your toilet area you can make elaborate chairs, support beams, or whatever you want, but make sure everyone uses the pit when they have the need to go. You can also screen the area in with a tarp, or just make sure it is in some bushes. Everyone wants some privacy when taking care of business.

Finally, let's discuss how first aid plays into the hygiene picture when we camp, fish, or hunt. Most of the injuries we sustain in the outdoors are very small cuts, punctures, or scrapes. You know the kind of injury I am talking about; you cut a finger fixing dinner, you get a fish hook in a thumb, or you fall and scrape a knee or ankle as you hike. It is important to immediately wash the injury with soap and water, and then cover it with a protective material. Now, there are liquid bandages out there, band-aid strips, and other material for coverings. You should use the one you prefer, as long as you use one. These steps are to avoid infection. I always carry a basic first aid kit when I am outdoors and recommend you do the same.

I have seen the smallest of cuts become major injuries due to infection. By washing the injury you are removing foreign matter and when covering the injury you are attempting to keep foreign matter out. If you keep your body clean, wear clean clothing, keep your campsite clean, and protect the injured area you will reduce the chances of infection. Of course, with any serious injury or infection seek medical treatment as soon as possible.

Camping or spending time outdoors does not have to be a painful experience. Use common hygiene sense and your time will be spent enjoying nature, instead of continuously answering "natures call." Remember, keep everything (including yourself) clean and you will do just fine. Enjoy your summer!

Chilled to the Bone!

While the weather was cool, the sun was shining brightly. There was not a cloud in the sky and the wind was very light. A figure soon appeared moving slowly over the distant skyline, down a trail that meandered from the pass. If you looked closely, you could see his camouflage clothing, his rifle, and his awkward movements. The man was swaying at dangerous angles as he walked through the woods. He appeared to be intoxicated as he bounced into trees and large rocks. His rifle fell from his shoulder, but the man did not seem to notice as he continued walking. After moving a few more feet, he took off his coat and discarded it in the bushes along the trail. He may have noticed his vision was blurred and he had a slight headache. As the man continued down the trail and out of sight, he was totally unaware that he was suffering from hypothermia.

Hypothermia is an injury not related to the most common injuries we think of when we go outdoors. Those of us who spend time with nature rarely consider this injury. But, it is a potentially deadly situation that can usually be easily prevented, if you know what it is, and how it kills. Hypothermia is the lowering of *the body's core temperature*. Most of us, let's say, have a body temperature of between 97 and 99 degrees. When our temperature drops internally to below this normal range, hypothermia sets in. If the core temperature is not brought back up, death usually occurs. We have all felt the beginning stages of hypothermia when we start to shiver.

Now, some of you are thinking, "I don't live in a very cold climate. I don't need to read any of this." Well, you may be wrong. *Hypothermia can happen in almost any temperature range and even indoors!* Keep in mind, most high temperature range hypothermia will occur with the elderly, but it can still hit others at any time. When your internal temperature drops to below 90 degrees you are in severe hypothermia. Confused? Well, now that you know what hypothermia is, let me share some other interesting information with you.

Your body heat can be lowered by any number of reasons; exhaustion, exposure to the elements, lack of food, poor diet, immersion (if your boat turns over or you fall into a stream), wet or damp clothing, and the list goes on. That is one of the reasons in my articles I often remind you to keep your clothing clean, in good repair, and dry. Most of us have experienced the beginning of hypothermia while hunting, fishing, hiking, or camping. We start to shiver and shake. Usually, we just add a sweater or jacket, or we just move closer to the fire. But, what happens when we fail to get warm? What happens in extreme cases?

Well, the symptoms of hypothermia are in stages and there are many sites online that offer additional information to those of you interested in learning more. I suggest you visit some of those sites and take a look at what they have to say. Keep in mind to stay with sites that know what they are talking about (see my recommendations at the end of this article). While I am not a doctor and other than some survival medicine classes I have attended, I cannot claim to be an expert on the subject. But I do know the symptoms, and they may start with a sudden burst of energy, then....

- A feeling that "everything is alright"
- The removing of clothing in cold or wet weather
- Shivering
- A slow response
- Uncontrolled shivering
- Loss of motor skills (lack of coordination)
- A headache
- Blurred vision
- Irrational behavior for the individual
- Abdominal pain

If these symptoms are noticed or felt, regardless of the ambient air temperature, treat for hypothermia. This treatment may be as simple as just warming the person up. This warming up may just require an additional layer of clothing, a hot drink or maybe a fire. In more advanced cases, other steps may have to be taken. Advanced treatment may require:

- Undressing the victim and placing them in a sleeping bag with another individual, cuddle and use body heat to assist in warming the victim. (Some disagree on this step, but I believe the additional body heat can help).
- Finding shelter in a warm building.
- Use warm (not hot) rocks and apply warmth to the pit of the stomach, small (lower) back, armpits, back of the neck, wrists, and between the thighs.
- Give the victim warm fluids and, if possible, increase sugar intake—but only if the victim is conscious.
- Avoid alcohol! Alcohol causes vasodilation (increase in surface blood flow), which leads to increased heat loss.
- Seek medical treatment immediately if it is possible in your situation.

Okay, now that we have a basic understanding of what hypothermia is, as well as some treatment, how do we determine at what stage a victim is? I suggest the old survival method I was taught:

With Mild Hypothermia

- Shivering (We have all had this from time to time)
- Goosebumps
- Hands may feel numb
- Hands shake badly enough that some tasks cannot be accomplished.

With Moderate Hypothermia

- Severe Shivering
- Stumbling
- Poor motor skills (poor coordination)
- Movements are more difficult to do and take longer
- Some confusion
- Difficulty speaking

- If the person cannot pass a sobriety test, i.e., walk in a straight line for 30 feet or so, they have hypothermia.
- And, in some cases the victim becomes depressed and withdraws.

With Severe Hypothermia

- Respiratory failure.
- The victim is in a stupor
- Skin color may become blue or puffy
- Irrational behavior for that individual (*compare to the person's normal behavior*)
- Shivering stops, but muscle coordination and motor skills are very poor.
- Pulse and respiration rate drop
- Overall confusion
- Inability to walk, even a short distance
- The victim may be unconscious
- Death

Do not give your victim food, but instead give them water and sugars. The stomach is not capable of processing foods at this point. Every fifteen or twenty minutes give the victim a warm drink. Also, your victim will need to urinate. If the bladder of the victim is full, the body will use some of its heat to keep the urine warm and not the body. Get your patient to urinate so the body can go back to keeping the major internal organs warm again. Have them urinate often.

Use carbohydrates to provide quick energy in mild cases of hypothermia, or you can use proteins and fats to assist as well. Both proteins and fats release energy slower than carbohydrates, but the heat generated will last longer overall. Use what you have, and that may be limited by where you are.

Do not give your victim alcohol, caffeine or tobacco. All three are to be avoided in any survival or emergency situations, because they increase heat loss and they dehydrate. So, remember in the old movies where a very cold or injured person is given a shot of whiskey to fight off the cold? Well, that is dangerous and foolish. Avoid alcohol, caffeine, or tobacco at all times when treating hypothermia.

Wrap the victim, once you have them dry, in layers and do not allow them to get wet. Keep them dry. I suggest using more than one sleeping bag, blankets and a "casualty" or "space" blanket. Remember that both the casualty and space blanket have a reflective side that can be placed toward the victim to reflect body heat and to prevent heat loss. In all cases, keep your victim warm and dry.

Do not just warm the outer portions of your victim and think it will work as a treatment. It is the inner core you should work on. *Placing the victim too near a fire may only compound your problems in treatment.* The warming of the outside of your victim may actually cause unwarmed, cold blood to start flowing. This flowing of cold blood may cause further chill to the inner core of your victim and lead to death. **Warm the victim from the inside out and do it slowly in most cases.**

Well, now we have an idea of what it is and how to treat it; how do we avoid hypothermia to begin with?

- **Dress for the weather**. Keep in mind that you should dress in layers so that you get heat from the trapped air pockets. Air equals insulation, which equals warmth.

- **Drink lots of hot fluids**. In a survival situation find wild plants from which you can use to make a tea with. I use a "pine needle" tea. Yes, you guessed it, made from pine needles.

- **Increase your food intake**. Keep in mind the positive aspects of carbohydrates, proteins, and fats in the treatment of hypothermia.

- **Limit your exposure** to the elements. If the weather turns bad, seek shelter. Do not force march or hike. Intentional exposure is usually a foolish idea.

- **Avoid shivering**. If you start to shiver, use common sense. Add additional clothing, have a hot drink, seek shelter, and start a fire.

- **Carry high-energy food** bars and hard candy in your survival kit.

- **Avoid exhaustion** when moving by taking frequent breaks.

- **Be aware** that anxiety, stress, or injuries may increase the potential for hypothermia.

Hypothermia is only one danger a person in the bush may have to face. Nonetheless, it can be a real killer to those who have no idea of what it is or how it works. By knowing the symptoms, proper treatment, and how to prevent it, the injury can be avoided in most cases. In some extreme situations, like a boat turning over in cold or cool weather, you will have to use speed and common sense in treatment. While hypothermia is potentially a very dangerous injury, for most of us it is caused by a lack of knowledge. Now that you know a little about the subject, I suggest you do some additional research on this potentially deadly injury. (When I typed in hypothermia I got 307,000 sites.)

Please note: *This article is provided as a motivational tool to stimulate the reader to conduct additional research on this subject. While I have prepared this article to the best of my ability, I am not a doctor or a competent medical authority by profession. The procedures I have used in this article are those taught to me, in basic first aid and survival medicine during my U.S. military survival training, and what I have learned conducting personal research.*

Hypothermia is a serious injury and requires serious research. When I typed in "hypothermia" to conduct an online search, I got more than 307,000 sites (and that was using only one search engine). As you conduct your first aid research, I recommend you concentrate on approved North American Medical Sites, U.S. Military Survival Manuals, or perhaps the medical departments of larger North American Universities.

Remember, Knowledge is Survival.

Tick-Borne Diseases and You

With the coming of spring, most of us will be spending more and more time in the woods. Hunters will be scouting new sites, or observing the movement of their favorite game, in order to be prepared for the coming hunting season. Hikers, campers, and fishermen will spend hours or days in the fields, woods, and trails of America. Often, we head off into Mother Nature without a serious care in the world, but we should have some concerns.

Most of us have encountered ticks on our wilderness treks and just add them up, like mosquitoes, as the price we pay to venture outdoors. But very few of us seriously consider the little pest to be much of a threat to us, much less our health (In the U.S. there is very little national concern over these dangerous diseases, or perhaps I should say, over tick-borne diseases in general). Usually we just pull the tick off and continue on our way, not realizing the potential danger the tick may present. A simple tick can carry a number of different kinds of diseases, all of which can cripple and even kill you. How much do you know about ticks, the removal of ticks, the symptoms of the various tick-borne diseases, treatment, and prevention?

Ticks infest the woods, fields, and front yards of many places in America. I can remember growing up in Missouri and finding ticks on me almost daily. These same ticks may be capable of transmitting a tick-borne disease. You may find it interesting that there are various types of ticks that carry the diseases, and tick-borne diseases have been identified in all states except Hawaii, Vermont, Maine, and Alaska. Those of us who live in the southern states are pretty much exposed to all of the tick-borne diseases, with the exception of the Babesia Infection, which has only been identified (so far) with the northeastern part of the United States.

So, let's look at a few of the tick-borne diseases and where they are usually found.

- **Lyme Disease** is found in a scattered manner all across the United States. However, it does not seem to be common in most of the plains states.

- **Rocky Mountain Spotted Fever** has been reported in all states except for Hawaii, Vermont, Maine and Alaska. *This illness is the most common of the tick-borne diseases.*

- **Southern Tick-Associated Rash**. This disease is common in the south and may be difficult, without laboratory testing, to separate from Lyme disease. To the eye, the rash may appear to be Lyme disease, due to the similarity of the rashes.

- **Babesia Infection** is very rare and only seems to be found in the Northeastern part of the United States. Unlike the other tick-borne diseases, which all have somewhat similar symptoms, this illness has malaria like symptoms.

- **Ehrlichiosis** is the newest tick-borne disease and is currently under evaluation. It was first clearly identified in 1994 and so far, it has only been identified in a few cases in Missouri, Oklahoma, and Tennessee.

Now that I have your attention, if you find a tick on you, don't panic. There are many different ways to remove a tick and the one that works for you is the best. *Do not grasp a tick and just pull it off.* The head may remain and cause an infection (even if the tick is not diseased). In the military, we often used a blown out and hot match head. We placed the hot end of the match near the ticks rear, it would release, and then it would back out. At that point the tick could be removed and dealt with properly. Also, we were taught to coat the tick with tree sap, an oil, or Vaseline, to cut its air supply. After a couple of minutes the tick will back out and you can remove it safely. Another good way to remove a tick is by using a commercial tick removal kit, which is available at many sporting goods stores.

Regardless of the method you use to remove a tick, *always clean your hands afterwards with soap and water.* Also, the area of the bite should be cleaned. There may be some itching in the general area of the bite following the removal of a tick. This discomfort is very common in a crotch area (genitals, armpits, or rear). Cold compresses, or a mixture of water and ashes, can greatly reduce the itch.

If you contact any tick-borne disease you will know within a few days. Do not wait for them to go away, but seek medical assistance immediately. The symptoms of most tick-borne diseases are (with the exception of Babesia, which has malaria like symptoms):

- A rash at the bite area; do not confuse the small red bite as a rash.

- You may develop flu like symptoms
- You may experience fatigue
- You may start having headaches for no reason
- Your neck may stiffen
- Your jaw may cause you discomfort
- A slight fever may occur
- Your glands may swell
- You may start experiencing swollen or stiff joints
- Your eyes may redden

If you do not see a doctor, and you go untreated, the disease will progress to the next stage one to three weeks after the bite:

- You may become dizzy
- Your heartbeat may become irregular
- And, you may experience a weakness of your facial muscles
- In the very late stage, the disease will affect your joints, heart, central nervous system, or other major organs.

Depending on the particular disease you have been exposed to, the symptoms for the late stages may vary. But in all cases, seek medical attention at the first sign of a tick-borne illness.

The treatment of tick-borne diseases depends on your doctor. In most cases, treatment involves the use of antibiotics. Your medical professional is very qualified to treat the illnesses, and will develop an individual treatment plan for your case. Keep in mind though; in many cases you can still experience recurring symptoms for a long time (perhaps years). Also, make sure you follow your doctor's recommendation for treatment to the letter. Lyme disease is very serious, and can adversely affect your overall heath.

Well, we have discussed ticks, tick-borne diseases, the removal of ticks, the symptoms of tick-borne diseases, and the treatment. But by now you may be asking, how do I avoid a tick bite to start with? Good question and a smart one as well. The best way to avoid a tick bite is to prepare before you go into the woods. Use common sense and:

Simple Survival

- Make sure all of your clothing overlaps and covers all exposed skin.
- Use commercial tick repellent on your clothing.
- Wear long pants and long sleeve shirts.
- Blouse your pants, or wear long socks that are pulled up to cover your pants.
- Keep long sleeves rolled down and buttoned.
- Always wear a hat; keep in mind that ticks love hair.
- Stop at least once, usually midday, and have a tick check. Check again before bedtime. Undress and check for ticks, remembering to check the crotch.

Our time outdoors should be fun and exciting for us. While the rewards of spending time with nature are great, remember, there are some risks. If you use common sense, dress properly, check for ticks at least twice a day, and know the symptoms of tick-borne diseases, you can feel more confident about your time outdoors. Knowledge is the key to really enjoying your time in the woods.

Simple Survival Tips

A casualty blanket makes a great temporary shelter. Just tie a rope between two trees (low) and drape the blanket over the rope. ...Use stakes to secure the bottom edges.

It's light and not expensive!

First Aid, You, and the Outdoors

As I looked down at the young man lying on the forest floor, I could see the pain in his dark eyes. His skin color was pale, his words were a mixture of fear and anxiety, and his breathing was rapid. I quickly looked around the area and determined his injury, a possible fracture of the right leg, was the result of falling from a ledge approximately six feet above us. I knew, from the symptoms, he was suffering from shock. Shock is a condition that results when the circulation of blood is inadequate for the oxygen needs of the body's tissues. What this means in a nutshell is a lack of oxygen to cells, which may result in cell death, and eventually it could lead to the death of the casualty.

Knowing the importance of reassuring the victim, I kneeled and spoke in a firm but kind voice to him. I kept talking to him as I determined his right leg appeared to be broken. I joked with him a little as I started treating his injury. I assured him that help was on the way, asked him about his pain, and eventually got him to talking about his new child. My goals of taking charge, assessing, and assuring, had been met. Three days later I passed him in the building we worked in. He had survived.

One aspect of the outdoors most of us pay little attention to is first aid. Why? I suggest that most of us think injuries will always **happen to you, but not me**. In psychology we call that attitude denial. It is an "it will never happen to me" attitude, and it is a very dangerous stance to have in the woods. See, all of us will sustain some type of injury eventually if we spend much time out of doors. It just happens.

Now, most of our injuries will be scrapes, shallow cuts, a fishhook in a thumb, or perhaps a small burn. These are easy to take care of and they usually never lead to larger problems. However, it is important to remember that the key in any emergency treatment is a two-step process (injury treatment and shock treatment).

First, you must determine the extent of the injuries and ask yourself if you are qualified to treat them. Obviously, if someone is seriously injured or near death, you may be out of your level of treatment. Nonetheless, in any situation you can do some things to assist the victim until help arrives. In a remote location during a survival situation you may be all the help that will be available for some time. *No, you should never attempt any medical treatment you are not qualified to do, nor should you sit on your duff and cry the "poor me" song out over and over.*

Your first step should be to assess the injury or illness. Take charge. But keep in mind the most qualified individual should be in control. If someone on the scene is more qualified than you, let that person control the situation.

If you are the one to control the emergency, ask yourself the following questions:

First, determine if there is still a danger in the area. Look around and ask yourself, what caused the injury and is it still able to hurt someone? This is important if the injury is the result of an electrical source, wild animal, human assault, weather, or other situations. I cannot cover all possible situations, but evaluate the cause first. You do not want to become the second or third victim of a mishap.

Second, is the injury life threatening? If not, it is a very simple process usually to treat the injured person. You can determine if the injury is serious by checking for breathing and pulse. Even if the victim is conscious, be cautious. Some injuries will not show all of their symptoms until later. Treat all victims for shock, which is covered further along in this article.

When you approach a casualty, look to see if they are breathing or choking. If breathing is not a problem, check to determine if there might be neck or spinal injuries. Is the body bent at an awkward angle? Is there a loss of feeling in the spine or neck area? Is there intense pain in one or both of those areas? Do not lift or move the victim until you are able to determine the extent of injuries. If you remotely suspect a neck or spinal injury, do not move the casualty, unless they are in extreme danger. Make them comfortable in place, if it is not life threatening to do so. At any rate, always remember your **a, b, c's**....Check the *airway*, the *breathing*, and the *circulation* (ABC).

Now, I cannot cover every type of emergency you could be faced with, but I will suggest you purchase a good quality first aid book and keep it on you at all times in the bush. You may never know when you will need it. If you suspect spinal or neck injuries, seek medical assistance immediately. But while you wait there are some things you can do.

In any painful or frightening situation you may encounter a victim going into shock (Just like the man in my opening paragraph). Early signs of shock are:

- Pale skin, lips may have lost color
- Cold, clammy skin
- Restlessness
- Weakness
- Increased rate of breathing or a shallow rapid pulse
- Anxiety
- Severe thirst or vomiting
- Confusion

In the later stages of shock the victim may:

- Show no interest or be unresponsive
- May lapse into unconsciousness
- Have vacant or sunken eyes

In all cases of shock you should do the following:

- Reassure the casualty. Speak to them often and in an assuring voice. Keep your own wits about you and do not panic. Your patient will know immediately if you lose control.
- Cover the individual to maintain body temperature. Remember to cover both over and under the injured person. Also, protect them, if possible, from the elements.
- If no spinal or neck injury, elevate the person's feet approximately one foot.
- Loosen all clothing. The key here is to improve blood circulation to all tissue, especially the vital organs.

- Do NOT give any food or water. Remember, there may be internal injuries and in that case, food or water could cause problems.

If the casualty is unconscious and you do not suspect spine or neck injuries, you can place them in a "recovery" position until help arrives. This is done by raising the person's closest arm above the head as you prepare to roll the individual towards you. Guarding the head, rotate the entire body toward you as one unit. Place the individual's other hand under their chin to maintain a clear airway. By doing this you will assist in keeping the head tilted slightly in the event the injured vomits.

All of the stuff above is a bit scary, but it can and must be done in serious cases. However, in most day-to-day situations you will be back to fishing, hunting, camping, or hiking in no time. **Keep in mind that the most common injuries are cuts, bruises, and scrapes.**

In cases of open wounds, cuts and scrapes, make sure you clean the injured area. I carry a first aid kid with items to clean and bandage open wounds. I usually use plain old soap and water to clean with, treat with a disinfectant, and then cover with a bandage. There, good as new! The key here is to clean the injured area and to cover it, to avoid infections. Small cuts and scrapes can become very serious if they become infected. And, very few of us are really that clean in the woods.

Another common day-to-day injury in the woods are burns. Most of the burns you sustain will be small burns, usually the result of picking up a hot lid to a pan or from touching a smoldering piece of wood. This type of burn is usually classified as a *1st degree burn* and while painful, it is a minor injury.

A *2nd degree burn* is identified by redness and the formation of blisters. This type of burn is serious and can be life threatening if large areas of the body are affected. Both the 1st and 2nd degree burn can be treated with cool water. This will lessen the pain and assist to lessen the amount of damaged tissue. Keep in mind that in the case of a 2nd degree burn, if the burn covers a large area it may not be possible to immerse the injury in cool water. In all burns, except minor 1st degree burns, seek medical treatment immediately.

The last type of burn is a *3rd degree burn* and it is by far the worse. The burned area will be charred or black in color. Surprisingly there may be little pain at first due to severe nerve damage. Use cool CLEAN water to treat the injury and cover the injury with a lint free cloth. *Seek medical attention immediately! Keep in mind to treat for shock as well.*

Most of us will cover many miles and sleep many nights in wilds of the world. We are usually as safe there as we are in our own bedrooms. But, just like at home, at times things can happen. Some of these things that occur cause bones to break, blood to flow, and skin to burn. You must know what to do and do it when the need arises. Remember to take charge, assess and assure. Be in control, evaluate the environment for other dangers, and assure your casualty that all is well. Treat the injury and then treat for shock.

By following my simple guidelines, reading more on first aid, taking course offered by the Red Cross or other organizations, you too can develop the knowledge needed to treat all types of injuries. Plan for the worse and expect it. Know that things can go wrong and usually will at the most inconvenient time. Remember, through preparation you too can be a survivor!

One aspect of this article that is important to remember is that these steps are for use in only in emergency situations until qualified help arrives. If you must apply any first aid, or use survival techniques, do so with extreme caution. The results of your actions will be yours and no one else's. And, remember, no two emergency situations are ever the same. So, it would be foolish of me to give you the impression that I have all the answers. I do not. Only the person on the scene can accurately make the difficult calls that are often made in emergencies. The whole purpose of these articles is to stimulate your thought processes and to motivate you to learn more. I hope we have succeeded.

Learn to Survive!

Fun in the Sun?

There is nothing more enjoyable than a fun filled day in the sun! Those of us who live in the United States are lucky to have the excellent weather we do. Our weather allows us to fish, hunt, hike and camp, knowing that most of the days will be warm and filled with sunshine. While our summers are excellent for outdoor activities, we should all be aware of one of the dangers associated with too much sunshine: sunburn. Now, I realize most of you have had some experience with sunburns, but how much do we really know about the injury?

Sunburn is simply overexposure to the sun's ultraviolet rays. And these rays can cause both temporary (a slight burn) and long-term (including cancer) damage to our skin. While our society identifies those individuals with a nice dark tan as being healthy, that perception is not accurate. Exposure to the sun's ultraviolet rays actually cause, besides the danger of cancer, premature aging of our skin. So, we may look good and healthy now, but in a few years we will begin to pay for our tan.

Children, especially infants, are very susceptible to sunburn. Also, those people with light or fair skin will usually burn before they tan, if the skin is not protected with sunscreen. Keep in mind, even those folks with dark skin can be sunburned, if the exposed skin is not protected. So, what I am saying in a nut shell, is all of us can suffer sunburn under the right conditions and if we are not protected from the sun's rays.

Sunburn usually occurs because we fail to cover exposed skin due to the temperature, humidity, and heat when we are outdoors. When the weather is very hot we may just put on a tank top and a pair of shorts, increasing the risk of sunburn. At times, we may forget the sunscreen or just decide not to put it on. Also, keep in mind that most sunburns will happen between ten in the morning and two in the afternoon, because that is when the sun's ultraviolet rays are the strongest.

Additionally, reflection from water, sand, or any light colored surface can cause sunburn. That is why fishermen are often burned after a day on the water.

All of us, at one time or another, have had a minor sunburn, with the red, tender skin that feels hot to the touch. Usually, after a few days, the discomfort disappears and we are back to normal again with no side effects. In more severe cases, blisters can develop and even "sun poisoning" (rash, chills, and nausea) can occur. In most cases we will lose a layer of skin that will peel off a few days after the burn. Also, some medications, such as doxycycline, can actually increase your chances of a sunburn. Ask your doctor about any medications you may be taking prior to heading out doors. If you experience a sunburn, how do you treat it?

Well, first let's look at what you should not do. *Do not* wash the area with a strong soap, or apply petroleum jelly, benzocaine, butter, or alcohol. These products can actually make your condition worse and prevent a normal healing time. *You should* take a cool shower or bath, apply a body lotion to the damaged area (Aloe gel is great for this). If you do not have a lotion on hand, you can add baking soda to your bath water to help relieve the discomfort. Also, the typical use of common pain relievers, such as Tylenol or Motrin, may help reduce the minor aches and pains associated with sunburn.

If the sunburn victim experiences dizziness, rapid pulse, pale, cool, or clammy skin, nausea, chills, rash, or fever, seek medical attention immediately. Other symptoms to watch for are if the victims eyes hurt or are sensitive to light, extreme thirst with very little, or no urine output, or sunken eyes. These may be signs of other heat and sun related injuries such as heat exhaustion, shock, or heat stroke. In case of any of these symptoms see a doctor as soon as possible.

Well, now that we have a better understanding of the dangers associated with the sun, how do we prevent the injury in the first place?

- Always use sunscreen and lip balm.
- When in the sun, wear a hat or ball cap to protect your eyes and face.
- Make sure your sunglasses have UV protection for your eyes.
- Avoid exposure to the sun between 10 am and 2 pm. Remember, that is the peak time for UV rays.

- Apply your sunscreen about 30 minutes before exposure to allow it time to be absorbed by your skin. Reapply the sunscreen after you have been swimming or about every 2 hours.
- The sunscreen you use should be rated at least 30 SPF (Sun Protection Factor).
- The higher the SPF the more protection it gives you.
- Pay close attention to nose, ears, neck, shoulders and face when applying the sunscreen, to get maximum protection.

Each year in the United States thousands of us will be sunburned. Most of us will suffer the minor discomforts associated with the injury and go on. But, how many new cases of skin cancer will result in future years? How many of us will visit emergency rooms for treatment of sunburns, heat exhaustion or heat stroke? I suggest this does not have to happen. Use common sense in the outdoors, always protect yourself from over exposure, use sunscreen, and most importantly, enjoy your summer!

A Hot Time

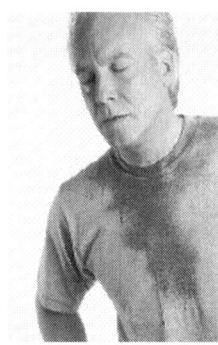
An older man of about fifty was walking along the bank of the stream, fishing pole in hand, when suddenly he collapsed in a heap. His face was red and dry as he immediately started vomiting. He had been fishing since early morning, did not have any water with him, and the high Missouri heat had claimed another victim. Can you imagine his chances of surviving if he had been in a remote survival situation? Since he experienced heat stroke, he most likely would not have made it if he had been alone. In this case though, he was given first aid, an ambulance was called, and he was transported to a nearby hospital. He survived. Heat related injuries can happen to all of us, regardless of age.

Most of us who live in the states are used to the high temperatures associated with the dog days of summer. The temperature rises, the wind quits blowing, and the humidity gets higher than normal. Outdoors things seem to just simmer in the heat. In the days of old, life almost came to a complete standstill as animals and people quit moving. Anything with a brain was seeking shade and cooler temperatures. Well, that is no longer the case since the invention of air conditioners. Most Americans don't even slow down much, when compared to the past. However, we should, because heat related injuries can be fatal.

Let's look at the most common heat related injury, heat exhaustion. This injury results from prolonged exposure or high physical activity during high temperatures. Additionally, high humidity makes us more susceptible. I saw many men and women pass out during physical training or parades when I was in the military due to heat exhaustion (that's why all the instructors made us drink a lot of water). When you combine high heat, high humidity, with low body fluids, heat exhaustion will occur. You can reduce the risk of heat exhaustion by staying in the shade as much as possible, traveling very little during the heat of the day, and drinking lots of water (water is not hard to find in Missouri, even in a survival situation, but make sure you purify it before drinking). Well, we know what causes it and how to avoid it, how do you recognize it?

- Weakness or dizziness
- Nausea and perhaps vomiting
- Clammy or pale skin
- Perspiration on the face and forehead
- Rapid breathing

Heat exhaustion is easy to treat, but a frightening experience for most of us. The victim should be moved to a shady area, if possible. Treat for shock, give small sips of cool water (if available), remove as much clothing as possible, and sponge the body with tepid water. Usually the injured person will be up and about in little time. However, if the person does not seem to "bounce back" seek medical attention. You may have a person experiencing a heat stroke.

A heat stroke is caused by overexposure to the sun and heat, combined with a high body temperature. This situation can be life threatening if not treated immediately. The victim may have:

- A high body temperature
- Hot and flushed skin
- Red and perhaps dry skin
- Restless or bizarre behavior
- Complain of a severe headache, having vomiting, or nausea
- If not treated, the individual will eventually lose consciousness

With heat stroke, move the person to a cool and shady place (out of the sun), check for breathing and pulse (use CPR if needed). You should place cool compresses around the person's head, sides of the chest, and armpits. If you have ice, use it to make the compresses and add a compress to the groin area. You should remove as much clothing as you can and fan the person, by hand if necessary. If the person is conscious and not vomiting or nauseated, you can give them small sips of cool water. Immediately seek medical attention with heat stroke.

So, we have discussed the two most common heat injuries; how do you prevent them?

First, do not stay exposed to the sun and heat any longer than you have to (seek shade). Keep your head (hat) and body (sleeves down) covered from direct sunlight. In a survival situation, move to a shady area and do your work at night, after the sun goes down. It will be cooler and you will sweat less, which will assist you in retaining body fluids. If you have it, drink more water than you usually do.

Also, when you urinate, check the color of your urine. Dark colored urine indicates you need to increase your water intake (dehydration is happening). Many survival professionals recommend that you have at least one-quart of water for every two lost. But remember, less fluid will NOT result in less sweat! In extreme heat, you may not even feel yourself sweat because the sweat evaporates very quickly. Always be on the lookout for sources of additional water, but avoid alcohol or caffeine; both will dehydrate you. And, purify all water that you suspect is unsafe with water purification tablets or by boiling.

Heat related injuries claim numerous victims each summer in Missouri. We are a state filled with people who just enjoy nature and hardly slow down when the temperature goes up. I suggest we understand the threat of heat related injuries, know how to recognize and treat them, and use good common sense. Armed with that knowledge, your summer will be much more enjoyable.

Note: This article is not meant to replace medical knowledge or expertise. It is provided to the reader only as a guide. The author has prepared it to the best of his ability from training received from the US military and American Red Cross. When in doubt about any medical emergency, always seek medical attention immediately.

SIMPLE SURVIVAL PSYCHOLOGY

When I was in the military and involved with search and rescue training, I often saw messages or reports pertaining to survivors and non-survivors. These cases were both civilians and military personnel. I was amazed while reading both types of correspondence. (We received this information to hopefully improve our survival training program). I read about people who had lots of gear, plenty of food and water, and they still did not make it. Or, on the other side of the coin, those who survived with little more than literally the shirt on their backs. Why the difference? Well, it is not that simple. There were many factors that contributed in both cases. There are many variables to consider when reading about survival situations. Nonetheless, in most of the reports I read the difference was usually survival psychology.

Take the case of the civilian pilot in Alaska that experienced aircraft problems and put his plane down on a frozen lake. The temperature was about minus twenty. When rescuers arrived at the site they were able to determine what happened easily. The pilot, now dead, had left a note. I cannot remember most of the note, but it read something similar to: "I cannot survive in this temperature. I am a dead man. I am going to smoke a cigarette and then end it all." It was very unfortunate. The aircraft controller had seen the aircraft go off radar and had been able to communicate with the pilot just before he landed on the lake.

Once on the lake the pilot had shut down his aircraft power and the controller was unable tell him that help was on the way. When the rescuer team arrived, they found two cigarette butts, a .38 caliber pistol in the pilot's lap, and blood not yet frozen on the side of his head. He had not even left the cockpit of the aircraft. Why? Why would a man take his life without a fight? I suggest he gave in to panic. He was not prepared mentally to face the situation.

I also read once about a man who crawled for more than 100 miles across the Arizona desert to safety. His car had broken down on a rural road and he attempted a shortcut to safety. It was over 100 degrees during the five days of his travels. He was burned black from the sun, very dehydrated, and near death when he walked out. He stated he was determined to be with his family again and used this determination to keep himself moving. Doctors and survival experts were surprised by his survival. The man should have, by all rights, died. He had done everything wrong (traveling during the heat of the day, not covering up exposed parts of his body, and not being properly prepared) and yet he made it. Now, I don't recommend you attempt that for obvious reasons, but it does show how human determination can aid your survival efforts.

So, what is the big difference in the two stories above? I propose it is frame of mind. One, the non-survivor, gave up before the battle even started. The other, the survivor, was determined to live. Of course pure determination may not keep you alive, but it sure adds to the odds. Lets discuss the steps you can take to stay alive when you realize you are in a survival situation.

Panic is a real killer. When you actually realize you are going to have to survive, keep your head about yourself. Stop. Find a place that offers you temporary shelter and think things out. Do not go stomping around in the woods looking for your way out. Stop. Consider the who, what, when, and where of your situation. Who knows where you are? Did you, as I always recommend, tell someone about your trip? This should always be done, even if you know the area very well. Tell any person (a boss, friend, wife, husband, etc.) the what, when and where of your trip. They should know what type of trip it is (fishing, hunting, hiking, or travel), when you left and when you will return (i.e., I will leave on Tuesday morning and will return seven days later on Tuesday evening), and where your trip is to be (to the Knockemstiff National Forest or to Lake Swampy). Make sure if you change your trip in any way to call or contact the person you informed. Many rescues are started each year because of a change in plans and no notification. If you have handled the who, what, when and where of your trip, rescue should be fast.

Get your thoughts organized. Unless you are suicidal, this step is a must. Take an inventory of what you have on hand. This step serves two purposes. First, it calms you down. The time it takes to inventory your gear will assist in de-escalating your panic. Second, most of us carry a lot of "junk" as well as needed items with us, and this is a time to see exactly what you have. All items on you can be used toward survival.

Keep busy. An active mind is less likely to dwell on the situation as hopeless. Notice I wrote hopeless and not helpless. In a helpless situation, there is no help. While you very well may feel helpless, you can help yourself. But in a hopeless situation there is no hope. I think you always have hope, as long as you are breathing. Keeping that hope is what makes a survival situation develop into a story of success. Concentrate on the little successes you experience and let the failures slide off. And, don't start feeling sorry for yourself. See, the more little successes you have the better you will feel. Start with something small, like a fire and a shelter.

Find a shelter and start a fire. Yep, even if you don't need either. Why? Well, once again for two reasons. The first is to keep you busy as I stated above. The second is they may be needed later when you are too exhausted or weak to make them. Additionally, there is a deep primal need for safety satisfied when you have shelter and fire. Ever notice how comforting a campfire is at night? The fire may not even be needed, so the comfort is usually just psychological. Anyway, get a fire going, construct a shelter, and sit for a bit.

Oh, I almost forgot; **avoid alcohol** when in a survival situation. It dulls your thinking processes and that is one thing you don't need (additionally alcohol dehydrates). Second, avoid cola's, coffee, and tea if you do not have a sufficient water supply. They can aid in your dehydration.

Now comes the difficult part, **waiting for rescue**. You noticed, I hope, I wrote waiting for rescue. Yep, I meant it. Let them find you. Nothing is more frustrating to search and rescue crews than looking for a person meandering somewhere in the woods. It is really like looking for a needle in a haystack and may lead to your death. Stay where you are. Once you realize you are lost and have established a survival camp, stay there. Being rescued is often compared to looking for someone in the mall. If you wander around looking for them, they are more difficult to find. But, if you plant yourself on a bench in the mall walk way, they will come by sooner or later. Wandering blind in the bush just uses up energy that you cannot afford to lose. Stay put.

The only exception to this is when you realize exactly where you are and know beyond any doubt how to walk out. If you do decide to leave a survival site, leave a note stating when you left (date/time), where you were headed (location you are attempting to get to), when you expect to get there, your heading (compass heading if you can), your physical condition (broken bones, cuts, overall general condition) and your full name. Make sure you post your note where it can easily be seen and in a waterproof container/bag. This info will aid the rescue team greatly. Remember, I recommend you leave the survival site ONLY if you are sure of where you are and know how to safely get out.

Well, now you are in a more prolonged survival situation; what comes next? Well, first stay off of your pity pot. Don't dwell on how rough you have it. Don't play the "poor little me" mind game with yourself. Make things happen. Let's look at what you really need to survive. First, you need air and water. Hopefully the air thingy is taken care of for you (if not, the next steps are not very important to you). Next, water is a primary concern. Purify all water not brought from home or purchased for your trip. All water. Even if the stream looks like a dream photo from the cover page of an environmentalist magazine. Much of our waters in North America are polluted or have "critters" (micro organisms). Don't take a chance.

You should always have a survival kit with you. These kits can be purchased commercially or made up at home. They can also vary greatly in size and weight. The kit I carry is very small (I use an old metal Bandaide box), but I have given great thought to the contents. It is just exactly what I need to survive on. I have included:

- A good quality pen knife
- Condoms for water storage, un-lubricated.
- Wooden matches in a water proof container
- Flint and steel and a metal match
- Water purification tablets
- A long strip of heavy duty aluminum foil folded up to cook with
- Fishing kit, i.e. hooks, sinkers, and some line. Nothing fancy. It can also be used to set snares or many other uses if you are landlocked and not near the water.
- A small commercial first aid kit (with instructions).
- One small pack of gum and one of hard candy for emergency energy
- A small survival pamphlet or book—keep it small and light

If you have a survival kit with you, it aids in your sense of well being. With the kit and your usual camping/outdoor gear, you know you have the minimum to survive. It helps you realize the situation is not hopeless at all. Do yourself a favor and practice using your survival items before you need them. Also, know your survival and first aid booklets. All of this pre-planning will make you more relaxed when you need to use the equipment.

What about food? Let's be honest here. Aren't most North Americans just a little overweight? Now, I am not saying a sudden starvation diet is healthy, but most of us could go a couple of days without food with no medical affects. And, why do most people immediately think of food when they think of survival? Keep in mind that most folks are rescued before serious hunger develops. It is psychological. If you think about it, it makes sense. Imagine a nice shelter, a warm fire, and a full stomach. Comforting isn't it? While no shelter, no fire and an empty stomach... I think you have the idea. Well, remember, people have survived for weeks without food but only days without water. You figure the priority out. (Before I forget, if you take prescription medications, always have them with you when you go outdoors. Not having them in some cases could be a killer). Nonetheless, if it makes you feel better trap, hunt, or catch something to eat. Make sure if you eat you increase your water intake, if your water supply allows for it. Keep an eye on your urine. If it becomes darker in color, increase your water intake to avoid dehydration.

Survival is never easy. If things can go wrong they usually will. I know people can survive in temperatures as low as minus thirty and as high as 110 degrees. How do I know? I have done it during training. The key is to stay active, concentrate on the tasks at hand, build up your successes while down playing your failures, and to face each obstacle with determination to overcome. Survival psychology is simple, when you think about it before you need it. I believe with the right psychological approach to any survival situation, you too can survive.

Take care and stay safe in the woods and on the waters of America. And, take a child hunting, fishing, hiking or camping.

THE WILL TO SURVIVE, DO YOU HAVE IT?

We all hear a lot about the phrase, "the will to survive." You notice, it does not say the will to live, or the will to die, it uses the word survive. I believe the word survive is there because it is the most important word in that phrase. See, at times in real survival situations, unlike a television show I won't mention, it is easier to just live, or give up and die, than it is to survive. I suspect I may have you very confused about right now. Well, he has finally lost it, you may be thinking. Perhaps, or, have I? Consider the fact that survival is very hard work. Death or living is much easier. Anyone can die or possibly live, but how many of us can survive?

You may be asking, living *is* surviving, isn't it? Not exactly, because survival means you live by reasoning, determination, training, and actions. Living simply means you continue to breathe until you are found. If you are in the bush long enough, without the will to survive or a lot of luck, you will move into category three, death. So, many people are considered survivors when in fact, they were just plain lucky.

The will to survive is a mental conditioning of your mind to survive **no matter** what man, nature, or luck throws at you. It is easy to think of survival and to say you have the will to survive, but do you *really* have it? The first thing to consider about survival situations it that no one wakes up in the morning and says; "I think I will be a survivor today." The trauma of suddenly finding yourself in a wilderness survival situation will require psychological acceptance. This acceptance is difficult because deep down inside you know you will now have to feed, cloth, shelter, and take care of your own medical needs. Even the professionals fight bits of doubt when it really happens (I suspect few would admit that though). It is the ultimate reality check. A failure to accept the seriousness of your situation will, without luck, lead to death.

We as humans, I think, are driven by some deep internal motivation and natural instinct to live in groups. I suspect this was a necessary part of our early evolution in order to survive. As a group we would hunt, pick foods, build shelters, take care of our medical needs, and protect ourselves. Additionally, it made it easier to select a mate. During that period any person placed outside of the group would soon perish. Perhaps that is why banishment from a group in those days was almost equal to the death sentence. Once a person was no longer part of a group, and isolated, they could only do so much alone. One of the first theories a psychology major learns in college is the need for mankind to belong (to a group or a society, if you will).

The total isolation we feel when forced into a survival situation is difficult for the unprepared to combat. Some people **_for the first time_** in their lives are honestly alone. Many of us do not even know ourselves very well, or deep down inside we may not even like ourselves. You would be shocked at how many people in our society do not like being alone, and actually try to avoid it. Once a person is placed in a survival situation, there are no cell phones, no computers, no friends, and no television playing to provide background noise. Survivors have commented about how "loud" this stillness in the field can be. As social beasts we all want, as well as need, to be with others. We are just social beasts. A survival situation isolates us quickly, and perhaps with a feeling of no immediate hope or help. So, how do we fight this feeling of pending doom?

First, before you go into the field, learn what needs to be done in most survival situations. Once you are forced to survive, think, then act. Stay focused on your task at hand. Let's say your first task is shelter construction (the priority of your tasks depends on the survival environment). If you have done your reading and had some training, you know what steps to take to make a good shelter for the type of environment you are in. Concentrate on making the strongest and best shelter you can with the materials you have on hand. Then, after that is done, work on another project. Stay busy. An active mind is a healthy mind.

Second, if you believe in a higher power, then it is to your advantage to pray or meditate. Do what your beliefs say you should do and as often as you need to. However, it is important to remember to _have faith_ in your higher power, but _help yourself_ at the same time. It is so easy to allow yourself to pass the buck to a higher power and no longer take any responsibility for your own actions. YOU are the one that must, with your higher powers help, survive. Most survivors I have talked to or read about prayed at various points during the situation, usually asking for food or water in some form. This communication with a higher power is good because it keeps your will to survive strong by giving you hope, and that is good psychological support.

Third, enter a survival situation knowing you will make mistakes or use bad judgment at times. All of us will. The key here, or so I think, is being prepared. See, an experienced outdoorsman will make mistakes too, but they will not be, usually, as severe as the novice. And, the inexperienced person will make not only more severe mistakes, but they will make more mistakes over all. This is due to poor knowledge or a lack of planning, both of which can cost you your life. In any survival situation remember to **think your actions out way before you act**. Use simple logic and use your mind. The best tool you have to assist you in survival is not a knife, matches, or a blanket, but the human mind. If you are preoccupied with self-pity, your judgment could be cloudy.

Watch your diet and water intake. If you can procure food and water, then do so. You never know when the opportunity may disappear. Learn to constantly look for sources of food and water. How, you may be wondering, does food and water apply to the will to survive? Well, simple. Man is better prepared to survive when he has a full stomach. See, a lot of our problems seem to go away in survival, or mentally they do anyway, if we have a shelter, fire, food and water. Sure, it is mostly psychological, but it helps. There is something mentally refreshing when sitting around a warm campfire, eating a meal and drinking water after a full day's work at surviving. We reap the efforts of our days work by having the fire, the food and the water. It is a "warm fuzzy."

Gradually build on your successful acts and down play the losses. If you do something well, remember how you did it. Think positive about all of your accomplishments. Don't consider it luck, though part of it may have been; you were still the person responsible for the end result. Often in survival a window of opportunity opens and the survivor fails to act. Failure to act on a golden chance is all too common. Each accomplishment needs to be rewarded in your mind.

Guts and determination are also important traits for the survivor. Those individuals who are "hackers" and not quitters will usually survive. They have an attitude toward life that helps them survive. They seem to feed on challenges and successes. Often, when I was in the military, the biggest guys, strongest guys, or the smartest guys would eventually quit. It was surprising to see the one individual who everyone would have picked to be the first quitter, complete training. Often they were of normal size and intelligence. It is all a mind game.

It was all about mind over the physical pain or difficulties. The human mind is the most wonderful tool you have, so use it often in the field. And remember, others have survived, and so can you!

One aspect I can speak on with some authority is nature. I don't ever remember being at any survival school where the weather was good, for the trainee anyways. Oh, it was perfect for training, maximum training as our instructors often said. So remember to prepare a shelter as soon as you can. Prepare your body for protection from severe weather, but just as important is the preparing of your mind. I have spent days isolated in shelters due to bad weather. Loneliness, remember the first part of this article, can be a real hard task to confront. I once spent a whole day doing math problems in my head and I remember a rough two days in Alaska where I made up stories in my mind. Keep your mind exercised along with your body.

The will to survive is an attitude. It is a deep commitment to survival. I suggest, while it cannot be learned, it can be reinforced by being prepared, with knowledge, and by developing a healthy survival psychology. Remember to downplay your losses while building your successes up. Confront your difficulties head on and with determination to accomplish your task, no matter what. Keep your faith in your higher power, and keep your mind active. Stay off of your self-pity pot and don't get into the "poor me" attitude.

If you have the will to survive, you will survive and not just live. You will be able to return to society knowing you, and you alone, kept yourself alive. You will know that you kept yourself alive where many others would have simply given up—and died. You will be proud of the fact you didn't just live, or even die, you were truly a survivor. The will to survive—do you have what it takes?

Simple Survival Signals

The day dawns with temperatures in the teens and a fresh blanket of virgin snow covering the ground. Your whole body shivers as you stroke the almost dead campfire back to life. You stop working with the fire when you faintly start to hear an aircraft approaching. Your excitement builds, and you start to yell and scream for help. Then, disappointment settles deep in your mind as you hear the plane pass overhead and then fly off away from your position. It only takes a few minutes for you to realize your site has not been spotted. You suddenly realize you will not be rescued today.

Let's take a look at how we attract attention in survival situations. We can stand on our heads, while we clap our hands, but I am not sure that would work. There are, however, other means of making sure we are rescued in a timely manner. Most, but not all, of these means of signaling are best done by using the senses of smell, sight, or hearing. Most effective primitive signals are made using the sense of sight.

One method that is not visual is the use of electronic devices. If you have an emergency locator beacon (ELT) or a cell phone, you are in good shape. Well, things are great and easy as long as the batteries last. Try to prolong battery life by using the radio or phone at certain times (When I was in the military we briefed our folks to transmit and receive at 15 minutes before and after each hour). Batteries will eventually die and then we have to revert to more primitive methods of attracting attention.

Your vehicle lights can be used to signal with as well. By flashing your lights on and off you will draw attention to your site. Lights work well when you are stranded in a car or truck and waiting for rescue. You can flash an SOS (Save Our Souls), international emergency code, by flashing three dots, three dashes, and then three dots. Dots are quick signals whereas dashes are longer (It would look like this, . . . ---. . .).

Signal mirrors, or shiny metal (Heliographs), are about as basic as a person can get. The best part of using something that shines is the lack of a battery that will eventually die. The drawback is you must have sunlight for the device to work. Nonetheless, most of the time the

United States has sunshine, with the exception of short periods of time when we experience adverse weather conditions.

You should practice using a signal mirror until you can pretty much aim the flash to strike any area you choose. You will be surprised how well you will do with just a little practice. A word of advice here, once you get a person's attention with the flash, *do not* continue flashing in their eyes. It makes rescue more difficult when your rescuers cannot see. Instead, aim the flash at the rear of an aircraft, truck, or group of people. That way, if your rescuers veer off course a bit, you can easily flash them in the face once more; then you should move the flash to the rear again. A piece of smooth metal will work almost as well as a signal mirror (I carry a small mirror in my survival kit).

Another way to attract attention is by using fires. At night the light from your campfire will draw attention. In the daytime your fire is a good signal, as well. By adding oil, cedar boughs or other things to a burning fire you will change the color of its smoke. Remember, three fires spaced in a triangle shape, is the international signal for help. It means you cannot move on, or, in other words you need assistance. *Do not let your fire get out of control.* A forest fire is dangerous and greatly reduces your chances to survive.

Placing a large "I" means you have a very serious injury in your group, while "X" means you are not able to proceed any longer. There is a whole group of ground codes and I will not get into what all of them mean, but the two above are the most important to remember (If you are interested in the other symbols, you can find them in most good survival books or manuals at your local library). You can pile wood or rocks to cast shadows, trample the snow, or else clear (or add) brush or grass to make the signal. Use a rough ratio of about six to one. I would suggest your width be 3 feet, minimum, while the length would be 18 feet. Have you ever driven by a handmade sign and discovered you could not read the print? Well, pilots looking for you could have the same problem with your signals! They have to be able to see it! The important thing to remember when making a ground to air signal is to disturb the surroundings enough to draw attention to your area. I like to think of it as contrast and the human eye

Three gunshots in quick order are also considered signals. The three shots indicate you need help and cannot proceed alone. The key here, if you have not guessed it by now, is the use of three of anything. It is just understood by rescuers as a signal of distress. If you are lucky enough to be a survivor and have a vehicle nearby, you have just hit the mother lode. While most cars, trucks, and aircraft make very poor shelters, they are a gold mine of resources for the survivor. In this article I am mainly interest in signals, so I will not address the various ways vehicles can be put to various survival usage. But, you can burn the fuel and oil to make signals (use extreme caution with the fuel), the insulation and tires generate smoke, and the mirrors, glass, and chrome make good reflectors. Even a headlight can be removed, rewired, and using the vehicles electrical system, be used to signal passing aircraft. The list is limited only by your imagination.

By day you should use smoke, and by night use light, to attract attention to your survival site. Remember you want to make a contrast against the background. If the day is dark and gloomy, you want light colored smoke. If the day is bright, use dark smoke. At night, of course, light is best.

You may not believe this, but one piece of valuable equipment is a whistle. Get a good quality one and keep it in your survival kit. A loud whistle can be heard for a long distance (at longer distances than a human voice) and it can be useful when you know rescuers are nearby. Additionally, you can use it to signal between members in your group if one of them strays off the beaten path for some reason. It is a good idea to blow the whistle in three long blasts (once again, a series of three).

If you have a vehicle, keep the snow off of the top and sides as much as you can. Depending on the color of the vehicle it can aid in your rescue. Do not use the vehicle as a permanent shelter because it will either be too hot or too cold, but as a signaling device. Additionally, have one fire burning all the time, and two others (numbers two and three of your fire signal triangle) ready to light. I would have the numbers two and three piled high with pine or cedar boughs. Be very aware of fire safety at these fires. The last thing you need is to start a forest fire. Also remember if you trampled down snow for a signal and it continues to snow, you will eventually have to redo the signal. The falling snow will fill your tracks quickly.

The key to signals is to draw attention. Look around you and think how you can make the area stand out more. It is helpful if you keep in mind at least three of our five senses, sight, hearing, and smelling, can be used to signal with. Disturb the natural surroundings; draw attention to your survival site, and you too will be a survivor!

FAMILY WINTER WEAR

With the fall and winter seasons quickly approaching, we need to consider how we will dress our family for all of our outdoor activities. Many times on my way to work, I see children waiting for school buses or walking to school improperly dressed for the weather. Now, I know at times this is the child's decision, but have you really considered how to dress in cold weather?

When I lived in Alaska, the first thing my family learned was to dress in layers. Usually the bottom layer was thermal long underwear or wool. Next, we would put on a long sleeve shirt and full-length pants. Make sure both of them are bigger than normal (trapped air keeps you warm) and are not tight. Tight clothing will restrict movements, reduce blood flow, and actually make you colder.

While you're at it, don't forget your feet and hands. I suggest two pairs of socks and I usually avoid the battery (heating) types. I have found the battery pouches get in the way and the batteries never last long enough. I usually don cotton socks first, to help whisk sweat away, then wool socks. There are many different types of socks on the market for outdoors use, so check them out. For my hands, unless I need my fingers for a task, I use mittens. Mittens will keep your fingers and hands warmer than gloves because they keep the air inside (surrounding your hands and fingers) warmer. I also suggest a good Gore-Tex® or Thinsolite® material. Both of these materials will keep you as warm as toast.

Next, if it is super cold, consider wearing a good wool or fleece sweater. It will help keep your upper torso warm in high winds and even in the normal air chill. Remember, it is better to overdress (you can remove layers if need be) than to under dress. Once you are outdoors is not the time to realize you do not have enough clothing on for good protection. You can always remove the sweater if you want later on. I prefer a simple v-neck sweater or crewneck. I do not like button sweaters because you can lose body heat between the buttons.

Another important item to consider is a good pair of boots. I suggest during times of the year where you may be exposed to snowfall or ice, you always use boots. Make sure you get the best quality boot you can afford. Once more I suggest Thinsolite or Gore-Tex, because I have worn them at minus 6oF and my feet have stayed warm. Of course, make sure you wear two pairs of sock as we discussed already (I buy winter boots a complete size larger than normal). This type of boot will allow your feet to breath, while keeping moisture out. I do not recommend the old "bunny boots" (arctic boots) or rubber boots, because both will trap sweat in the boot and that can lead to problems with your feet cracking or the skin tissue being damaged. Leather boots are fine, unless it is extremely cold or wet. In both cases leather boots just don't do the job.

Two items that are very important and often overlooked are a scarf and a good hat of some kind. Up to ninety percent of all body heat can be lost through the neck and head area of the human body. Wear a good wool scarf that is long enough to wrap around a couple of time and then tucked in the coat. Your hat should also be made of wool, Thinsolite® or Gore-Tex®. In extremely cold weather a hat with earflaps that can be lowered (sometimes called a "mad bombers hat") can be used. They are usually lined with animal fur and are very warm. I have worn this type of hat in minus 6oF and it kept my head very warm. But a good stocking cap or facemask will also do the job of protecting you. It is a matter of individual preference.

The last two items are another scarf and a good quality coat. I use the scarf to cover my mouth and nose when the temperatures drop way down low. It keeps my lungs from hurting when the chill is just too much. Plus, the heat from your mouth and nose will help keep your face warmer. If you wear glasses, like I do, make sure you coat them with an anti-fog spray before you go out. Your breath can make the glasses fog up. Your coat should have at least two layers, an internal layer of heavy fleece or wool and an outer layer of nylon, Gore-Tex® or Thinsolite®. The outer layer will keep the cold winds from blowing your body heat away and help keep you warmer. I prefer a coat with a hood as well, to add to the warmth of my head. Just be cautious when walking because some hoods, when pulled tight, may restrict your vision.

Now, you have heard me harp on wool, Gore-Tex® and Thinsolite®; why? Well, all three will keep you warm when they are wet. All three of them will also allow you to sweat and still stay warm. In cold weather sweat can actually freeze and kill you in very little time. You do not want to wear clothing that causes you to sweat and have it retain the moisture, because moisture is very dangerous. If you ever feel yourself getting too hot while out in very cold weather, remover a layer of clothing. Do all tasks slower in cold weather to avoid sweating, because it will freeze. Take frequent breaks and if you are with another person, check each other periodically for white or red patches of skin on exposed flesh (this may be frostbite).

One consideration here when it comes to children. *Make sure they help you pick out the winter wear they will use.* I have found a child is more willing to use clothing they picked out. Parents may not choose the design or style that a child wants to wear and then the clothing will not be worn. Remember, children want to wear what other kids are wearing, not necessarily what is warm or even safe for them. But, trust me on this, they know exactly what they will wear, so invite them on the shopping spree.

With the coming winter take time to get the clothing you need now. Make sure your children are properly dressed any time they venture outdoors. If you hike, fish, or hunt during the cold season, use the suggestions I have made. Remember to dress in layers, so you can remover unneeded clothing. Also keep in mind that dead air will help insulate you once it warms up from your body heat. Winter does not have to stop or even slow down our usual activities, but we do need to use common sense. Take care and stay safe.

What to Wear

Most of us who hunt, fish, hike, or camp rarely give much real serious consideration to what we wear. Usually, we don whatever clothing is available and meander off on our trip. No, I am not suggesting we worry about the latest fashions, or that we only buy brand name clothing. What I am suggesting is that we spend some time making sure we not only have clothing that is comfortable, but clothing that is made for our sport. Just like those who participate in other sports and have a uniform, so do we in a matter of speaking.

Lets take a look at your hat. It should have a wide enough brim to shield your eyes from the sun and rain. Also, during cold or cool weather it should be of a solid construction and not any part of it mesh. During cold weather most of our body heat is lost though the head. Just adding a hat during low temperatures can make a person warmer. Of course in the summer or during hot weather, a hat may not be needed or a mixed mesh construction can be worn. I like a hat when I am outdoors because it shields my eyes and I like the feeling. Make sure the hat you have fits your type of hunting. For me, I can never use a real wide brim when I bow hunt because it causes me problems when I release the arrow. At any rate, always try using your weapon with a new hat, just to see if it interferes with your technique.

A good outer garment is needed most of the time. Even in the summer I often have at least a light nylon windbreaker in my fanny pack. If the weather turns cool, I have it available. In extremely cold weather you will need a heavier garment. I suggest a coat constructed of Gore-Tex® which is excellent protection for wet or cold weather. This material is lightweight and is every bit as good or better than wool for cold weather. I also prefer a coat that has adjustable wrists, a flap (that folds over the zipper) that buttons, and a hood with a drawstring. All of these features add to the warmth of the wearer. It keeps your body heat inside where it does the most good.

If you are hunting, hiking, or moving around a lot, a parka is not usually a very good choice. I have found them to be cumbersome to wear hunting and slows my reaction time. Also, if I move much in a parka I will start to sweat, and sweating in cold weather can kill. The sweat may freeze once you stop moving, and that can lead to hypothermia and other related injuries. A parka is great for general camp use and chores but not, in my opinion, a good choice for moving any great distances. I know the coat can be removed when you get over heated, but it is difficult to hunt or hike with a coat you cannot wear. My feelings on a coat is, if I can't wear it most of the time, then I should consider replacing it with something else I can wear.

Another layer of clothing to consider is your shirt and pants. I know many of you prefer jeans and flannel shirt, but that is not adequate for extremely cold weather. When the weather turns really cold, you should dress in layers to retain body heat. Tight jeans will not allow the undergarments to be worn and, while durable enough, jeans just don't have the exterior pockets for storage of gear. Jeans, however, are suitable for warm weather, if you have a backpack, buttpack, or other type of bag for gear storage.

In my opinion, the best clothing for the outdoor wear is military surplus, or new, Battle Dress Uniforms (BDU's). BDU's come in different camouflage (woodland camouflage and desert camouflage) designs and have six pockets. Also, the BDU is constructed in a lightweight or heavy weight style, so you can use them during the summer or winter. Both designs have reinforced knees and elbows for long wear. Additionally, the BDU is a comfortable uniform to wear and has a proven success record in combat. Of course, other surplus military clothing will work as well and the best part is the uniform has been tested by thousands of men and women. Usually you can find surplus uniforms from other countries that work pretty good, as well. The Europeans usually have a long line of wool and wool is an excellent insulator during cold or wet weather. At any rate, military surplus clothing is not very expensive, easy to obtain, and does the job very well.

There are hundreds of undergarments available on the commercial market. The key here is one of comfort. Most do an excellent job of keeping you warm, so you need to select underwear that allows you freedom of movement, insulates, and is comfortable. I usually wear cotton "Long Johns" and they do a very good job of keeping me warm if I dress in layers over the undies. In cool weather, you can wear boxers or briefs if you wish. Just make sure they are not too tight or chaffing may result as you walk and sweat. Many older Vets I know do not wear underwear in hot weather because it causes heat to build up at the crotch (and the chaffing issue is eliminated). Your decision on undergarments is an individual choice, but in cold weather you will need long underwear.

During winter or cold weather I suggest you wear two pairs of socks. I usually wear a pain of nylon socks and then cotton or wool socks over them. I like the feel and comfort of the nylon on my skin and the second pair of socks are the ones that really keep my feet warm. Also, the nylon will reduce friction with the boot as you walk. During the warmer months I usually just wear one pair of cotton socks. I have found cotton to be comfortable and durable enough for most of my summer needs outdoors. There are many commercial types of socks on the market, from Gore-Tex ® to electric socks heated by a battery. The choice is once again an individual choice, but choose well because problems with your feet can greatly influence the success or failure of your trip. Also, make sure your feet are always dry and in good condition. Change your socks daily or whenever they become wet. It makes good sense to look for blisters or injury to your feet each time you change socks. Nothing stops a great trip like bad feet.

You choice of boots is very important, because good quality boots will keep your feet dry, warm and in excellent condition. On the other hand, poor quality boots can cut a trip short due to injury to your feet. During cold or wet weather I prefer to wear a high top, lace up boot, constructed of Thinsolite®. Thinsolite will keep your feet dry and warm, even in very poor weather. I have worn boots made of this product in Alaska when the ambient air temperature was way below freezing, and my feet remained as warm as toast. I also suggest you avoid the "Bunny Boots" if you plan to do much hiking. I have found this rubber-insulated boot to cause my feet to sweat excessively and that can lead to freezing. Nonetheless, "Bunny Boots" are fine to sit in hunting blinds, in tree stands, or for around a campsite. In the warmer months a leather boot will work just fine, as long as the boots are not brand new.

Any boots you take to the woods should be well broken in. New boots will almost always rub, pinch, or chaff the skin causing blisters. A good way to break in leather boots in a hurry is to get the boots wet and then wear them until they are dry. Now, use some common sense here. Obviously you cannot walk around the house in dripping wet boots, so take a short walk and remain outside as much as possible. (This suggestion may reduce the amount of verbal abuse you are exposed to by your spouse). But this procedure does work. Of course it is not to be used in cold weather, but in a few hours your new stiff boots will fit much better. Make sure after the boot is dry you take steps to preserve the leather, or the boot will dry stiff and hard. I usually rub the leather down with saddle soap and then apply a thin layer of polish.

Hiking boots are okay for most folks, but I prefer a high top boot. I want protection for my ankles and the extra support a high top boot provides. Once again, this is an individual choice. Often during the summer months I will use a pair of Vietnam Jungle Boots as I trek through the woods. I have found them to be comfortable, they add ankle support, and they have two holes on each boot that allows water to drain from the inside of the boot. But the biggest reason I prefer this type of boot is because they are light-weight and comfortable.

Other cold weather accessories you should consider are scarves, mittens, gloves, ear protection, and perhaps face coverings. Once again, I suggest Thinsolite®, Gore-Tex ®, or wool construction of your accessories. All three will keep you warm even if you get wet.

Make sure your scarf selection is long and wide. This will allow the scarf to be tucked into your shirt or coat. I prefer a long wool scarf that can serve as a head wrapping if needed. Also, I usually purchase a bright orange or red scarf that can be used for signaling if I am forced to survive. Try to buy your outdoors gear with double uses in mind at all times. This will cut down on the number of items you have to carry as well as weight.

Also, mittens are warmer than gloves (body heat from the fingers is shared in mittens), but if you are a hunter, you want mittens that have been designed so you can extend your shooting fingers. Keep in mind, however, in cold weather exposed flesh can stick to metal. Gloves, on the other hand, may be a better choice for folks who hunt, ice fish, or want to be able to grasp objects. Each finger in a glove is covered and while there is some loss of dexterity, they will suffice in most cases.

When it comes to ear protection you should consider what you are doing outdoors. If you are hunting, and need to be able to hear well, then you may not want to cover your ears. Or, perhaps, you would prefer to use the hood on your coat or maybe a very light headband that you can slide off quickly. Hikers, campers, and others may want to wear earmuffs or maybe a wool watch cap (stocking cap). Once again I suggest a bright color that aids in your being seen. Since hunters all are required to wear some international orange (with the exception of those hunting turkeys or fowl) a stocking cap will just assist you in being seen better. Check your state's hunting laws to determine the legalities of various types of clothing colors in certain hunting situations.

Face and head protection often comes as one. Face masks, or hoods, are sold in most sporting goods departments of large stores. Again, I suggest you consider Thinsolite®, Gore-Tex ®, or wool because they provide protection against the cold and work well even when wet. A face mask has an advantage in that the design allows the wearer to roll it up and wear it like a stocking cap. Then, in extremely cold weather the face protection feature can be rolled down to cover the face. Usually this design has openings for the eyes and mouth only, though some do have a nose opening as well. Hoods, on the other hand, usually cover most of the face and nose, leaving a large circle open for the eyes. Hoods are a better choice for those of us who wear glasses.

If you decide to get a full-face semi-rigid mask, usually military surplus, keep in mind they are known to cause itching to some wearers. This design is similar to the face protection some hockey players use and is worn with straps that go around the head. Usually the outer material is water resistant and the lining material is of wool or blend. I have found them to be too hot, they cause me to itch, and my vision is greatly limited while wearing it. Also, this design does not remain very flexible during very cold weather. Another problem I had, when using this piece of individual gear, was with my glasses. But, as with most outdoor wear, it is an individual choice.

During the warm months, always carry sunscreen and keep your legs and arms covered by your clothing. Ticks, chiggers, and other insects are motivation to do so, as well as sunburn. While shorts and a t-shirt may be cooler and even look better, you should be aware of the risk you are taking by wearing them. Outer wear should be worn for protection, not looks.

Outdoor wear is very important when it comes to enjoying our time spent with nature. A good selection will keep you comfortable, cool, and protect you from the elements, insects, and minor cuts and scrapes. A poor selection often makes the trip shorter or very unpleasant at least. Take the time to evaluate your clothing and boots closely, looking for protection as well as comfort. Buy the best outdoor wear you can afford and keep your gear in good condition. Remember to try to buy your equipment so it serves more than one function. But, most importantly, get gear that will allow you to enjoy your time outdoors and to do so safely.

Make Your Own Clothing

There may come a time when you are forced to make your own clothing or accessories you need in the field. When I attended survival school, we had to make packs, goggles, some small pouches, and other gear. Generally, it is not that difficult to do, but it does take some serious thinking. For instance, what you may need is never a problem to identify, but how to make it may take some time. Then, you must also consider what to make it all out of.

Those of us in the Air Force usually had access to parachutes from crashed planes. Or, perhaps we had bailed out and at least had one "chute" with us. A personnel parachute, when I was in the military, was twenty-eight feet in diameter. That, friends, is enough to make your shelter and all the accessories you may need. But what about you, the average civilian who does not have a parachute? What do you have to use for emergencies? Well, each survival situation is unique and your equipment and supplies may be limited in some cases. However, you always have something available.

If you car breaks down, you have unlimited resources available to you. Everything from the battery to the car seat covers can be used. You have many miles of wires (for snares maybe) and insulation you can use to your advantage. The key here is to use your mind and consider unorthodox ways of using what you have available. I once read of a man and woman who survived subzero weather by using crumpled up newspapers to line their coats with. In another case, I read about a man who used his hubcaps to shine the sun on a rescue aircraft (he didn't have a signal mirror). Think and survive.

Let's consider what items you can make that can be worn in some fashion. Headgear, Arab style, can be made from a towel or large piece of cloth. Just make sure there is a headband of some sort used with it, so it is held firmly in place. Also, goggles can be made from cloth, wood, or plastics. Just cut two small slits where your eyes will be and have a hole on each end of the goggle. It can then be tied around the head so it is held firmly in place. Goggles are very important for eye protection in both the desert and arctic environments.

In cold weather you can construct insulated socks by taking a pair of socks, placing dried grasses in them, and then inserting a sock covered foot. Make sure the dried grass cover the foot 360 degrees. Then, the sock with insulation may be inserted in a boot or handmade moccasin. The key to insulation against the cold is dead air spaces. These spaces heat up quickly and retain heat very well. Of course, once the grasses become pressed or compact, they need to be changed. Check them at least twice a day.

Moccasins can be made from a large triangular piece of cloth or leather. Keep one tip of the triangle at the front of the foot and the other two tips outward on each side of the heel. Then, raise all three tips and secure in place with rope or string. While there are better and more durable moccasins that can be made, this type can work well in an emergency. Remember, we want working clothes, not fashion here.

Puttees or gaiters, can be made from just about any cloth or leather. They are merely wrappings that go around the ankles and up the legs. In the military, during World War II, they were referred to as "leggings." I suggest you cut your material in strips, about 2 or 3 inches wide, and wrap the legs. Gaiters can keep insects out of your pants and offer some protects from brush and briars as you travel. Keep in mind, green or uncured leather will shrink if it gets wet. So, if you use fresh uncured leather to wrap your legs with, try to keep your gaiters dry.

Another item that is easy to make is what my grandfather called a Mule Collar Pack, or some folks call it a Horseshoe Pack. Regardless of the name attached to it, it is a very simple pack to make and is very easy to wear. It resembles a rolled up blanket, and you may have seen photos of Civil War soldiers wearing them. All you need is a blanket, or large piece of cloth or material, and some cord or rope.

Spread the pack material out flat and place your equipment at the top. Leave a good 6 to 12 inches of material on both sides of your gear. Be sure and put your large and flat items down first, then the smaller items on top. I suggest once your gear is on the pack material, you fold the sides up, keeping the fold straight on both sides. Then, starting at the equipment end, slowly roll the material down. You should attempt to keep the roll as tight as you can.

Once the rolling is completed, tie the roll in at least three places. Tie one spot at each end, and one in the middle. Then, I usually use a larger piece of rope to tie the opposite ends of the roll together, forming a crude horseshoe or mule collar. Then, to wear it just slip the "hole" of the pack over your head and shoulders. When worn properly the pack should cross from a shoulder and go down to the opposite thigh, both front and back. This type of pack is easy to make and a breeze to carry.

Another item that is easy to make is a survival serape, or poncho. Just take a blanket, or large piece of material, and cut a hole in the center large enough for your head to fit through. Don the serape, and tie the loose material at your waist. If the material you constructed your serape is waterproof (plastic or nylon) you may have made a rain poncho. If the material you used is a wool blanket, you will have a very warm piece of clothing for cold weather use, even when your serape gets wet. Wet wool retains its insulating properties even when damp or wet.

In some situations, depending on where you are, you may be able to use reeds, grasses or other natural resources for clothing. You can weave grasses or reeds into cloth like material that can be fashioned into crude clothing. Additionally, make a few large sheets of material and you can use them to reinforce your shelter if need be. Also, in some areas of the world, large leaves (like the banana leaf), can be used to make clothing. Furthermore, between the hard outer bark of many trees and the wood itself, is a thin layer of material that can be removed and woven into material as well. Or of course you can use animal skins, both cured and "green" (uncured). In an emergency almost anything around you can be used.

If you are forced to survive, look around you. What do you see? Reeds can become a new serape, grasses a new loincloth, or tree bark can make a pair of sandals. Also a floor mat from your car can become a sleeping mat. An old blanket can become a pack, head covering, or a survival serape. A gallon of motor oil can be used as fuel if the need be. And a fishing kit can be used for other purposes besides fishing. The line can be used to make snares and a baited hook works well for catching birds. Keep your mind active, observe, evaluate, and survive!

FOR GOODNESS SNAKES

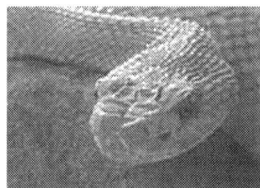

Snakes was a word spoken when I was young that was right up there with the boogieman. I was especially scared of the name of one local snake, the Copperhead. Over the years though, I have learned that snakes do not really live up to the terrible reputation they have acquired. I have also discovered that most will avoid you, if they have a choice. Yep, I know all the old stories of snakes that catch their tails in their mouths and roll, I heard about the snakes that "spit" at you (there is one of these, a cobra, in other parts of the world), snakes that fall apart when you strike them, and snakes that chase you. Well, they may be out there, but I have not seen them in my forty plus years of meandering through the woods. But, I learned a few things on a recent outing that can help make a hunting trip, survival situation, or camping trip safer.

Wally and I had taken four teenage boys on a combination fishing and camping trip. The evening was warm, but we were all huddled up around the campfire as Wally started talking about snakes. Immediately he had the boys attention. There is something about the subject of snakes that always seems to grab attention. Not a word was spoken as Wally told us about a creature that is hated by some, and feared by most.

"There are about 2400 different types of snakes in the world." Wally said as he lifted his old beat up coffee cup and took a sip, "And, you might be interested to know that only a few, near 200, are actually dangerous to man. That means that less than 10 percent of the snakes in the world are harmful. But people are usually very fast, too fast in my opinion, to kill a snake because they think it is dangerous.

I know all about the poisonous snakes in the United States. And they all, but one, belong to a group called pit vipers (The other group is called short fanged snakes, or Elapidae, and they are coral snakes). Now, some folks call pit vipers long fanged snakes, or Crotalidae. The Copperhead group, Rattlesnake group, and the Cottonmouth (Water Moccasin) are all pit vipers. Of all the snakes in the United States, I am concerned about these three, because we have all three of them in this area. Remember, though, snakes are to be respected, not feared. And, regardless of the type of snake or its group, most will avoid man if given half a chance.

So, what else do I know about snakes?" Wally gave the boys a big crooked grin and continued speaking. "Actually I don't know very much, but I have never been bitten and that makes me an expert in my mind. Snakes are usually inactive during really hot weather and during the cold season. During the winter they actually hibernate, or sleep, kinda. Keep in mind now that a snake will move to the shade during the hot part of the day and move into the sun during the cooler part of the day. So, where do these snakes live?

Snakes like to stay around stacked firewood (all the boys turned their heads toward our wood pile for the fire), under and around old lumber and junk piles, along stream and pond banks, under rocks or logs, and in or around old worn out buildings. They may even be in holes or on ledges during the day. Well, now that you know just a little about snakes, what about a snake bite? How dangerous is it?

Statistics show that less than one half of one percent of people bitten by a poisonous snake will die from the bite, even if left untreated. Or that was what the Army told me when I went through military training. I'll tell you how to treat snakebite in a minute. Why am I going to wait to tell you? Because snakebite is very unlikely if you use common sense when you are outdoors.

First, dress for the outdoors. Wear high top boots, heavy pants (like jeans or heavy military surplus fatigues), a shirt, hat, and wear gloves when you pick up wood, or when you have to place your hands in places that could be a living room for a snake. Also, *if you know* there are a lot of snakes where you will be, wear snake chaps. You can purchase them at many stores and they can make your trip less stressful.

Second, make noise as you move. Now, I realize when you're hunting you won't want to do this, but then be extra cautious. Normally though, when moving through grasses or weeds make as much noise as you can. This will alert the snake and it will know you are coming. Stay on trails as much as possible and keep the kids close by. Be very cautious when you step over logs or large rocks. Notice I said cautious, not paranoid. Snakes hear by vibrations and the more noise you make the more vibrations that are in the air, so warn them you are coming." Wally gave a chuckle and looked around the campfire at each boy before he continued, "Usually, with kids around noise is not a problem. Also, snakes smell you by using their tongues. That is one reason a snakes tongue is always flickering in and out. When they smell prey with their tongues they go after dinner.

Third, be aware of what is around you. In the military this is called situational awareness. Keep your eyes on the trail and watch the kids. I also keep an eye out for movement where it should not be. A well-camouflaged snake, with its natural colors, can be very difficult to see. It sounds like a lot to do and it is. I constantly scan the walkway and keep a conversation going with the kids. That makes it easier for me, because it warns the snakes we are coming.

Fourth, watch where you put your feet, hands, and body. Walking should be done with your eyes open and you being alert for any movement. Additionally, as you pick up wood for the fire, watch where you place your hands, and wear gloves. Many people are bitten each year as they pick something up. Never place your hands in a hole or place you cannot see into. Snakes often use dens, holes, or lie under rocks. Also, people think snakes come out by the thousands when it gets dark; this is not true, but they are harder to see. Always carry a flashlight after dark.

So, if you experience snakebite, how would you know? Perhaps you will see the snake strike, or feel a sudden pain from a bite, but not always. Also, Rattlesnakes do not always rattle before they strike, so you may not hear a warning either. You will start to swell around the bitten area, usually within 3 minutes or so, and you may continue to swell for almost an hour. But, wait, there is more."

I noticed the boys were all ears as Wally continued, "During this time there is usually severe pain associated with the bite. If you check the injured area you will see the fang marks (normally two punctures, but there may be only one if the snake did not get a good bite), some bleeding, intense swelling, and there will be blood in the victim's urine. This blood is from major organs that are injured by cell loss and tissue damage. Your patient will experience a bad headache, and a lowering of their blood pressure with an increased pulse rate. Usually they suffer from severe thirst as well. Medical treatment should be sought immediately, because death can occur within 24-48 hours if left untreated for some individuals. If you consider all the snakebites around the world, the pit vipers cause most of the deaths.

Well, now you know even more about snakes, what do you do if you get unlucky and experience snakebite? As I said earlier, you will find most bites occur to hands, feet, and legs. You should cut the pant leg (or any clothing) or remove the pants (clothing). This should be done in case the swelling becomes severe. Then, most doctors will tell you to wash and clean the bite with soap and water, immobilize the bite, treat for shock, and immediately seek medical attention. Also, various doctors will tell you to not cut the bite like they do in the movies, not to suck the poison out, and not to put a tourniquet on the injury. According to some doctors those television techniques might just compound the damage done. It makes sense to me. It all sounds easy, huh?"

"All right, let's review some of the rules about snakes and the outdoors.

- Watch where you walk at all times in snake country.
- Make noise as you move, especially in tall grass and slow moving water.
- Watch where you put your hands and feet at all times.
- Wear heavy pants, high top boots, and gloves in snake country.
- If you corner a snake, make no sudden moves. Back off very slowly. The snake may strike at quick movements.
- Always check for snakes in your sleeping area, including your sleeping bag, and clothing before using them.
- Use sticks or shovels to move logs, fallen leaves, or rocks. Snakes love to stay in those areas.
- Never handle a live poisonous snake. If you must use a snake for food, kill it and remove the head before you handle it.
- Treat all snakes with respect. They are part of nature and should not be played with, tormented, or abused. Leave them alone and most of the time they will leave you alone."

The boys all looked around the campsite and not a word was spoken for a long time. Wally had really educated them and they were thinking about what he had said. The lesson must have taken hold because a few hours later one the boys approached me and asked to use the flashlight. He said he had to use the bathroom. As he walked down the trail to the port-a-toilet I could not help but notice he had his jeans and boots on and was sweeping the light from side to side on the trail. I slowly shook my head and thought "Yep, Wally surprises even me sometimes."

It doesn't matter if you hike, fish, camp, or hunt, you should have a basic understanding of snakes. While they actually pose a small threat to those of us who enjoy the outdoors, they can harm you. And, those of us who hunt often go off the beaten path in search of game, so we need to be extra cautious. Dress properly, use good common snake sense, and your trip should be uneventful.

Wild Survival Weapons

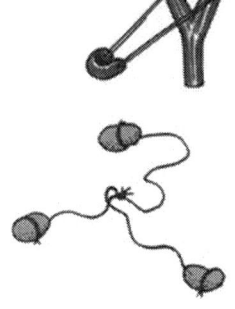

For some people, the idea of being in the bush without a weapon is very scary. In fact, folks often ask me, "How do you defend yourself?" I always have a chuckle at this question because I am likely to say "defend myself against what? Wild attacking rabbits, squirrels, or even ducks?" Unless a person is attempting to survive in a combat area, the actual need for a weapon for personal protection varies. In most cases no weapon is needed at all, unless it is being used to assist the survivor in procuring food or in camp chores. In most of North America, the need to have a weapon for protection against wild animals is not very great. However, in some states, a weapon is good to have against bear, moose, or other large game.

Most critters in the wild know man, and wisely they shy away from us. Nonetheless, we have all seen the television and movie scenes where large packs of wolves, wild dogs, or other animals, attack a campsite. It is pure nonsense. Now, if an animal is rabid though, anything is possible. Oh, I am not saying campsites are never attacked, but when it happens, it is usually by a solitary bear, cougar, or other type of large meat eater. And, they are generally after sources of food (keep a clean campsite), or your horses, not you. And, of course, at times humans can become part of the menu. When I lived in Alaska one danger to many campers, hunters and fishermen was not even a meat eater, but a moose. It is important for you to keep all of this in proper perspective and to have a basic understanding of survival or camping safety. If you don't, you will never have a good night's sleep in the wild.

So, you feel the need for a weapon? I agree it is a good idea to have one at times, but mainly to kill game caught in snares, traps, or caught cornered. If you feel the need for safety and security and desire to have a large weapon, you can make those as well. A lot of the weapons you make will depend on how and where you ended up in a survival situation. If you are a hunter and become lost, or in some manner are faced with survival, you may have weapons with you. Or, you may not.

Simple Survival

A lot of different situations can occur in the wilderness. Weapons can be lost or broken.

If you are the survivor of a plane crash, a sinking or overturned boat, (and the boat you were on washed up on shore, you will be in luck.) or a stranded vehicle, you may have more materials to work with. Keep in mind; in cold or hot weather never use the interior of any vehicle for shelter. It will be too hot or too cold. The wings of an aircraft will provide you with shade and protection from the sun. But, vehicles can provide you with many items to make tools, weapons, and other needed items. The weapons you can make from wreckage or a stranded vehicle will be limited only by your imagination. Without any wreckage the task of making weapons is harder, but not all that difficult.

Almost anything around you can become a weapon. Those of you who have attended self-defense classes know that a pencil, car key, bottle, book, comb, or even a thumb can become effective weapons. Regardless of the type of weapon you may want, you will be limited by the sources around you. In some areas you may not have many stones, rocks, or even wood (arctic conditions north of the tree line). In other survival situations you may not even be on land, you may be at sea. In all cases, look around and take inventory of all of your equipment. I have known survivors to use the sharp edges from a ration can to make a crude knife to gut fish with. I have known others who used a sharpened belt buckle to cut with, and still others who field dressed small game with their teeth. You have weapons all around you, so look for them. Keep your imagination active at all times.

One of the most handy survival weapons is a simple club. It is very useful in killing small game and for general camp use. It is simple to make and can be constructed of many different materials. Using a forked piece of green limb (hard wood works the best), a large rock or piece of bone, and some vine, wire, or rope, you can make a club in next to no time (I always carry about 25 feet of parachute 550 cord in my survival kit).

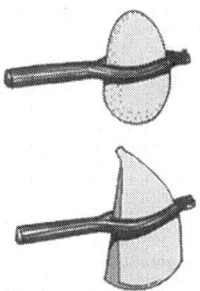

Make sure the limb has a Y section on it and fit the rock into this section, then secure the stone or bone in place using wire, rope, cord, vine, or wet rawhide. Wet rawhide is the best because it will shrink as it dries and holds the stone securely in place.

A simple knife for stabbing with can be made from pieces of bone or from an antler. Just break off or locate a piece that is large enough to hold securely and has a sharp point. While you will not be able to cut with it, it can be used to stab with. Or, you can use a sharp tipped piece of wood.

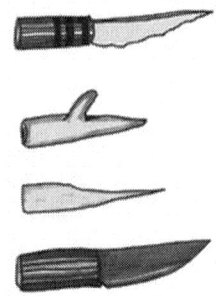

If you need a knife to cut with, consider using sharp edged bones, hard stone, metal from a wreckage, wood, or even glass for the blade. In a survival situation you may have to use what you can find to make tools and weapons with. Almost any sharp edge from any hard material can be used. Find a piece of green hard wood, split it slightly, insert your blade, and then wrap the handle *tightly*. Once again, wet rawhide makes the best wrap because it shrinks when it dries and will hold the blade firmly in place.

Another weapon that is easy to make is a spear. It is very useful in killing any game you don't want to touch or get too close to. An example might be a snake, porcupine, or any injury causing animals.

In the injury causing category remember horns, antlers, teeth, fangs, and hooves can all cause injuries. A spear can be made as simply as sharpening the end of long green piece of wood and hardening it in a fire. Or, you can attach a blade point using the same types of materials you used for your knife blade. And, the spear point can be attached exactly like your knife blade was, using wire, vine, string, cord, or wet rawhide. An easier way to attach a point to a spear shaft is to simply tie it on. Place a knife parallel to and tightly up against the shaft of the spear. Then lash it on securely.

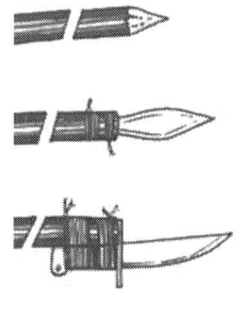

Two more weapons that you can make, and use mainly against small game, are the slingshot and bola.

For the slingshot you start by cutting a Y-shaped piece of green wood, cutting two strips of rubber (from a tire or rubber tubing) about eight inches long, and a pouch that can be made from cloth or leather. Secure the two strips of rubber on both sides of the Y on the wood near the top, tie the pouch to the open ends of the rubber strips, and you now have a weapon. You can use small pebbles as ammo. I assure you, with practice you can procure a bird or rabbit for dinner. A hint here, use two or three small pebbles when you shoot (makes it more likely to hit a target).

The bola is much more difficult to use but is simple to make. Tie all three ends of the pieces of string or cord (I use parachute 550 cord) together at one end. At the other ends, tie a stone on each piece of line. You now have three cords with a stone on each end that meets and is secured at the other end. To use the bola, grasp the tied end, twirl it over your head, and release it toward your target. Once you release the bola, it opens up and covers a very wide path. While it is very effective against birds, it can also wrap around the legs of larger game and trip it. Then, using your newly made spear and knife, you can kill it and process the meat.

While the making and using of primitive weapons takes some time, it can be done. I suggest using your spear to stab with, not for throwing. If you only have one spear and you throw it, what do you do if the animal turns on you? Do not throw the only weapon you have available, keep it in your hands. Plus, depending on the type of blade your spear has, you may break it. These same weapons were used by early man many years ago and they were deadly in the hands of a person who knew how to use them. The Native North Americans kept their families alive with such weapons by providing both food and protection. If others can do it, so can you.

There are unlimited sources around most survivors for use as weapons. Keep in mind that some of these sources may not be recognized as such by most survivors. Bone, glass, and rough metals, stones, antlers, horns, and other materials can be modified for use as weapons. Keep your survival mind active and evaluating all material at hand. I realize there may be many more different types of weapons made from natural materials, but as usual, my purpose for writing this article was to stimulate you thoughts. I want you to think about making weapons from materials you have on hand. Some of the weapons I have explained here can be done in many different, and perhaps better ways. I have only shown you the basic methods.

Anyone Can Use An Ax, Right?

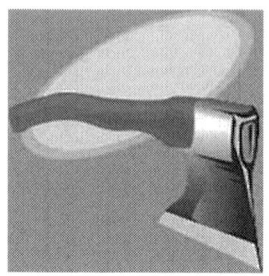

When I was a kid growing up, I thought everyone knew how to use an ax. Since I spent the first eighteen years of my life on a farm, using an ax or a hatchet was as common to me as using a fork. I have since learned that many people today do not have any experience on how to properly use an ax or a hatchet, and in most cases, they don't need to know. But, those of us who camp, hunt, fish, or backpack, will eventually have a need to use this excellent cutting tool. Even those of us who travel by mobile home, will eventually need to use an ax or a hatchet.

One of the biggest mistakes most folks make when having an ax or hatchet around is not keeping them stored safely. Both the ax and hatchet I carry come with leather sheaths that I use to keep the cutting edge covered to avoid injury and also to ward off damage to the blade. I would never think of carrying either of my cutting tools without the sheath. Many serious cuts are sustained each year when folks fall on cutting blades or use them in unsafe ways.

Additionally, many people suffer severe cuts when they come in contact with their legs when using an ax. Always be aware of the position of your feet and legs! And, never use an ax or hatchet that has a broken handle. If the tool is not safe don't use it, and never tape a cracked handle (that is an accident waiting to happen). You can easily replace a broken handle in the field by trimming a piece of wood to fit the ax or hatchet head. And, never use an ax or hatchet after consuming alcohol!

Also, keep in mind that a hatchet and ax are designed for two different jobs. While you can cut a tree down with a hatchet, eventually, it will take a very long time to do so. A hatchet is just not made for the job of cutting down trees, but rather for general campsite chores. Besides, it is very rare for a person camping or in a survival situation to have the need to remove a tree, so a hatchet should be your tool of choice for most general uses. It is smaller and lightweight when compared to an ax.

If you must cut down a tree or cut a log in two, make sure you strike the face of the tree at an angle and not at 90 degrees, or straight on (you will just whack at the wood that way and make very little progress). And, vary the location of strikes of the blade from top to bottom (or left to right if the tree has fallen). Additionally, if you must trim wood to make a point for a tent stake (a more likely project), place it on a stump or log before you do so. This will protect the cutting edge of your hatchet and keep it sharp.

One of the most common tasks when using a hatchet or ax is the removing of tree limbs to use for various projects. Remove the limb from the underside and not the top. If you attack the limb in the crotch of the limb and not the underside, you will split the wood and also find the task is much harder to accomplish. Vary the angle of your strikes on the underside of the tree from left to right and you will find it much easier to remove the limb. Also, I suggest if you have a lot of limbs to remove from the same tree, start at the base and work your way to the tip of the tree. And keep in mind, it is very difficult to cut through a limb with one swing of an ax or hatchet, so concentrate on cutting from left to right.

Also, one of the most common tasks associated with axes or hatchets is splitting or cutting wood for a fire. Make sure you use caution to avoid damaging the blade. I usually place my wood to be split on a stump to keep the head of my ax from contacting the ground, or hitting rocks, and dulling the blade. Small limbs or wood can easily be cut in two pieces if you lean it against a log and strike the wood where it rests firmly on the log. Or, you can hold small pieces of wood with one hand, place the wood on a log, and strike the wood where it meets the log. If you hit wood leaning against a log (down and away from the log surface), the wood may bounce up and cause injury, or bow in sharply and cause the blade to slip, both of which can cause an injury to you. Make sure all contact with the wood you want to cut is resting on a steady and secure surface.

Now, a dull blade is much more dangerous to use than a sharp one. A dull blade will bounce instead of cutting cleanly, and that often leads to injuries. Keep your blade sharp and you will discover the task is much easy to do. Use a file to remove burrs or nicks on the cutting surface. Move your file blade from the handle toward the cutting edge (or outward). Then, once you have the nicks and burrs removed, use a wet stone (with a little water or oil) and slowly move in a circle as you apply it to the blade. Keep the angle consistent as you move the stone.

Ax or hatchet use does not have to be difficult, and with a little practice all of us can use either effectively. The key is basic safety, work from side to side as you cut, keep your blades from contacting rocks or the ground, and keep your blade sharp and in the right shape. Also, remember to never use an ax or hatchet if you have been drinking alcohol, and keep your ax stored in a sheath. Ax or hatchet use is no mystery, but it does take some basic knowledge and common sense.

IF YOU AX ME

Those of us who enjoy hunting often spend long periods of time camping. We drive or hike to our hunting location and then setup camp for the hunt. If we take a vehicle, we will usually have more equipment with us than when we backpack. However, in both cases we will usually have a good quality hand ax or hatchet with us. Most outdoorsmen find them to be valuable tools for chopping firewood, clearing brush when setting up camp, or even chopping ice when drinking water is needed. But, how much do we know about this versatile little tool?

First, a hatchet must be kept sharp to do its job well. A dull tool will often bounce and that could cause a severe injury to the user. So, keep your hatchet or ax sharp! To sharpen a hatchet or ax, prop it up against a log with the cutting surface of the blade up. Then, place a wooden peg against the head, where it rests on the ground, to secure it against the log.

Take a file, and remember, files work best when pushed and not pulled, and remove any burrs alone the cutting surface. Start pushing the file from the cutting edge toward the body of the hatchet head. Wear heavy-duty gloves if you have them and always use a file with a handle. Try to keep the angle consistent as you move the file over the cutting edge. Once the burrs have been removed, use the rough surface of a wet stone, lightly oiled if possible, and repeat the process the same way.

When the burrs have been removed and the cutting surface of the blade is smooth, use a wet stone to put an edge on the blade. The stone should be moved in a circular motion and the stone should be kept firmly against the blade. It is easy to allow the stone to fall from the surface, but try to avoid this. Then turn the hatchet over and repeat the process, but this time circling in the opposite direction on the blade.

The first rule in using any cutting tool, especially an ax or hatchet, is to never swing the blade towards you. You want to make sure if you miss your target, or the blade bounces, you are not struck. Also, tree limbs are easier to remove if the underside of the limb is struck and not the top. Additionally, it is safer to cut thin pieces of wood as it rests on a log. However, make sure you strike with the blade where the wood rests on the log and not at any point between the log and the ground. If you do, it is possible the blade will either bounce, or the wood, if cut, may fly into the air. And, at any time you are cutting wood on a log, watch where you place your hands and your feet. Do not hold the wood leaning on a log with your foot or hands.

If you must cut a large piece of wood with your hatchet, do not continuously strike the wood straight on. You should strike the wood at an angle, let's say 60 degrees, and vary impact from one side of the cut to the other. Alternate the sides you hit as you strike the wood. A properly used hatchet will start producing wood chips from the cuts very quickly. I do not recommend the use of a hatchet to cut down trees, unless it is an emergency. The handle is not long enough to give you the force you need and it will take an extremely long time to even cut a small tree down. Over all, using a hatchet to cut a tree down will also use up too much energy, something to consider if you are in a survival situation.

While many hatchets come with steel handles, how do you replace a wooden one if it breaks in the field? (And keep in mind, a hatchet with a cracked or taped handle is very dangerous to use). Most of us don't carry spare hatchet handles, so we will have to make a temporary substitute. I suggest you do this only in emergencies, because it can take time and the process will frustrate some people.

Now, most professionally made handles will have a slight curve to the handle, but in an emergency a straight handle will work. Your first step is to find a piece of hard wood (oak, hickory, etc,) that is knot free. Then cut the new handle to about the same length as the broken handle.

Remove the broken wood in the hatchet head by burying most of the blade (cutting edge) surface in the ground and building a fire on top of it. The broken wood in the blade will then burn out. Keep the fire small. Allow the blade to cool before the next step.

If you have a pencil, you can outline the hole in the head of the hatchet onto the new wooden handle. Then, place the head against the top of the new handle and see how far down the handle the blade will come, mark that spot. Once you have the shape of the hole in the head outlined and the width of the head, you can start removing excess wood. This step should be done carefully to allow a proper fit between the new handle and the blade. I call this the "fitted" part of the handle.

Once you have the new handle properly shaped for the head, you are still not finished yet. Make a notch in the portion of the new handle that will fit into the head. Make the notch with the width of the head in mind. I suggest the notch be more than two thirds of the distance down the fitted part of the wood, or from the top. As soon as you have the notch completed, you will need to cut a wooden wedge. I generally taper a piece of wood that is the same width as the notch in my "fitted" part of the handle.

Now, insert the new handle into the head of the hatchet or ax. Use caution here so you do no cut your fingers. As I suggested with sharpening the blade, wear gloves if you have them. Once the handle has been installed into the head, then tap the wedge into the notch you previously cut. Make sure the wedge goes in firmly. Once the wedge has been placed into the handle, remove the excess portion of the wedge with a knife.

Your final step is to soak the head and wedge insert in water over night to tighten the head onto your new handle. Once you have removed it from the water, dry the head and apply a very light coating of oil. This oil will assist in preventing rust on the blade.

Some safe considerations with hatchets:

- Never leave a hatchet on the ground
- Keep a hatchet in its sheath
- If you do not have a sheath, bury the blade straight down in a log
- Never run with a hatchet in your hand
- Never attempt to catch a falling hatchet.
- Keep your hatchet sharp, a sharp blade will cut smoother and not bounce back as often.

Hatchets; we often carry them, but rarely give them much thought. A good quality hatchet or hand ax can make our lives much easier in the field. Good dependable tools allow us more time to hunt by allowing us to spend less time in camp. Remember to keep your hatchet sharp and in good repair and I will see you in the field.

Wanna Bet Your Knife on it?

As a hunter, I have found a good sheath knife can be a real lifesaver. We have all seen the movies where the main character is carrying a knife with a blade a foot long (Bowie or Rambo types). While it looks impressive, it isn't really very practical. As an experienced hunter, it is always easy for me to spot the newest member of the hunting group who usually has very little experience in the woods. They almost always show up wearing a knife modeled after their favorite action movie star. And, unlike the movies, our hunter had to "live" with his or her knife selection for the duration of the hunt. In many ways they are lucky, because there are more experienced hunters around them.

Knives; how much do we really know about them? I cannot make you a knife expert in one small article, but I can give you a few pointers that may assist you in selecting a knife that will work the best for you in the field. Also, keep in mind, there are many different kinds of knives on the market and they are all designed for different uses. But let's look at the components of a typical sheath knife.

A knife is made up of these important parts:

1 - The Blade, the metal blade that extends from the handle. The blade has the cutting surface ground onto it. It also comes in various lengths and shapes. Each blade shape is designed for a particular task. Some knife blades are for filleting, skinning, chopping, and so on.

Additionally, some blades are made of better steel than others. (If you are interested in the metals used for knife blades, the Internet has a lot of information). I won't get into all the different metals that can be used to make knives, except to say, I prefer a 440C blade. I have found it to hold an edge well, be strong enough for about any task I would require of it, and to be a good metal. Cheap knife blades will either be impossible to sharpen, or will not hold an edge. Also, at least make sure your knife is made of stainless steel (reduces rusting and corrosion). If you are interested in more information about the metals used in knife construction, I suggest you conduct a web search (I typed in knife blade metals and had 19,000 sites listed).

2 - The Point. I think most of the readers know this part of the knife. This part is usually used for gutting game, piercing, or stabbing. It is also a very dangerous part of the knife. It should always be sheathed or covered when not in use. Never walk or run with an uncovered knife in your hands.

3 - The Tip. The forward one fourth of the blade. It does most of the cutting and separating. The tip also includes the point (#2).

4 - The cutting edge, well, it is just that. It is the tapered length of the blade that is sharpened and designed to cut. There are many different types of edges available, but I prefer a straight edge. I have found they are better in the field for me because I can sharpen them quickly and keep them sharp with less effort. The type of edge, just like the metal used in the blade, is an individual choice.

5 - The Guard or Bolster tip. This part of the knife protects your hands from the blade in the event your hand should slide on the handle during use. Knife guards come in various shapes, sizes, and designs. Some of them can be too big and actually make the knife more difficult to use. Select a knife with a guard design you find practical, not beautiful.

6 - Handle. The handle of a knife can be constructed of many different types of material. I have seen them made of wood, plastic, polypropylene, and one even made from an old truck tire (rubber) in Southeast Asia. I avoid metal handles like the plague. I find them too cold to use much in severe winter weather and could actually stick to your hand if it is cold enough.

7 - The Butt. This is the handle end of the knife, opposite of the tip. It is, for all practical purposes, the 'end' of the knife. In some survival knives this may contain a metal cap that can be unscrewed to reveal a hollow storage compartment. I, personally, see no need for the compartment. I carry my survival gear in a survival kit. But, it is an individual preference.

There are other parts to a knife, but these are the most important ones for our discussion. I want to suggest how to select a good knife, not how to make one. A good quality, well designed, sheath knife will contain all of the parts I have just explained. Please understand, I am not discussing penknives or jackknives. They are dogs of a different color. *I am only talking about sheath knives.*

Ok, you have found a knife that is made of a good metal, has all the required components, now what? Simple, pick it up. A well-designed knife *should feel natural in your hand.* Does it feel balanced? The distribution of weight between the blade and the handle affect the balance a great deal. You do not want a knife with a blade that is too heavy, just like you don't want a blade that is too light. Spend some time and find a properly balanced knife for your hand.

The knife, if ergonomically designed, will feel like it is one piece and actually, you should not be able to feel the differences in the weight of the blade and handle. It should *feel natural, fit the hand normally, and be light* enough to use for a prolonged period of time. Avoid knifes that feel too heavy, too wide, or feel "wrong" to your hand. Here again, it is a matter of choice.

Once you see the knife you want, look at the sheath. Is it made of a good quality material? Sheaths can be constructed of metal, plastics, leather, cloth, and the list goes on. I prefer a leather sheath that is re-enforced with rivets. I also make sure all sheaths are double stitched. I once lost a knife I had because the sheath was poorly constructed, so I take extra care in selecting only quality work.

Whether or not the sheath is designed so it can be tied to my leg, attached to my web harness, or secured to my ankle, matters little to me. I prefer a knife sheath that attaches, securely, to my web belt. I have found knives that I attach to other points of my body either, a) get in my way, b) cannot be reached when I really need them, or c) aren't in the sheath when I want them.

Ok, once you have a good quality knife with a sheath, that's all there is to it...*right?* Wrong. You also need to know how to sharpen your blade and how to keep the blade in good condition.

In an emergency, many different types of stone may be used to sharpen your knife blade: quartz, sandstone, or granite are very good examples.

If you use a professional sharpening stone, make sure it has two sides. A good quality professional sharpening stone has both a rough side and a smooth side. Use the rough side first, then the smooth side.

Hold the handle of the knife in your right hand and apply even pressure on the blade with your fingertips. Many experienced hunters have a preferred angle to hold the knife blade (usually 13-16 degrees, or the just about the thickness of your blade), but I suggest you, as a beginner, just work at keeping the angle constant. Remember also to keep the stone wet. You can sharpen your knife by pushing the blade down a wet stone, in a slicing motion. Then, turn the knife over and pull the blade towards your body. Use caution here to avoid injury. Another way to sharpen your knife blade is to move the blade in a circular motion. The key to a sharp knife is keeping a constant angle, using a wet stone, and using your fingertips for even pressure.

Your knife can be preserved by wiping it down with vegetable oil after you are finished sharpening it (even stainless steel will rust, it just takes longer). Many folks use other oils, but I prefer to use a vegetable oil since I may at some point use the knife to eat with. Not to mention I use the blade to prepare an animal carcass after a kill. I just feel safer using a vegetable oil. Additionally, I also feel I should explain some basic knife safety with you.

- Never run with a knife in your hand. It is too easy to fall, or trip, and stick yourself with the tip. If you feel like running, place the knife in the sheath, or drop the knife.

- Never throw a knife that is not designed for throwing. You can break the blade, bend the blade, or, yep, stick yourself. Keep the knife either in the sheath, or in your hand.

- Never use the blade as a screwdriver to pry things open with, or to cut metal. Use a knife only for its designed purpose, to stab or cut. Using the blade improperly may cause it to break or cause injury. The last thing you need in the woods is an injury, regardless of how small it may be.

- Never use the butt of the typical sheath knife as a hammer. It is not designed to hammer with and you may damage your knife. (There are some knives on the market that have a butt designed for hammering, but I don't trust them). If you need a hammer, then get one. Would you use a hammer to field dress game? A knife is designed for cutting, not hammering. Remember the old military adage, *"Use the proper tool for the job."*

- *Never* attempt to catch a falling knife! I have seen some nasty injuries as the result of people attempting to do just that. If you drop a knife, let it fall, while making every effort to ensure your feet are not near the impact point. You don't need an injury.

Keep the edge of the blade sharp! A dull blade causes many more injuries than a sharp one. You should never have to apply undue pressure or force a blade to make it cut. Also, you should not have to "saw" with a blade to cut. If you do, you need to sharpen the blade or use a different type of cutting tool (perhaps you need a hatchet or ax and not a knife). Take care of the edge on your blade and it will take care of you when you need it.

Sheath knives come in all sizes, shapes and designs. I suggest a small or medium blade, easy to maneuver, with a nice even balance. Once more I will hype the 440C blade with a straight edge as my blade choice. When you evaluate a knife ask yourself a very important question, "could I trust my life to the quality of this knife?" In some extreme situations the quality of a good blade could do just that, *save your life*. There are good knives out there that are not expensive, of good quality, and will last a lifetime if properly cared for.

Now you should have a better idea of how to select the one you want, with the quality and design you need. Remember that most experienced woodsmen carry a penknife or a jackknife in their pockets as well as a sheath knife. I also carry a good quality jackknife in my survival kit.

When you are hunting, or faced with a survival situation, the quality of your gear can make the difference between life and death. As my old sergeant used to say in the military, "carry quality gear, keep it in excellent condition, and it will always work when you need it, as often as you need it." Once your game is down, or you are isolated, what you have on you may be all you have to work with. Wanna bet your knife on it?

HOW TO SELECT A GOOD POCKET KNIFE

Since the beginning of time, mankind has had both the desire and need for good quality knives. Earlier in history this need was often hunting or protection based. In the beginning knives were usually made of flint or crudely shaped from wood, but as man developed, so did the knife. It was only natural as man discovered and put new metals into use the knife blade was soon made of these fresh materials. History has recorded common man-made knives of flint, copper, bronze, and iron. And, of course, the current use of steel has completely changed knives to the point that they are now not only useful but very high in overall quality. Additionally, as new metals and materials are discovered, who knows what the future holds for the development of simple knife?

Most of us who spend time in the outdoors carry at least one knife and many of us carry more than two. I suggest we all carry a sheath knife along with a pocket knife of some sort, so we have a back up or a knife for special uses. Keep in mind neither the sheath skinning knife nor the pocket knife was designed to do the same jobs. Since I covered the skinning knife in an earlier article, let's look at pocket knives.

There are many different types and styles of "pocket" knives on the market today, but I want to discuss the pen knife, jack knife, and multi-purpose knife, all three of which are very common designs. We have all seen them, but do you know the difference and which design is the best one for you? If you are like most outdoors people, you just pick up a knife that happens to attract your eye just as long as it has a good design. But, there is much more to it than simple visual attraction, especially when your life may one day depend on the selected knife.

A jack knife is simply hinged at one end, but it may have more than one blade at the hinge. I prefer a jack knife with more than one blade and I carry one as a backup in my survival kit. Of course the blades fold into the handle and the knife is safe to carry, either in your pocket on in a small pocket knife sheath. A jack knife is thought to be the most popular type of pocket knife among backpackers, hunters, fishermen, campers, and the military.

The Multi-blade knives (Boy and Girl Scouts knives, Swiss Army knife, and Tool Pocket Kits) are the second most purchased pocketknife design sold today. Usually they have scissors, corkscrew, screwdrivers, can openers, perhaps a wrench, tooth pick, and everything else but the kitchen sink. We have all seen them, and I dislike them due to their bulkiness and additional weight. Some of these multi-bladed knives can have dozens of various blades, most of which will never be used in the woods. I know some of these knives are made to very high standards and are of excellent quality, but I still question how that can be with so many attachments. I guess each of us can decide which design is best, but as a frequent backpacker, I refuse to pack weight I cannot benefit from at some point. I want a sharp knife blade, not a tool box.

Another knife, the pen knife, is hinged at both ends of the handle, and most have two or three light blades at each end. It is a good knife for those that want more than one type of blade. It was originally designed years ago to cut or shape pen quills that were used in writing at the time. One positive aspect of a pen knife is it is smaller and very light weight when compared to a jack knife, which may vary greatly in size and weight. The pen knife is considered by many to be the third most commonly carried pocket knife in the world today.

There are variations of these knife designs with such features as locking blades, one handed opening and closing blades, assisted opening blades, and the list goes on and on. I suspect the design of the common pocket knife will always be under revision and we will see many changes as new materials are developed in the future. I know that in just the last twenty years or so many new designs have been developed and some older designs improved on. Personally, I think it's great.

Now that you know the difference in the basic pocket knife designs, what kind of blade steel should your knife have? Many knife experts consider S30V the best steel on the market for blade construction, but there are many different grades of steel and at different price ranges. I personally prefer a blade of 420HC, which is stainless steel (this only means it is resistant to rust, but it will rust if not properly cared for), takes a good edge and is easy to sharpen. Different blade steel has different hardness ratings and different edge retention considerations, so look around a bit and compare.

There are a number of different grinding styles used in making knife blades. The most commonly used (of factory made larger knives) is the semi-hollow grind, which combines a sharp edge with good dependable blade strength. Also, another good blade grind is the flat grind (or sometimes called the V-grind, is used most often in small pocket knives), which produces both good strong blade and a sharp edge (it is easy to sharpen, too). There are a few more styles of grinding, but these two are the most common of the factory grinds found in both small and large knives.

In the long run, look for quality steel that will hold a good edge is easy to sharpen, and resists rust. Also, the grinding style of most blades is not of much interest to the typical user and most are factory applied now days anyway, which leaves you with little choice. However, avoid cheap imported knife blades (usually from third world nations) that are of poor quality, potentially dangerous to use, and are basically useless in the field. Nothing is more frustrating to me than a knife that will not hold or take an edge, or is poorly constructed.

The handle of your pocket knife should feel comfortable and solid in your hand. I can assure you, you will not use an uncomfortable knife for a long period of time, unless in an emergency. Rubber and textured handles can give you a better grip in wet or damp conditions, while plastic or composite handles are extremely durable in severe weather conditions. Then again, I like the beauty of natural wood in a handle design. Avoid metal handles in extremely cold weather because the metal will stick to exposed flesh if the temperature drops low enough. Make sure the handle you select is the best one for your intended use and select it for feel and comfort.

Once you have your knife at home the work starts. Like all of your outdoor gear, your knives will require frequent attention if you want it to work when you need it the most.

- Keep the blades of your knife clean and dry, with no fingerprints or moisture on the blades (these can cause stains).

- Wipe the blades down with a light film of oil or silicon, remembering that most stainless steel knifes can both rust and stain if not cared for properly. Use a soft cotton cloth to do this.
- Keep the hinged ends of your knife clean and free of pocket debris or dirt.
- Oil the hinge points with a drop of oil to assure a smooth and easy opening, with a noticeable snap when closing. My grandfather called this the "walks and talks" part of a knife (the blade "walks" open smoothly and "talks" when it loudly snaps shut).
- Keep the blade sharp; dull blades are dangerous to use because they need more force to cut. If you have to force a knife blade when cutting, it either needs sharpening or perhaps you may need an ax or saw instead of a knife.
- Never sharpen your blade on a powered wheel, which will raise the heat of your blade's steel and ruin the temper of the steel.
- Always cut with the blade of a knife moving away from your body. I have seen many injuries result from poor knife usage or a simple slip of the knife.
- They were not designed for throwing.

Most of us who travel in nature's back yard would never dream of going out without a good quality pocket knife. There are many different designs, sizes, colors, and types on the market today. If you are like most of us, you prefer a good quality pen knife or jack knife, and now you know what to look for when you purchase your next one. Just remember the number of hinge points you want, the construction of the blade, the number of blades, the type of handle you need, and a few simple safety factors.

Picking a good pocket knife is not that difficult, but it does take a little time. I suggest you avoid the cheap models.

Making Your Own Survival Kit

Each summer thousands upon thousands of people attempt to spend some time with Mother Nature. They may hike, fish, hunt, walk, boat, or participate in any of a number of outdoor sports they enjoy. Often, they may be miles from other people and in some very remote corners of the country. Some people even have emergencies come up in designated campgrounds. A few, yes, jest a few, will become lost, or maybe forced to survive. Often they are ill prepared for even an overnight emergency, much less for longer periods of time. Most emergency response teams, professional outdoorsmen, and survival instructors highly suggest that anyone who spends much time in the field carry a survival kit.

While there are professional survival kits available commercially, for less than fifty dollars, a small compact survival kit can be made. Also, for a little more money a larger survival kit can be assembled. While many of you may have a lot of experience in the woods, constructing a survival kit takes a lot of pre-planning. Your first consideration is the type of kit you want to construct. It is obvious that a large kit will have more components (great for families), and thereby make survival easier, but at the same time a large kit will weigh more. While smaller kits will weigh less, they will not have the creature comfort items you may want. So, step one is to decide two things; first, how experienced are you in the woods, and second, based on your experience, select the components for a kit. The more experience you have the less items you need to carry.

In all situations you should have a minimum survival kit on you. For only a small investment you can buy all of the components needed, or you may find some survival kit components in your home. However, I suggest you never skimp on quality. Get the best components you can afford. Here are the absolute minimums I would recommend:

- A good quality pen, or jackknife.
- Two unlubricated condoms, or unpowdered vinyl disposable gloves, for water storage.
- A metal match (magnesium striker) and/or flint and steel.

- Half a dozen assorted band-aids.
- A disposable lighter.
- Small button sized compass.
- Scalpel blades, two different sizes.
- Very small flashlight, key chain size and type.
- Four tablets of a pain reliever (acetaminophen, 500mg).
- Six fish hooks of various sized, but mostly small.
- Approximately thirty feet of 2 lb test fishing line, wound around the disposable lighter.

All of the components listed above will easily fit into small container. I use an old metal band aid container, but any rigid, water resistant, container will do. I have seen military mess kits, plastic containers with snap on lids, and many other containers used for storage of this survival kit. I then tape the kit closed, using a length of electricians tape, which can also be used in the field. In an emergency, this minimum survival kit will keep you alive. Granted, it will be rough, but you have what you need to start a fire, store water, and procure a meal. However, I only suggest this kit to the most experienced woodsmen. This kit depends more on the users knowledge than it does the components to survive.

If you want or need a larger kit, there are a number of options available to you for containers, as well as components. But, let's consider the containers first, because you have to decide how you want to carry a larger kit. Two of my favorites are fanny pack survival kits and survival vests. If you are backpacking, a survival vest may not be comfortable under the straps of your backpack, especially if the pack is heavy. In a case like that, I suggest you use a fanny pack worn backwards, with the storage case in front of you. If your upper torso is free, then a survival vest is by far the easiest and best way to carry all you may need.

While there are professional survival vests available (like the US Air Force 21/P), I suggest you save some money and make one from an old fishing vest. Or, even a new fishing vest is less expensive than a commercial survival vest. If you use a fishing vest, all you have to do is maybe sew a couple of the pockets flaps with Velcro closures on them. Additionally, you may want to sew two large pockets inside the fishing vest to hold your large soft items.

Regardless if you use a fanny pack or a vest, you will need the items I have listed above along with:

- A plastic whistle, with a lanyard for your neck.
- A large plastic trash back for water condensation.
- A large plumber's candle.
- A bottle of water purification tablets.
- About fifty feet of parachute cord, 550 cord.
- An emergency strobe light.
- A space blanket.
- A casualty blanket.
- A first aid kit.
- Soap, small hotel size.
- Needles and thread.
- Powdered sports drink of some kind, in a zip lock bag.
- High-energy bars, or a dehydrated ration, or Meal Ready to Eat.

Additionally, you may want to include items that you feel you would personally like to have. I have added a poncho (I hate being wet), a large piece of heavy-duty aluminum foil folded up, a small aluminum cup, six beef flavored bouillon cubes, snare wire, flexible thumb saw, anti-diarrhea tablets, and a small survival manual. For me, this kit does the job. All of the components will fit easily into a vest or a fanny pack, with room to spare.

I have some suggestions for packing a vest that will add to the overall comfort level of the wearer. Place the soft flat items (casualty blanket or a poncho) in the inside pockets. Keep all bulky or items with sharp corners in the outside pockets. After a few hours, if your vest has been packed incorrectly, the components will start to "dig" into your body. Keep the soft items near the body and this is not a problem. Also, keep the nice to have items to a minimum. Don't get carried away, or your survival kit will become too heavy.

As you head out to the woods this summer, take a couple of minutes to prepare a survival kit. A fanny pack is the easiest survival kit to construct, while a survival vest is simple and inexpensive to make. All it takes is a vest, some very basic survival gear, and a sewing machine (you can go with just the standard vest pockets if you don't have a sewing machine). In less than an hour you can have a survival kit you can wear. A survival vest or fanny kit is always ready to go and you can just pick it up as you walk out the door. Within no time you will even forget you are wearing it. While survival is never easy, it does get easier when you have the needed gear along with you. Prepare for emergencies, and you too will survive.

Simple Survival Tips
Heat Reflector
During high winds, use a heat reflector. Your fire will burn better.

Make a Simple Survival Vest

When you need survival gear is not the time to discover you don't have it with you. Years ago, while in the Air Force, I learned how to turn an old fishing vest into a hunting/survival vest. It is easy to do and doesn't take very long to construct. You will be surprised how organized it is, as well as inexpensive to put together. All you need is a fishing vest — I used an old one, and some survival components. Just make sure you do not use a vest with built in flotation. It would be too bulky to use with a backpack.

I used my wife's sewing machine to sew three large pockets inside the vest. I sewed one large pocket on each side, inside front part of vest, and one larger one in the back, on the inside. You can make the pockets as large or small as you like. I also sewed a bit of Velcro® to the vest and the top of the pocket. I did not add a closing flap to the pockets, so they actually looked like deep pouches. The Velcro ® will keep the pocket (or pouch) closed. You can add as many or few pockets as you like. However, most fishing vests come with enough pockets to store all of the survival equipment you would ever need.

My vest is packed all the time and ready to go. That means any time I can just pick it up and I know my gear is there. I keep the following items stored in the outside pockets.

- A quality penknife or jack knife.
- Condoms for water storage, unlubricated.
- Water proof matches in a plastic container.
- Flint and steel and a metal match.
- Water purification tablets, small bottle.
- A long strip of folded heavy-duty aluminum foil folded up to cook with
- Fishing kit, i.e., hooks, sinkers, and some line. Nothing fancy.

- Commercial backpacking first aid kit (with instructions). I carry a very small one.
- One small pack of gum and one of hard candy (energy).
- Approximately 30 feet of parachute nylon cord (550 cord).
- A very small penlight flashlight.
- Five beef bouillon cubes wrapped in a plastic sandwich bag.
- Five tea/coffee bags wrapped in a plastic sandwich bag.
- An emergency strobe light, with an extra battery.
- Whistle, plastic

Other small odds and ends that make life more comfortable for me, (i.e., thin space blanket, an additional knife, mechanical fire starters, and so on).

Inside the vest, in the large pockets, I store the softer and bigger items. The pocket at the rear of the vest contains my good quality casualty blanket. In the right, inside pocket, I keep a pair of dry socks and a poncho. The left inside pocket has my boonie hat and Nomex® flight gloves. The hat protects me from the sun and rain, while the gloves are great heat protection when I cook or work with the campfire.

When you consider adding survival components, consider what they are to be used for. I try to break my gear down into categories when I consider adding anything:

- Foods (examples are candy, coffee, teas, bouillon cubes, etc.)
- Signaling equipment (strobe light, silver lined casualty blanket, Matches for signal fires, signal mirror, flares, and a whistle)
- Food procurement (parachute cord for snares, fishing kit, perhaps some wire)
- Water (water purification tablets, condoms, maybe a collapsible two quart canteen as well).
- Shelter items (poncho, casualty blanket, space blanket, and cord to make a shelter).
- First Aid (a small general first aid kit and first aid manual)
- Fire starting (metal match, storm proof matches, lighter, etc..)

- Nice to have: (sewing kit, Nomex® gloves, boonie hat, and other comfort items)

All of this sounds like a lot of gear, but it is not very heavy. I can wear the vest along with my backpack very easily. The key is to put a soft object in the inside rear pocket to help cushion the backpack. Also, make sure the item is flat in the pocket. If it is bunched up, you will experience some discomfort with a backpack on. Also, some of these items serve more than one purpose. For example, my casualty blanket to construct a shelter, and even to signal with (one side is bright silver in color), and can be used to wrap up and sleep in, or treat an injured person.

So, there you go. Use your imagination to design your own survival vest. Or, you can go down to "Joe's Survival Surplus" and purchase a used or new aviators vest. It is pre-made and ready to go. The commercial one will have about the same number of pockets, but it will be made of mesh and all the pockets will have Velcro closures. Also, a commercial one may have line tied to the vest that allows you to secure each survival item. This is ok for some people, but I dislike the idea.

The idea of securing your survival equipment was developed by the Air Force to keep equipment attached to the vest in the even of a high speed bailout or from being lost due to turbulence during a parachute freefall. Also, if the aircrew member had to open his vest, perhaps to get a radio out during a parachute descent or while hanging in a tree, if he dropped it the gear would not be lost.

I like the idea in some ways. If you drop your gear it is no further than the end of the cord attaching it to the vest. Plus, the cord can be removed from the vest and put to other uses.

I dislike the idea because after you remove a few items to use them you start to look like a spaghetti pot that has exploded with lines everywhere. This happens because most people, me included, are too lazy to wrap the item up properly once they use it. The piece of gear goes back into a pocket poorly wrapped and with part or all of the line hanging out. Then, I can see the lines getting entangled in brush and on limbs as the person moves. Or your hands may catch on a dangling line.

The choice is yours to secure your items or not. I don't plan on making anymore parachute drops, so I have removed the line. If you are worried about losing your gear consider it. It is an individual preference and you can try it out if you are interested.

A survival vest is easy and inexpensive to make. All it takes is a vest, some very basic survival gear, and a sewing machine (you can go with just the standard vest pockets if you don't have a sewing machine). In less than an hour you can have a survival kit you can wear. It is always ready to go and you can put it on as you walk out the door. Within no time you will even forget you are wearing it. While survival is never easy, it does get easier when you are wearing a survival vest.

Understanding Rescue and Recovery

Some of us who hunt in remote areas may one day be forced to survive in the woods for a period of time, due to becoming lost or perhaps an injury. Keep in mind that once we are missing and it has been reported, a rescue operation will start very quickly. Most people who are forced to survive in the United States are rescued within forty-eight hours. This quick action is due to the excellent abilities and training of our rescue teams. They fully understand their capabilities and responsibilities. But, it is not just the rescue teams who have responsibilities. We, as survivors, also have responsibilities prior and during a rescue and recovery. We must prepare for a rescue attempt.

One aspect of survival that I always found hard to understand was the number of rescues that developed severe problems during the actual point of pickup, or recovery. It seemed most of them were routine, then when they were in the process of actually saving a person, something would go wrong. You, like me, are most likely asking, what could happen that would foul up an actual rescue?

The most common problem with the rescue and recovery of survivors is with the survivor, not the rescue team. Often, due to the deep psychological relief of being rescued, the survivor would make a serious mistake and the rescue would either have to be aborted or it would fail. The most common problem with a rescue, in my opinion, lies with the survivor not following instructions, survivor panic, or getting impatient during the recovery. Keep in mind, unlike the movies, a helicopter does not always land and just pick you up. There are many different kinds of equipment used in rescues, from a Horse Collar (a teardrop shaped device with a metal seat and safety straps) to a Stokes litter (resembles a long basket), and depending on the terrain, any device could be used. In some cases, the device may be as simple as a rope.

First, let's consider some ways you can signal for rescue. It is generally understood in the survival world that three of anything may indicate an emergency. This can be three individual fires burning in the shape of a triangle (a fire at each corner), three gun shots fired one after the other, or even three loud blasts from a whistle. Keep in mind the number three. Additionally, you can make more elaborate signals by piling rocks, brush or snow, so it creates a shadow. Most of the rescue people I had talked with suggest the shadow signal be about 12 feet long and at least 3 feet wide. This size seems to cast the best shadow. However, there may be times that it is not possible, so do the best you can. The idea here is to draw the human eye to your signal.

Well, if you decide to pile brush to make a signal, what should your signal look like? There is a simple code, found in most military survival books or manuals, with usually five or more signal designs. I always stress the big three: require assistance (V), need medical assistance (X, for unable to proceed), and going in this direction (a large arrow indicating direction of travel). Of these three, the second one, need medical assistance, is the most commonly used signal. Why? When most of us are forced into a survival situation, much of the time injuries have been sustained from aircraft or vehicle crashes, falls, cuts, or other injuries. And, depending on the weather (severe heat or cold), terrain, and other factors (water and food supplies), you may have a medical situation on your hands. I usually instruct students to simply use the large X, because most survival situations will have medical concerns.

If possible, as soon as practical after you have organized your survival site, prepare or evaluate the area around you for landing zones, or drop zones, for a rescue team. If there is a large field near you, place your fire signals near it. Look for obstacles (loose brush, limbs, etc.,) at the recovery sight and clear them from the area. If the surrounding area is too dense for use, you may, if it is physically possible, be forced to move to a better spot. Do not go too far from where your vehicle stalled, the aircraft crashed, or the mishap occurred. Rescue teams will start the search from your last known position and then gradually work out from there.

Once sighted by a rescue team they will notify you that you have been seen. If you have a survival radio, they will do that on an emergency frequency, say 243.0. Not many of us in the woods carry a survival radio and the rescue team knows this. If it is a fixed wing aircraft (a plane) that spots you, they will raise and lower the wings in a rocking motion (up and down) at day or night. Do not panic if the aircraft rocks its wings and then leaves the area. They may be low of fuel, or may even be leaving so a helicopter can come in to do the actual pick up. In all cases, your position will be quickly fixed and radioed back to the rescue base camp.

Now, as you prepare for the actual rescue attempt, secure anything that could be sucked up by helicopter rotors or into an aircraft engine. This means all ropes, tarps, blankets, clothing, and so on, should be stored. If a chopper comes to rescue you, do not approach the aircraft unless instructed to do so. This instruction will be by a crewmember on the rescue aircraft. And, always approach a helicopter from the front if possible. Approaching from the sides and especially the rear can be very dangerous. Try to go to the aircraft from a 9 to 3 o'clock position, from the pilot's viewpoint. This is safer and also allows the pilot to keep you in sight.

Usually, in most rescues, a crewmember will leave the aircraft and come to your assistance. In severe cases, where the aircraft cannot land, they may lower a rescue technician by a hoist cable to the ground. If a crewmember is lowered, follow the instruction given by them to the letter. These people are the experts and getting excited and doing things on your own could result in severe injury or even death.

In remote areas the rescue helicopter may just lower a rescue device to you. It may be a complex looking affair, or as I said earlier, something as simple as a rope. There are some simple rules to follow that the US Army and Air Force recommend;

- Stand clear as the device is lowered.
- Wait for the device to touch the ground, to ground out static electricity.
- Sit or kneel, facing the device while getting into position and donning it.
- Always, if they are available, put the safety straps on first.
- Place any straps under the armpits, **as you face the device.**
- Always keep the hoist cable on any device in front of you.
- Make sure your hands, legs, and feet are kept clear of excess cable.

If you do not have a radio for communications with the pilot, give a one handed thumbs up, or shake the cable vigorously from side to side to indicate you are ready to be lifted.

Do not do anything from that point on, except to hold on to the device firmly and follow any orders from rescue personnel. Do not attempt to climb into the chopper, because you may fall.

Many survivors have been lost just as they reached the door of the rescue aircraft due to failure to follow orders, or panic. It is common, so remember this for you will be lifted and turned as you are pulled into the aircraft. That step may give you the sensation you will fall, but as long as you are holding the device securely, you are safe. Do not let go of the device until you are well in the chopper and instructed by a crewmember to do so. In the military we were instructed to hold onto the device until the rescue tech pulled our hands off of it.

Survival is always difficult and often very dangerous. While rescue is the least dangerous aspect of survival, or so survivors often think, it does take some thought to do so safely. At times survivors will survive for long periods of time, only to be lost during the rescue and recover stage. This almost always happens because the survivor fails to follow orders or panics. By using good common sense, understanding how a rescue takes place, and following orders, you too can survive the most critical aspect of survival, rescue and recovery.

Camouflage, Now I See You, Now I Don't

Camouflage is much talked about and used, but rarely understood. Part of our misunderstanding of camouflage is the result of watching too many action type movies. In the movies our hero generally has a specially designed camouflage uniform, as well as a very detailed and uniquely designed face pattern. While all of that adds to the excitement of the movie, it is hardly suggested for most hunters or military members. So, what is camouflage, why is it used, and how can you use it properly?

Camouflage is the art of blending into your natural surroundings, thus giving you the ability to remain unnoticed (this is especially important for turkey hunters). Sounds easy, but it is not that simple to maintain good camouflage. Your first consideration is determining what you want to remain concealed from. If it is an animal, determine first if it is colorblind. It is easier to camouflage from an animal that is colorblind and you can actually use international orange, red, and other bright colors without any loss of concealment. This may be an important safety factor if you wish to use camouflage patterns, and yet remain seen by other hunters. But, what if you are camouflaging against animals or humans that are not colorblind?

Your concern at that point is making sure your camouflage matches your surroundings well enough that you remain unnoticed. It would, for instance, not be to your advantage to use desert camo in a woodlands environment (unless your game is colorblind perhaps). Also, if you attach plants or bushes to yourself for camo, make sure they match the area you may be in. Nothing will grab the eye more than the wrong color, or type of plant, in the wrong place, unless it would be when that object is moving. Your goal with camouflage is to blend in and become one with your surroundings. This is done effectively by simply breaking up the human form.

Additionally, take a look around you as you move with your camouflage (situational awareness the military calls it). If you have bushes attached to you and you are moving over a field, you will be noticed. Additionally, any plant life you use as part of your concealment should fit the area. By that I mean if the area has only pine trees and you are wearing oak or long grasses as part of your camouflage, you will stand out. Many military members will stop when they enter a new area and apply fresh camo to match the area. Keep in mind also, your greenery will die after a short period and start to droop. You will have to cut and attach fresh camouflage at that point. You want to look natural, not like you have been ill.

One area that many people, including the military, overlook is the proper use of camouflage paint, or makeup. We often smear a few streaks of paint on our face and call it done. This mistake is common, but isn't an effective use of camouflage. No, I am not suggesting you spent hours putting on your "make up," rather I am saying it should be applied properly. Poorly applied camo may draw attention to you and actually hurt your concealment efforts.

As you apply the camouflage makeup, make sure the high features of your face (nose, forehead, cheeks and chin) are covered well. It is usually a good idea to apply a light layer of baby oil or a lotion to your skin prior to applying the camouflage makeup. This tip will make it much easier to remove the camo when you need to take it off. Also, you can use a blotch or slash-pattern design of camouflage as you put it on. I prefer to cover high points of my face in black or dark brown. Additionally, it may be a good idea to cover your eyelids as well. I have seen a perfectly concealed individual with his eyes closed located easily at night through the use of a high-powered light. His eyelids actually shined when the light hit them. Don't forget to cover your ears, both front and back, as well as your neck.

Another area we frequently forget to camouflage is our hands and fingers. Your skin color will stand out on your hands, if the rest of you is well camouflaged. Take the time to cover your hands well, including the skin between your fingers (the webbed area). If you are wearing a short-sleeved shirt, do not forget to cover the arms as well. Have another hunter or member of your team check you closely for exposed skin once you have applied your camo.

Keep in mind that camouflage does not make you invisible, especially when you are moving. It just makes you harder to see. In other words, it breaks up the natural form of the human body. If you must move while wearing camo, make your movements very slow and do not skyline (be seen against a sky background) yourself. Usually, it is a good idea to stay to low lying areas and to move in the shadows. This type of movement will make you much harder to see. If you are hunting game, and near your target, move only when the animal is feeding (and has its head down) or when it is looking away from you. Be prepared to freeze at any second. If you freeze, at times even when in clear view, you may not be spotted. Movement is what attracts the most attention when you are attempting to remain unseen. Move only when you must, and then very slowly.

Other considerations with camouflage is making sure you have nothing exposed that can reflect sunlight or shine at night. Remember that eyeglasses, necklaces, bracelets, and watches can shine and give your position away. Even at night, a light shined on you may result in a shine from one of these items.

When you must move and remain unseen, as I said earlier, use shadows, but remember the sun is constantly moving so the shadows will be changing as well. Be aware of your natural surrounding and use rock formations, trees, and brush to assist in your concealment efforts. Move as little as possible, or as I stated earlier, move slowly when you do move. Remember to break up the "V" of all crotch areas, between the legs and your arms. Make any observations you have to do in the prone position. Once again, remember, if you think you are seen, freeze. Most of the time you will not be seen for what you are.

One last area of camouflage we often forget is scent. Humans, as well as most game, will smell us way before they ever see us. Make sure you do not use perfumed soaps, shampoos, shaving creams or shaving lotions (and we are a smell good society). Also, gum, candy, or the use of tobacco may give your position away. One aspect of scents we rarely think of is smoke (both from cigarettes and campfires). I once knew a hunter that would purposefully stand in the smoke of a campfire prior to going hunting. He claimed it masked his odor. He also claimed it was an old trick he had learned from a Native American. Well, he was correct in this view, *it would cover his odor,* but he failed to realize any critter in the woods would smell the smoke way before it ever saw him. And animals, just like humans, associate the scent of smoke with man. Use caution when around smoke from your campfire or when around smokers to avoid absorbing the smell. Oh, by the way, I never knew that man to ever bag any large game.

In the military they taught us the acronym BLISS when considering camouflage. BLISS stands for Blend, (keep a) Low silhouette, (keep a) Irregular shape, (stay) Small, and keep to Secluded areas. Essentially, BLISS along with good camouflage makeup, situational awareness, and scent control, will do the job of assisting you in your concealment efforts.

Camouflage, now I see you, now I don't, is simple to use but few of us use it properly. By remembering what I have suggested in this short article you too can blend into the background. Camouflage is BLISS.

Camping is Fun with Kids!

One of the best ways of getting a child involved with your outdoor activities is to have them involved from the start. When I take a child on their first overnight camping trip, we start getting ready days in advance! Let me give you an idea of what I do, and perhaps it will work for you. Keep in mind each child is different, so approach them differently. I do know if the child is in the early stages of planning for a trip and stays active in all phases of it, they really have a good time. And, I have been camping with kids for more than thirty years.

The weekend prior to the trip I will sit down and just talk to the child about what they can expect on a camping trip. Many kids will be concerned about things that may never enter your mind. For instance, my oldest daughter was concerned about bathrooms, while my nephew was worried about how and what we would eat. Both are valid concerns, but hardly anything to be seriously worried about. But not just children have vivid imaginations. When I was in jungle survival school in the Philippines we had a lieutenant that sat up all night around the fire, because he had seen spiders the size of cars in the old Tarzan movies. No way he was going to sleep with any critter that big running loose! And, kids today have much better imaginations that most of us adults could even consider. But talk to each child and explain what you know about their concern and be honest with them.

Also during the same week as the trip, I will pull out all of my camping equipment and double check it. This does two things; first it makes sure the equipment is still in serviceable condition, and second, it gives me a chance to show the child how the equipment works. I will even have the child assist me in erecting the tent in the back yard, pack up the first aid and survival gear, double check the mess gear and so on. I use this time to teach the child and do so in a controlled environment. You will find the average youngster is fascinated by the different kinds of gear and equipment that you may have around.

Make sure your gear, food, and other supplies are in good shape. Nothing discourages a young camper like a trip that has been poorly planned. I once spent a rainy night in the Missouri Ozark Mountains because my uncle could not put up our tent. That was over forty years ago and I still remember how miserable the trip was. Prepare and plan; that way the child's first impression is a good one.

The night before the camping trip, we prepare our dinner for the next day. I have each child assist and believe me they have a lot of fun doing it. Remember, some kids have not done much camping so it excites them. I have each child select a meat item (chicken, pork, or beef), two veggies, and a piece of fruit for dessert. I place one square of heavy-duty aluminum foil down flat and have the child center the meat and veggies. I then have the child fold the aluminum over the food. We then place the folded meal in another piece of aluminum and seal it well. Now the meal has been double sealed in aluminum. Next, we take the fruit, apple, banana, or pear, quarter it and wrap it in aluminum as well. The next day your child only has to place the meal with dessert on the hot coals, not flames, and the meal will cook in its own juices (pierce the metal covering with a fork prior to cooking). An Adult should turn the meal about every 5 to10 minutes to keep it cooking evenly. The children love these meals, because "they made it."

Once I arrive at the campsite, I assign camping chores to each of the children. I have found they enjoy the responsibility and it actually makes it easier on the adult leader. I have one wash the dishes, one rinse and dry, and another gather water and so on. I think you have the idea here. Then, before we get down to having fun, all of us gather up as much firewood as we can. It is important here to explain to the children to gather dead and dry firewood. Also, it is a good idea to discuss the danger of snakes with them before you start. I hope all of you noticed I said, discuss and not scare (less than 10% of the world's snakes are poisonous). Teach children to respect snakes, not to be paranoid about them.

I also think each child should be warned of certain dangers that are just natural when we camp. For instance, explain to the child:

- Do not wander off away from the camp, and give each child a whistle to blow if they do become lost...my son once sounded like a train moving through the woods when he became lost as a youngster.

- Explain to each child that only an adult can make the fire, add wood to the fire, or cook on the fire (of course this depends on the experience and ages of the children). Keep a fire extinguisher on hand or a couple gallons of water.

- Remind children that wild animals are just that, wild. They are not to be petted or fed. Bites, scratches, and claw marks can result from children attempting to pet a wild animal, not to mention the dangers of rabies.

- Make sure each child knows they are not to drink any water that is not from your water container, no matter how clean it may look in a stream or lake.

- Show each child where your toilets are. I have found girls will usually go to the designated spot, for privacy, where boys just use the first tree. Enforce the use of your bathroom area, even late at night. Hygiene is very important when camping.

- Stress the importance of keeping clean. This means clean clothes each day and the reporting of all cuts, scrapes, and scratches. In the woods, small injuries can quickly become infected. Make sure an adult cleans and covers each injury.

I am sure there are other rules you may have in your mind as well. If you think they are important, then explain them to the children. But, I have to warn you, they will ask you why, so be prepared to answer them. The idea here it to keep the list of rules short, we don't want to restrict the fun, but safety should never be compromised. Plus, I have seen children that followed the rules much better than most adults. So, be sure you set a good example for the younger ones.

Plan the day's activities with children. I usually get up early and have them help me prepare pancakes and eggs. Pancake mix can be placed in a large zip locked bag, water added, and then the child can mix the whole mess. I do the actual cooking, but they can hold the plates, hand me the mix and eggs. Make them part of the preparing the meal. They love being a part of it all.

After breakfast is done (and the chores) I usually take them on a nature walk. On this type of walk we hope to see some wild animals, flowers, and beautiful countryside. Keep the length of your walk short enough for the smallest child you have along. Also, move at the slowest child's pace. Point out different aspects of nature as you walk. The more you know about the outdoors the more excited they will become. If you can keep them quiet long enough you may even see a deer or two. I also try to have a small snack for each child as we hike. We usually stop and eat near a lake, stream or in a field. This serves two purposes, it feeds the little guy or gal (they are always hungry in the woods), but it also teaches them that we do not litter the trails. I have each hiker place the empty paper and containers in their backpack to carry back to camp.

Once I return from the hike, I give each child time to just play around the campsite. Usually a game of tag, or catch will break out. If not, and they become bored, then I use my old secret...I take all of them fishing! Fishing always works, but you may not get much fishing done if you have a small group of kids with you. They constantly need the hook baited or help getting the line untangled. I enjoy the excitement when a child catches a small fish, though my daughter once caught an eight-pound bass drowning a worm in some nearby reeds. The important thing is to just let them have fun!

For lunch I usually (depending on the age of the children) let them cook hotdogs over the fire (under close supervision), have chips, and veggies sticks (carrots, celery, and so on), and milk (if you have an ice chest). Our dessert is usually fresh fruit. Fresh milk is never an issue for short camping trips; on long ones you can get the milk that does not require refrigeration. I tend to eat the same types of foods camping as I do at home.

During the afternoon if the children are old enough we take another hike in the woods or go looking down by the water. I do not let them get too close to the water's edge, but they can still see frogs, an occasional snake perhaps, and small fish feeding. Most children are scared of the large dragonflies when they first see them. This is normal. My niece thought they were large bees! You can have almost as much fun as the children just by watching them!

Start dinner early. Most kids I have taken camping build up a terrible hunger during the day. Just like at home, I tend to control the amount of snacks they have during the day (except fruit and veggies), but feed them often and a lot! On my last camping trip the boys and I had grilled steaks, real baked potatoes, fresh green salad, and a can of peaches for dessert. They ate every last bite and then as soon as it got dark the real fun started!

Children, and most adults, love a campfire at night. I can't sing, but I do when I camp. I teach the kids old country songs, funny songs, or we take turns making songs up. Often, after the kids have some experience camping, the subject will turn to scary ghost stories. We take turns going around the campfire telling the best scary stories you have ever heard! I wish I had a dollar for every time I have told (and I made it all up in my head) of *"The Hand That Won't Die!"* Keep the stories down if you have a new member or an inexperienced camper. The idea is to have fun, not scare a child so badly you are up all night with them (I know this from experience). However, use your own judgment here about the horror tales. They may not be appropriate for your age group of kids.

At night I let the girls go to one tent and the boys to another. You can, usually anyway, expect a night raid by the boys. I usually sit between the tents and wait. Most of the time the raid comes very early because the children are tired and can't wait long. I have caught more boys that way! Though, I did once catch a group of young girls. As I said, usually they will raid early, because they are tired.

In the morning I will wake them at a reasonable time, let's say around 7am. I get them up early for a number of reasons (they may be difficult to get up if they are still tired from the day before). The first reason is so they can help me with breakfast, and then all of us can clean the campsite. Second, I will have some activities planned for the day. I usually ask the children on the second day what they want to do. Listen to their plans and ideas; they may have a great suggestion. Now remember, you want just enough things planned to keep them from getting bored, but don't plan every single minute! Allow the children to have time to do things as a couple or alone. This is healthy and good for them to have some unstructured time. But, keep them safe and know where they are at all times.

Also, bring along some books and board games the children have chosen. It is important for the children to pick those items and not you. I refuse, personally, to allow a child to bring electronic games, radios, or cd players. I feel camping is the time to get away from those things. Of course, you may decide differently, but I have never had a child miss them if they had other things to do. You should bring these books and games with you so the child has something to do if the weather turns ugly. I once spent three days in Alaska with a 10-year-old boy and nothing for him to do as it rained, rained, and then rained some more. *I will never do that again.*

When you depart a campsite make sure the fire is out, trash has been picked up and stress the importance to each child of "leaving only your foot prints." I have found that most children who are taught good camping skills, responsibilities, cleanliness, and safety, make excellent campers as adults. It is you and I who can motivate these youngsters and turn them into great responsible campers!

Camping with children can be a great deal of fun. But, as I have said, the big secret is to get the child involved from the very start. Keep them involved too during the whole process! Make them feel as if they are part of the trip and not just excess baggage. Give them camp responsibilities and explain why the chores have to be done. Let them do as much as they can for their age. Stress safety, hygiene, fun, and turn the trip into an educational time for them. Teach them the wonders of nature, preservation of our woods and streams, and a deep appreciation of what America has to offer our campers, hikers, and outdoor families. ***But, most of all, teach them we can all, regardless of our age, have fun outdoors!***

CAMPING WITH A CHILD

Camping with children is not like camping with adults

Those of us who enjoy sharing nature with children often mean well, but at times we fail to accomplish our goals of motivating, educating, and eliminating fears. I feel it is our responsibility as adults to teach our children properly. I have discovered that unlike adults, most children are unafraid of the real dangers from nature. This may be due to the fact that most children are trusting of most things, and what fears they have in most cases are unrealistic. Now, this still does not mean that a child will not be scared on an overnight camping trip, but if approached properly by an adult, this fear can be great reduced.

Prior to your camping trip spend some time with the child and discuss what will take place. Be honest and speak about insects, animals, bathrooms (or the lack), foods, and so on. Find out what the child's concerns are. Discuss the concerns with the child and be honest here. It is important that the child learn to trust your suggestions and explanations.

I also suggest you start your children camping at an early age. All three of my kids started very young, by the age of one year old. Granted, we only took them to designated campgrounds and in fair weather, but they "grew up" camping and now are very experienced campers, and very comfortable sleeping in the bush with just a campfire and the minimum amount of supplies. It is a learning process, and with this learning process came not only experience, but a total acceptance of nature as it really is.

Another very important aspect of camping with children is setting a good example for them. We want our children to grow up protecting our natural resources and keeping nature clean. I have a few simple child educating rules that I enforce when I camp with a child.

Keep the campsite clean at all times. Trash and waste goes into the proper containers *immediately*.

Use only dead wood for fires. Stack the wood up neatly and explain to the child why it is not placed too close to the fire.

Require all campers use the designated toilet area. Boys, I have found, tend to want to sneak behind a tent.

Teach the child about the animals you see. I believe you will find them fascinated by the small creatures, rabbits, squirrels, ducks, birds and so on.

Make certain your child knows that wild animals are wild. Stress to them that the animals you see are not pets and *under no circumstances* should the child attempt to feed or pet any animal.

I always stress to any child just before we leave a campsite that we need to make sure **the area is cleaner than when we found it**.

Another aspect of sharing nature with a child that should be addressed is safety. Make sure to always stress camping safety with each child. Explain why it is dangerous for the child to leave the campsite alone (may get lost, encounter a snake, or dangerous animal). Give each child a plastic whistle and make sure they understand to blow it only if they are lost.

Inform each child that the only water to drink is from your water source. Many kids want to taste stream or river water, and that is not safe to drink.

Warn, but do not scare, each child about snakes. Pit vipers, the most common type of poisonous snake in North America, are found throughout the United States and Canada. *I explain the role that snakes play in nature and that most (about 90%) of the snakes in the world are not poisonous.*

Camp safety is another good subject to discuss. Explain that only adults can make a fire, add wood to a fire, or cook on a fire (unless supervised by an adult). Keep a container of water or a fire extinguisher near the fire and show the child how to use it.

You should also make sure all of the kids know to report any injury, regardless of how small, to an adult. All cuts, scrapes, or punctures should be cleaned and covered to avoid infection.

Another area to discuss with children, and not a very popular one, is hygiene. Explain to the child that regular bathing, the brushing of teeth, and good overall cleanliness is required. Nothing can ruin a camping trip faster than an illness resulting from poor hygiene.

Keep the children involved in basic camp chores appropriate for their ages. They can assist by doing dishes, washing their clothing, airing sleeping bags or blankets, picking up litter, or any other needed tasks. Also, older children and teens can actually do some camp cooking with supervision. I usually start them out with hotdogs on a stick, marshmallows, or helping me prepare and cook pancakes for breakfast. As the child ages, so does the type of cooking.

Another good idea is to have a few hobbies, books, or games along to give the child something to do when they want to stay close to the campsite or during bad weather. If you have games or books along they can pass the time until the weather clears. Just be sure and allow the children to pick the games, hobbies, or books before the trip. It should be things they are interested it, not you.

While camping with a child is not difficult, it does require a little planning on your part. Just remember to have some basic safety rules, chores, and activities planned for your trip. Take care, stay safe, and I hope to see you and your family at the campgrounds soon!

*C*AMPING WITH *C*HILDREN

It is a time for sharing

There was a slight chill in the air and a false dawn was just visible through the trees. A deer suddenly appeared and slowly made her way down the field, feeding slowly as she moved. A young fawn followed the doe, seemingly without any fear. My eight-year-old daughter gave a slight sigh as she watched the  beautiful animals moving slowly toward us. I felt a special closeness with my child and nature as the scene unfolded in front of us. It is a special memory that neither of us will likely ever forget.

In my many years of camping in Missouri, I have yet to enjoy it more than when I share the experience with a child. The sparkling eyes of a youngster as they watch a deer feed along a fence or seeing a flock of ducks take to the air over a lake is very rewarding to me. I see the wonder and beauty of Missouri as something to be shared with all of our children. I also think each of us as adults have a responsibility to teach the younger generation about caring for the natural resources of our state. It is up to us to teach our children to enjoy nature, respect it, and at the same time take care of it. The task sounds easy, but it does take some planning to do properly.

One of the best ways to teach a child about nature is to take then on a hike, an afternoon of fishing, or an overnight camping trip. Most children are interested in nature and love to see the various plants and wildlife. But, let's discuss how to take a child on an overnight camping trip, my favorite way to introduce Mother Nature.

Make sure you talk to the child prior to the trip to prepare them for what they may experience. Try to find out if they have any unrealistic fears or concerns. Often times they may worry about snakes, toilets, or unlikely concerns like bear attacks or monsters. Keep in mind, a child today is exposed to countless types of media and they may not have an accurate idea of what nature is really like.

Remember, many children who are in the woods for the first time will, even if they are not aware of it, copy your behaviors. This is a good thing to consider, because it can assist you in teaching them. Before the trip it is extremely important that you set some rules, and during the trip make sure you follow them as well. You should be consistent when you enforce them. These rules are designed with the child's safety in mind, not to restrict their enjoyment.

The campsite must be kept clean of litter and waste at all times. Make sure each child and adult is reminded to pick up empty cans, papers, or other trash and place it in an appropriate container. It is an excellent time to teach the new camper about camp hygiene.

Use only dead wood for your fires. Not only will the wood burn better and give a hotter flame, it will also smoke less. Stress to the child that the killing of a tree for the fire is a waste since there is so much dead wood around, and dead wood burns better.

Show each person the designated toilet area. If it is a remote camping site, the toilet should not be near your water source. You should establish it down wind and a good distance from your campsite. Stress that all members are to use the toilet area only to relieve themselves. I have found boys, especially at night, will attempt to just go behind the tent.

Assign each child chores to accomplish around the campsite. This may mean washing dishes, gathering firewood, hanging sleeping bags and blankets to air out, or whatever is needed. Chores assist in developing a good responsible camper.

Get up early in an attempt to find deer or other game feeding near your campsite. Often in the early mornings or late evenings animals will be feeding or moving toward water. I have yet to see a child that was not fascinated just watching a deer feed. Share the wonder of wild animals with a child.

At the same time teach the child these wild animals are still wild animals and not pets. *No child should ever be given the impression that they may touch, pet, or feed a wild animal*. While it is not only dangerous to both the animal and the child, it may lead the animal to depending on handouts for food.

The rules listed above are not your only concerns. You not only want the child to enjoy the trip, you want the trip to be safe. There are other issues you need to address that will make the trip safer and add some needed structure.

The only water that any one should drink is water that is clean and purified. This can be water from a designated safe source, bottled (bought), or water that has been purified by chemicals. Regardless of how clean a stream or lake may look the water is not safe to drink. Bad water can make you very ill.

Snakes are an issue that all adults and kids in Missouri need to know about. Although most snakes in the state are not poisonous, there are a few you should keep in mind (rattlesnakes, copperheads, and water moccasins). Usually I just remind the child of the dangers of snakes, I do not try to scare them. Stress the need for the child to watch where they walk, where they place their hands and feet, and to use a light at night. If you over do it, the child could become paranoid of snakes. And, snakes should be respected, not feared.

All injuries, regardless of how small, should be reported to an adult. The injury should be washed with soap and water and then covered. Small injuries may become infected very quickly when outdoors and not kept clean. *I suggest all non-minor injuries be evaluated and treated by a doctor.*

Personal hygiene is an issue that also needs to be discussed. Most children, and some adults, feel that keeping clean is not that important while out camping. I disagree. It is more important than when a person is at home. I require the child to change clothes daily, bath, and brush their teeth just like at home. I go further and checks hands and fingernails prior to meals. It is a good habit for the child to get into, because many camping illnesses are the result of poor hygiene.

Campfires seem to mesmerize kids of all ages. *This is an area that requires close supervision constantly.* Young children should not be allowed to add wood to a burning fire, play with lighters or matches, burn sticks in the fire, cook on a fire, or get near the fire at any time. I do suggest that older kids and teens be taught how to start a fire, how to maintain it, and cook on it. Each child is different and only you can decide when a child is old enough (and responsible enough) to learn about using fires. Make sure in all cases you keep a supply of water or sand available for emergencies, or a commercial fire extinguisher.

When your camping trip is over and you are preparing to leave, make sure your fire is out, all litter has been picked up, and you leave the site cleaner than when you arrived. Explain to each child the importance of what you are doing. Teach all children that only footprints should remain when they leave a campsite. The camping habits we instill in a young child while outdoors will last them a lifetime. Be a good example, educate, and motivate a child. The future of Missouri's natural resources is in your hands. Invest in our state's future, and take a child camping today.

CHILDREN AND SURVIVAL

The Added Stresses of Surviving with Children Along

Have you ever talked to your children about child survival? I mean, what to do if the car breaks down during bad weather, or what to do if suddenly forced to survive for any reason. I have, and the results surprised me. While most of you may think a child would not be interested in survival, they are, or at least the ones I spoke to were. The children I have spoken to were my own, as well as others in a classroom, and believe me, they all showed an interest. The classrooms I have spoken in were always quiet as if they were hanging onto each word as I spoke.

If you are out with children and suddenly find yourself in a survival situation, stay calm. If the children are very young, they may not notice any changes in your behavior. But, there will be changes. Just the sudden realization that you may have to survive will cause a slight (or great) change in all of us. However, older children may pick up on it immediately. While each situation, as well as each child, is different, I do have some suggestions.

Stop. If your car breaks down, you won't have a choice here, but if you are hiking or walking you do. Stop and think about your situation. Do you have any idea where you are? If not, do not panic. You must, at this point, use your mind to survive. If you do panic and begin to meander around in the woods, you may die and those with you as well. Stop and think. Who knows where you are? Who knows when you should return? Who did you tell about your trip? All of these things should have been told to someone before any hike in the woods, or even a simple car trip in isolated country.

Next, if the children are old enough to understand, explain what has happened. I would suggest you simply say, "We have to stay here and wait for help. I am not sure where we are and I need you to help me." Older children, in their teens, can be told openly, "We are lost and need to stay here until we are found. I need your help to make us comfortable. Can I depend on your assistance?" The last statement will make them feel needed as well as part of the "group." Depending on the child, you may use different phrases, but the idea is there. Convey you need to stay where you are, you need to wait for help, and that you need them to help you. With the younger kids you might even be able to make a game of it all, or perhaps say very little.

Attempt to gain control over your initial inner fears. It is important for you to stay strong and to provide good leadership for the group. Of course, I realize you may not be a survival expert, but you don't have to be. The key here is to maintain the image of trust the child has for you already. As children, they see us as those who provide food, water, comfort, and safety for them. While the sudden responsibility to care for a child in a survival situation will be very stressful, you must do all you can to keep an adult image portrayed at all times.

If you need to cry or feel as if you are going "to pieces", leave the group. Insure an adult is with the child at all times if you leave (so, leaving may not be possible). Make the excuse of needing to using the "toilet" or to gather firewood, then walk off a little ways. Do your thing and then return once your composure is regained. Survival is tough and it is rare an individual does not break down if they are out there long enough. If you are a religious family, then pray together. Most survivors pray at some point in their situation if they are out there long enough.

Okay, now that you have control and are maintaining your image, now what? Due to length restrictions and the complexity of this article, let's use older children in our situation (8-14 years old). As I stated earlier, you can make a game of your situation. I would suggest you and the child **go through your equipment**, all of it. You will be surprised what a child may have in a pocket or a backpack. Often you will find gum, candy, a knife, and other goodies. I know a man who found a small pocketknife and two cans of soda pop. Regardless of what you will find, inventory all of your equipment. Have the child assist you. I would have the child go through my pack as I went through theirs. Then, change packs and do it again.

As you find gear, ask the child what it could be used for, besides the obvious. Remember, just because they are younger and smaller does not mean they can't have some very good ideas. I think you would be very surprised what they can come up with. See, they don't know that certain things are expected to be used only in certain ways. Consider all of their ideas. Discuss the practical uses of the equipment with them and make sure they know exactly how to use each piece. This step is critical in the event you sustain a serious injury or death.

One aspect of being in the woods with a child that I feel is very important is being prepared. Once you are forced to spend the night in the woods with a child is not the time to discover you don't have matches. Or, that you don't know basic first aid or how to use some of your survival gear. Prepare. Be a scout and remember the scout motto, **always be prepared**. I never go out without my survival kit with me. No, it is not very big and it does not weigh much, but it could prove to be a life saver. I actually carry most of it in a small plastic box about three inches wide and about five inches long. I have it in my right pants cargo pocket at all times (or in my car). What do I have in it?

- A quality penknife or jack knife.
- Condoms for water storage, un-lubricated
- Latex gloves if you prefer not to have condoms.
- Water proof matches
- Flint and steel or a metal match
- Water purification tablets
- A long strip of heavy-duty aluminum foil folded up to cook with
- Fishing kit, i.e., hooks, sinkers, and some line. Nothing fancy.
- Commercial back packing first aid kit (with instructions). I carry a very small one.
- One small pack of gum and one of hard candy (energy)

Also, I carry three other things on my person. I carry a good quality space blanket, a casualty blanket, and about twenty feet of cotton cord. I have found I can survive with the above items, and all of this stuff weighs almost nothing. I carry it all in one cargo pocket and still have lots of room left. It is my insurance policy.

One other area I need to discuss is how **you and the child should dress** when you are in the woods. I usually wear military cargo pocket styled pants and shirts. These can be purchased for you and older children in surplus stores at a good price. I also suggest good boots, warm socks, and you both should have a belt. I wear a wide brimmed hat to shade my eyes from the elements and the child should have a hat of some kind (the head loses a lot of body heat when it is not covered in cold weather). Of course you know I also have a poncho but not much else is really needed. If you want to get the two of you a fanny pack and wear jeans, all of the equipment I have listed will easily fit into one container. Once you are in a survival situation with a child is not the time to decide you need the gear. You have it with you, or you will do without.

Establish some very general, but important **safety rules for the child**. You may expand or change this list as you see needed depending on your individual situation.

- *Never* leave the campsite alone
- *Do not drink* any water that is not in a container (streams, rivers, ponds, etc...)
- *Report all injuries*, regardless of how small to the adult (clean and cover all injuries to avoid infections)
- Only the adult is allowed to **make a fire and maintain it**. Older children may be taught to start a fire and "feed" the fire with supervision. Make it clear to the older child they are to do this alone only in an emergency.
- Make sure the child knows **not to eat any plants, insects or animals** without your approval. Some plants may be poisonous, some insects may bite or sting, and some animals may injure the child.
- *Do not scare* the child with stories about snakes, but cover the subject. Make sure the child knows to make lots of noise, not to place their hands in holes or under dead trees. Warn them to report immediately when they see a snake (two reasons here, you don't need a snake bite, and second, you can eat the snake if needed).

Keep the child and yourself busy (this helps avoid the "poor me" syndrome). As soon as the gear is inventoried, have the child assist you in making a fire. The two of you should gather twigs, small pieces of dead wood, and other kindling. Then, working together, gather up as much dead wood as you can find near you. Stack the wood in a pile no closer than 10 feet to your fire pit. Show the child how to stack the twigs in a tee-pee shape over dry moss or small torn and crumpled up pieces of paper. Only the adult should light the fire. The child, nonetheless, if old enough, should be shown how to do it. Make sure, if possible, you keep a source of water nearby, or loose soil or sand, to assist you in putting the fire out quickly if you have to. Instruct the child on the purpose of the soil, sand, or water.

Once the fire is going, have the child assist you in preparing a shelter. You will be surprised how quickly two people can make a place to sleep. I suggest, if the weather permits, you run a rope or vine, between two trees about three feet off of the ground. If you have a blanket, poncho, tarp, or casualty blanket, you can then drape it over the line and secure the ends in the dirt with wooden stakes. Make sure your door faces your fire and that your fire is not too close (less than 10 feet in my opinion). Then the two of you should cut fresh pine boughs (most states have pine trees or leaves can be used) to line the floor of your shelter. This will insulate the shelter floor and help you stay warm as you sleep. Remind the child to keep a look out for snakes, but don't scare them.

You may or may not have sleeping bags, depending on how you reached the situation you are in, but if not, feed the fire as often as you need to. In warm weather you may not even need a fire to survive, but I strongly recommend one for psychological reasons. Both you and the child will feel much better with a fire burning. There is some deep unexplained satisfaction about a fire at night. Perhaps it suggests safety from harmful animals or just having the light may make us feel as if we are in control of our situation. At any rate, always have a fire at night.

Perhaps, if the child is not ready to sleep, you can tell "good" stories, or share a piece of candy. Avoid the typical ghost or scary stories if you are in a survival situation. This will assist in keeping the child's fears of uncertainty down. Most likely, I would even sing a few songs to convey that things aren't that bad. If the child is scared or terrified, you may have a very difficult time of it. Try a few words of love and maybe some hugs. I am sure some children, perhaps those that hike or camp a great deal, will adjust to your situation very quickly. **They may even enjoy the great adventure!**

Water may or may not be a problem. There are many variables involved with water procurement. You may have water with you, or you may have to find it. If you can, boil any untreated or unknown water. You must do this regardless of how clear and clean the water seems to be. Explain to the child that the water, if not treated or boiled, can harm them. Be sure and drink plenty of clean water. Dehydration can be a real problem in any survival situation. Instruct the child to tell you when they have dark or brown (in color) urine (a sign of dehydration). Then, increase the child's water intake.

If you backpack a lot, carry water purification tablets with you. A small bottle of 50 or more takes up very little space and weighs little. Have the child assist you in water procurement and treatment regardless of what procedure you have to use. They need to learn how to do it properly.

I think by the end of the first day of survival, your little helper will be worn out. It takes a lot of work to prepare a proper survival site. Keep the child active in assisting you. This helps wear them out and that helps them sleep better. But keep in mind; one of our goals is to also teach them. As a child, they may not think they should give suggestions or help an adult. Attempt to draw out what they are thinking and feeling as often as you can. Involve them in your survival plan and your actions. Help them to adjust to the trauma of survival as well as you can. You may not have the right words, or even know what you are doing at all times, but if you honestly listen to the child and try to do the right things, they will know. Honesty and a good hug will go a long way.

The thought of survival with a child is frightening to most people. Even the thought of survival with adults scares most of us. Survival is never easy, and the added stresses of having a child along can be overwhelming for most people. You must face the psychological and physical aspects of your situation. Remember to make the child a part of your team. You should strive to build teamwork. Involve the child, listen to the child, and most importantly, be yourself and do the best you can. The stark reality of all of this is you have no choice. You must do whatever needs to be done so you and the child can survive. Finally, keep in mind that most survival situations in the United States will last less than 48 hours. This is hardly long enough to starve to death, or die of thirst. Your only goal is for you, and the child, to stay safe and survive until found. You can do it.

Hiking with Kids

When my children were barely more than babies, I took them hiking on designated nature trails. Each of them had a small pack they would carry, full of their favorite snack or drink. Now, obviously, you cannot cover long distances with young children with you, but you can expose them to the wonderful world of nature. By the age of one year, all three of my children had been camping. As they aged, our hiking trips covered much longer distances. So, the next time you consider leaving the kids at home with a sitter or dropping them off at mom's house, reconsider.

However, most children (even some out of shape teens) will not be able to walk far and some will have very little fear of the outdoors. This means they can be a bit of a problem for the adult that takes them, but it is well worth the hassles. I usually start with very short walks around the campgrounds and acclimate the child to the pack, boots, and to learn to listen to the adult (regardless of the age of a child this is a good idea). The listening part is crucial, if you want a safe trip.

As far as safety is concerned, I have found most youngsters, in spite of age, do not like to hold hands when they walk on a trail. I suspect, just like us, they enjoy the independent feeling that comes with hiking. So, you can expect trips, falls, and minor injuries. I always carry a small first aid kit, filled with disinfectants, band-aids, and other necessary medical supplies. Now, I have been taking children hiking for more than thirty years, and I have yet to see a child experience anything worse than a scrape. I also keep a few suckers in my pocket, as a treat to reward the bravery of a small injured child.

Now, keep in mind, it is important to treat any injury as soon as you see it. Small cuts, scrapes and punctures can become infected very quickly in the woods. Make sure you wash the injured area with soap and water, apply an antiseptic, and then cover the injury with a band-aid.

While some people may think my hikes with young children are silly and dangerous, they really can be very rewarding. The eyes of a child come alive as they see the blooming flowers, hear the birds chirp, and perhaps see a small animal. Due to the amount of talking most children do as they walk, you will be very lucky to encounter a deer or other large game. Nonetheless, the idea is to get the child associated with nature, so they are not frightened being in the woods.

At the same time keep a close eye on the little tykes. They have a tendency to want to pet or feed small wild animals, catch grasshoppers, or even snakes. They have no fear at all, so they need constant watching. Make sure you set the rules about wild animals before you leave the camp area (i.e., no touching animals, no petting or feeding, and no attempts at catching any animal or snake).

Also teach your children not to play with, or pick up, any plants. Some, like poison ivy, or sumac, can cause rashes and require medication. If you see a child touch a plant you are unsure of, immediately wash their hands with soap and water (usually it is the oils or sap in a plant that causes the rash). Some plants are poisonous if eaten, so instruct the child to eat only what is in their backpack. If a child ingests a plant and has a physical reaction, seek medical attention immediately.

Keep your initial hikes short, perhaps only a hundred yards or so. Stop at the halfway point and have a short picnic. Let the child open their pack and remove their snack. Have them sit on a blanket or ground cloth as they eat (this will cut down on the number of invited insects you have). I have found most of them really enjoy drinking from a canteen, and my son had his own plastic mess kit he used when we hiked. The idea here is for the children to enjoy the trip and gain confidence in the field. And, trust me, you will have to be patient. They will seem to talk endlessly about what they see around them. They will ask about the plants, the trees, and any small game they may happen to see. It makes them aware of a new world away from a television, computer games, and movies. It opens up a whole new world for them, and you are the one to do it.

My children are grown up and the two oldest are out of the home now. David, my son, hunts, fishes, and winter camps in Alaska. He has developed into a very experienced outdoorsman, and I had very little to do with it. I merely introduced him to nature and then let him go. Sure, I offered suggestions as he grew, but at times I let him learn on his own. My daughter Lisa and her family camp often. They have turned some weekends into family trips, and they have loads of fun. Amie, my youngest daughter, camps, and fishes with the best of them. Your child can learn to do the same things.

If you want your child to grow up knowing nature and not fearing the outdoors, expose them now, while they are still young, to the wonders of woods. Take them on a hike and watch their faces as they see a whole new world open up. After all, don't we owe it to them?

My Child is Lost is the Woods!

One of the biggest fears most parents have while camping or hiking with a child, is that a child will become lost. Well, while it is rare for a child to become really lost, it does happen at times. There is no way to protect your child to the point of this not being a possibility and have the child still enjoy the outdoors. Oh, sure, you can keep little Billy or Sally on a restraining strap, but how much fun would that be for them? I suggest, that instead of worrying about the possibility of your child getting lost, we teach your child what to do if they become lost, as well as what you can expect as a parent if it happens.

My children have been camping and in the woods since they were about a year old. Yep, it sure cut down on my enjoyment when they were younger, because they required constant supervision…at all times (young children require you to be with them at all times when they are in the wild). But, once they were around eight years old, I could relax a little. I still kept an eye on them, but by then I had them conditioned to a certain degree. By the age of eight, I had also trained them on what to do if they became lost.

The first thing I taught each child (there were three of them) was to always carry a canteen and a survival kit. The canteen will provide safe drinking water for the child in the event they become lost. The survival kit contained:

- Trail mix and a high-energy bar; pick the child's favorite flavor of bar.
- A plastic whistle; teach the child to blow the whistle for three long blasts, then stop for a while.
- A large signal flag, cut from an orange garbage bag, or use a bicycle safety flag.
- A signal mirror made from aluminum foil and cardboard.
- A bright orange garbage bag with a hole torn in the top, so it can be used as an emergency poncho. Do not cut the hole, or it may tear further when used by the child.

It is important for the child to be taught how to use these items. Have the child practice with each component of the survival kit until they can demonstrate how to use it properly (you can have the child demonstrate the proper use of the gear in the back yard).

Another area to train the child in is what to do it they become lost. Often, a child will wander around because they are scared of getting in trouble or because they don't know what else to do. This can cause real problems for search and rescue teams, because the child is constantly moving with no sense of direction. Here are some suggestions for a child if they become lost;

- All children (if more than one is lost) should always stay together.
- You should stay in one spot, do not walk around.
- Wait for help to come to you (remember, we love you and want you back).
- Try to keep warm; if with another child or a dog, cuddle up close to conserve body heat.
- Find shelter. The easiest shelter is under the lower limbs of a tree, but try to stay where there is an open spot or field nearby.
- Signal when you see an aircraft. The simplest way is to run out in the field, lie down, and pretend you are making snow angels...that way you are a bigger target for search aircraft to see. At the same time, hold your signal flag in a hand, so it is moving.
- Do not drink any water, except what is in your canteen. Any other water can make you very sick.
- Try not to lie on the bare ground (except to signal), because it will make you much colder. Dead leaves or grasses should be gathered up and you can sit on or sleep in them. But, watch out for snakes.
- Instruct the child to avoid snakes, but try not to scare them.
- Do not touch any animals in the wild, none!
- Stay away from rivers, lakes, pond or cliffs.
- Keep as clean and dry as you can.

- If you hear a noise at night and it scares you, blow your whistle five or six times, real loud! The whistle will scare off any animals that may be near you.

Remember, lots of people are looking for you and we will find you. You can expect to be scared and to feel lonely, but follow these rules and you will be ok. There are a number of things parents can do also. First, when hiking, stay on designated trails. Second, until your child has some experience camp only in designated campsites. Always keep an eye on the younger kids and know where they are at all times. Finally, don't wait very long to call for help when you notice the child has disappeared. Don't spent hours looking for a lost child. If the child is actually lost in the woods, you may not be able to find them on your own.

Search and rescue teams use everything from helicopters to dogs and are very highly trained in what they do. So, once you have reported the missing child, stay out of the way. Let them do their job (I know you will be concerned, but let them handle it). But, you can expect to answer some questions from the police as well as the rescue team leaders. They are not trying to put you on the spot, but some information is essential to speed up the recovery of your child. They may ask you about the child's medical history (are they on any important medication), what they were wearing (important depending on the weather), how much they know about the woods, and so on. Be as honest as you can, because some of this information can impact the rescue.

Each year, thousands upon thousands of families spend time with nature. In almost all of these trips to the woods the child returns home safely. Nonetheless, make sure you and your child have been trained on what to do if the child becomes lost. It only takes a few minutes to make a survival kit, teach a child how to survive, and to prepare for the worst case scenario (it takes less time than that for a child to become lost). Make sure you and your family are properly prepared to enjoy your time in the woods safely.

There are Only Three Kinds of Hunters...

While many of us spend time in the woods hunting, few of us really know where we are. We often meander around in circles, or go where we wish, and then return. I suggest there are only three kinds of hunters in the world today, *those who have been lost, those who will be lost, and those that lie about it*. And, I guess I fit all three categories. Honestly, how many of us really know how to read a map or use a compass? How many of us can actually survive if we do become lost? Or, is it really important to know how to do those things? I am not saying these skills are actually needed for our short runs into the backward bush, but they should be learned by all of us who spend much time in the field. In an emergency, these skills can save your life. Let's look at navigation first.

First, look at your map of the area you plan to go to (*you can usually get a map at the local US Geological Survey, order them online, or from an appropriate state office*). Look at the contour lines and determine the type of terrain you will be walking over. Depending on the type of map you have, size wise (scale), the lines will indicate the amount of climbing you will have to do. Keep in mind that it may be wiser to go around certain parts, rather than over it. Why climb a hill when it may be faster to go around it? But, you must also have an idea of the distance involved.

A good way to keep track of how far you have gone is by counting your steps. For X number of steps tie a knot or slip a bead. There are commercial beads on a string for you to use, or do like I do and use a cord; I tie a knot every 100 paces. One hundred paces are about three hundred feet. Now, keep in mind that your length of step will affect the number of feet you indicate when you knot or slip down.

Another thing to keep in mind is the pace of the slowest walker. Not all of us move at the same speed, especially if we are carrying a large backpack. So, pace your walk to the slowest person in the group. This allows the group to stay together and makes a much better (and safer) trip overall. I have been on hikes where the group was poorly organized and people were scattered all over the place. Stay together and your trip will be much more enjoyable for all concerned. Plus, if there is an emergency, you can work better if you know where all of your hikers are.

A compass is useful, but only if you understand its usage. Remember, there is a difference in magnetic north and true north. Your local Geological Survey has the true north for you, which depends on your location, so give them a call. Depending on where you are in the world, you can be off as much as 12 degrees if you take a magnetic north heading when you travel. Pay attention and know where the real north is when you plan a trip. Look at your map and plot your trip. You can make compass headings and notes right on the map, if you wish. I find that method of keeping notes the best for me.

One last thought here on travel. Do not, unless it is an emergency, travel at night. Once, in the Philippines during survival training, I almost walked over the edge of a cliff moving at night. I had to be moving, due to the escape and evasion part of the survival course, but it sure woke me up quickly. It is dangerous to be moving around when you cannot see. Use some common sense here and travel only during the day.

If you cannot tell a map from a ballgame handout, take a course in map reading. Many colleges, state conservation agencies, or other organizations offer the training. There is nothing more dangerous than a person with a map, thinking they know how to use it, and they know nothing. It is not a shame if you don't know how to read a map, but it is down-right dumb to not admit your ignorance and then pretend you know how to.

Nature is there for us who hunt to enjoy. But, before you go out, make sure you have at least a basic understanding of the dangers you may be facing. While most of us encounter few problems, all it takes is a wrong turn or misunderstanding and you could have a serious problem on your hands. Knowing where you are and how far safety is could mean the difference between life and death. There are other considerations to keep in mind if you become lost, too.

Your first step is to stop. Find temporary shelter if you can, sit on a log, or just stand there. Stop. Look around you. Do you honestly know where you are? Do you know beyond any doubt? You must be totally honest with yourself at this point; believe it or not, your life could depend on it. If the weather is wet and cool, notice I did not say cold, you might even have the beginning symptoms of hypothermia and not be aware of it. (If you are not aware of what hypothermia is, you should not be in the woods. It is the lowering of the body's core temperature and can kill). If the weather is cold, your safety may depend on your next step. I suggest you take a look around and decide then what needs to be done. If you are honestly lost, relax. All is not hopeless nor may you even be in serious danger. But, plan as if your life depends on it, because it may. As long as you keep your wits about you and have planned in advance you should be all right.

Take a look around and find a place for a shelter. An ideal shelter would be a cave, but those can be few and far between. If a cave is not available you may have to construct a shelter. Now, in a survival situation, a shelter is not hot and cold running water, a heat lamp, or a set of bunk beds. Many nights I have slept under a shelter made with a tarp or rain poncho. These types of shelters are easy to construct, are somewhat water resistant, and keep you safe.

The key in constructing your shelter is its location. Avoid making it under dead tree limbs, in dry streambeds, on low spots, or too close to running water. High winds, rain, or other weather conditions could make them very dangerous. Two trees, eight feet of cord or line, a poncho and you are set for the night. Merely tie the cord to the trees, drape the poncho over the line, and secure the bottom of the poncho so it does not blow around. I usually tie the end of a piece of line to the poncho grommets and the other end to sharpened wooden stakes I hammer into the ground. A kind of poor man's tent, but it does work.

In cold snowy weather, you should insulate your shelter. Place pine boughs on top of the tarp or poncho (as constructed above) and then add about six to twelve inches of snow on top. This snow will act as insulation and actually keep you warm. Have the opening to the shelter facing your fire. Do not have a fire inside the shelter (carbon monoxide poisoning). Keep the shelter well ventilated to avoid carbon monoxide poisoning. (I have used a shelter of this type in Alaska when the temperature was minus twenty degree Fahrenheit for three days.) Of primary concern is to conserve your energy and to keep out of the wind. Wind chill can be a real killer.

Next step, usually for purely psychological reasons, is a fire. Keep it small and keep your firewood dry. Wet or green wood is difficult to keep burning and a waste of energy to gather. Also, I usually keep a small bit of kindling in my shelter as well so it stays dry. Dry kindling will make it easier and faster to start a fire in the mornings. Also, keep your fire small. You will use less wood and a small fire is much easier to cook on. Well, it is easier to cook on If you have food. A good fire will also assist rescuers in finding you, especially at night. A small fire in front of your shelter and you out of the wind will really make you feel much better. You can even construct a heat reflector is you wish.

Once you have a shelter and fire the battle is half won. Stop once more and relax a minute and **take inventory of the equipment you have on hand**. Look at what you have, how it is to be used, where it is to be used, and who is to use it. I mean, fishing equipment will not do you much good as fishing equipment if you are land locked. However, the line and the tackle are priceless. You can make snares with the line or use the fishing pole to catch snakes for dinner if need be. Look at abnormal uses for all of your gear as well. Let your imagination take over. I once saw an Alaskan Native start a fire by using his bootlaces and a piece of wood (he made a fire bow). I have even seen women's sanitary napkins used as dressings when a person sustained a serious cut. Keep the mind active. Your will to survive and your mind are your best tools. Keep them both finely tuned.

Once inventory is completed, start on the most serious task you have; **procuring drinking water**. Not all water found in the woods is good for drinking. When you camp, hunt, fish, or hike, always have some fresh water on you. I carry a small baby bottle filled with water, and it fits into my cargo pocket of my pants. But, for long term drinking, carry water purification tablets or boil your water. It is funny, when you think of survival most people think of the lack of food, not lack of water. Most of us, especially me, can do without food for a long time with few ill effects. No, I am not suggesting it is healthy, just that water is more of an immediate need. If you have adequate shelter, fire, and water, you can survive for a surprisingly long time. Food, for most of us anyway, is a habit. We eat too much. Besides, the odds are you will be found within forty-eight hours if others know where you went. So, get comfortable and relax.

When you are surviving you will get dirty. This cannot be completely prevented. Nonetheless, attempt to **stay as clean as you can**. Dirty clothing loses its insulating properties and will not keep you as warm as clean clothing. Beside, good sanitary conditions will assist your body in fighting infections from small cuts and scratches you will receive. Keep your clothing and yourself as clean as you can under the conditions. Keeping your clothing dry is important as well. Try to wear wool, Gore-Tex®, Thinsolite®, or other commercial products that are known to keep you warm even when wet. There are lots on the market so get the best you can afford. Wool is one of my choices.

Once you have a shelter up, fire going, and perhaps dinner on the grill, **stay there**. *It is much easier for folks to find you than for you to find them.* Additionally, I NEVER go out into the woods without someone knowing where I am, when I left, and when I expect to return. You can tell a family member, girlfriend, or a buddy. It is safer to do this and will assist the authorities if they have to launch a search and rescue effort for you. Consider this; have you ever wandered all over a mall looking for someone? It was difficult to find them, huh? But, if you take a seat on a bench they will walk by you sooner or later. Two trains of thought here, 1) let them come to you, 2) you use less energy. This energy thingy is very important when you don't know when your next meal is coming from. Conserve your energy and let them find you. Besides, you have already established all the comforts of home, right? Why leave it, then?

One aspect of all of this I have saved toward the last is **being prepared**. Once you are forced to spend the night in the woods is not when you want discover you don't have matches. Or, that you don't know basic first aid or how to use some of your survival gear. Prepare. Be a scout and remember the scout motto, *always be prepared.* I never go out without my survival kit with me. No, it is not very big and it does not weigh much, but it could prove to be a lifesaver. I actually carry most of it in a small plastic box about three inches wide and about five inches long. I have it in my right pants cargo pocket at all times. What do I have in it?

- A quality penknife or jack knife.
- Two Condoms for water storage, un-lubricated.
- Water proof matches in a waterproof container
- Flint and steel or a metal match
- Water purification tablets (50 tablets)

- A long strip of heavy-duty aluminum foil folded up to cook with.
- Fishing kit, i.e., hooks, sinkers, and some line. Nothing fancy.
- Commercial back packing first aid kit (with instructions); I carry a very small one.
- One small pack of gum and one of hard candy (energy)

Also, I always carry three other things on my person. I carry a good quality casualty blanket, dry socks, and about twenty feet of cotton cord. I have found I can survive with the above items, and all of this stuff weighs almost nothing. I could carry it all in one cargo pocket and still have lots of room left. It is my insurance policy.

One other area I need to discuss is **how you dress** when you are in the woods. I usually wear military cargo pocket styled pants and shirts (battle dress uniforms). These can be picked up in almost any surplus store at a very good price. I also have good quality boots, warm socks, and always have a belt. I wear a wide brimmed hat to shade my eyes from the elements. Of course you know I also have a poncho but not much else in the way of clothing is really needed. If you want to get a fanny pack and wear jeans, all of the equipment I have listed will easily fit into the container. Once you are in a survival situation is not the time to decide you need the gear. You have it with you, or you do without.

With today's electronics and gadgets it is very difficult to really become lost. GPS (Global Positioning Satellite) systems, cellular phones, and other devices make it safer. But, many people, me included, prefer not to carry those things out of doors. I go out to avoid noise and technology, not to carry it. Keep in mind, all it takes is a touch of bad weather, a serious mishap, or a wrong turn, and you may find yourself in a survival situation.

As you hunt, you are isolated and may often be in some very remote country. Learn to read a map and how to use a compass. And, if you become lost, stop, and then act. Frequently, what you have with you will be all you have to use for survival. Remember, your mind is your best tool. Your determination to survive is your best motivation. With a survival kit, your mind, and determination, you too can survive until rescued.

My Aching Pack

When hunting for caribou in Alaska, we often trekked through miles of extremely difficult country to get to game. And, as you may guess, the weather was always terrible, or at best headed that way. The equipment I used in most cases was the best I could afford, but I often experimented with ways to save money (These days, while I do make some gear, I prefer get the best outdoor gear I can afford to purchase). I noticed during our hunts that all of our backpacks were very heavy and would dig into our shoulder blades. What really got my attention was how difficult they seemed to be to balance correctly. My time big game hunting in Alaska taught me that you could improve on the gear you carried. Most importantly, those trips taught me how important it is for your pack to have proper weight and balance.

All of us who hunt learn that improper weight and balance is a problem after only a few hours. How many times have we taken stuff along that we really didn't need? *Well, what do we take and what do we leave?* I have developed a system that always seems to work for me. After each hunt or overnight camping trip I lay all of my equipment out for cleaning. I make a list of all items. As I go over my list I make a check mark on things I did not use at all. Then I make an x mark by the name of items I used only once or twice. I then consider if I could really do without the item in the future. An exception to my rule is my survival manual and my first aid kit. They are emergency items and will always be taken, used or not. I then remove those items not used at all or very often. I do not take them on the next trip. If on the next trip I find I need them, they go back into my inventory for re-evaluation on a future trip. Each item is constantly being evaluated for usage versus weight.

Another way to cut down on weight is to consider your water supply. Ask yourself two questions; where will my water come from and how much do I need? If you are going on a short afternoon or morning hunt a canteen will do. However, for longer periods of hunting you will need more water than a canteen full. If you hunt or camp in public designated areas water may, or may not, be found on the site. If you want, you can even purchase water in plastic bottles or pouches for your trip. Remember to keep the weight idea in the back of your mind. If you decide to use stream or other water sources make sure to purify it using water purification tablets. You can purchase water purification tablets from any sporting goods store.

Many foods can be unpacked and then repacked in plastic bags in many cases. If you use dehydrated or freeze dried commercial meals they are usually very light. Meals Ready to Eat (MRE's) are military surplus (cost is around five to seven dollars a meal) and they come in a heavy-duty plastic pouch. I cut the pouch open, remove the individual items I will eat or need and then repack them in large zip lock bags (Do not open the food pouches in the main pouch. I am talking about removing the main heavy-duty plastic container and then selecting your choices). A typical MRE package will contain gum/candy, toilet paper, a main meal entree, crackers, and other little goodies. One of my favorite items in the MRE's is the small bottle of hot sauce, which can be used to spice up any meal. MRE's can be eaten hot or cold and have been designed to give you lots of calories for any activity.

Additionally, if you take dry goods, i.e., powdered milk, coffee, tea, sugar, beans, oatmeal, pancake mix, pasta, or other such items, repack them in zip lock bags. You can actually premix some foods, so all you have to do is add water. I often do this with pancake mix and powdered milk. At the campsite, I just add water in the morning and soon have the smell of fresh pancakes in the air. Make sure to mark the contents of each zip lock bag with a permanent marker. You can use this hint for any powdered or dry foods. Keep in mind, cardboard boxes and metal or plastic cans have a tendency to poke into your back, and for sure add to the weight.

Two items that are always with me are my first aid kit, with emergency treatment manual, and my survival book. Both of these items I purchased at a military surplus store. The survival book is Air Force Pamphlet 64-5 and my emergency medical manual is a pamphlet put out by the Red Cross. You can find many different kinds of publications out there, some free and some at a small cost. Make sure they are well written, easy to understand, and small. Once again consider weight. Read, not scan, both of these pieces of information. This is so you know what to do before you do it. Besides, it is not comforting to the victim of an injury if you are beside them reading a manual as you treat them. That seems to leave a bit of doubt as to your proficiency in first aid procedures.

Always have a good quality compass and a map of where you are going. Most importantly know how to use a compass and read a map. Know the difference in magnetic north, grid north, and true north. Learn to triangulate your position and how to count steps to give an idea of distances traveled. While many folks can read a map they have some problems with the contour lines on them. These lines indicate increases or decreases in terrain. That is especially important for hunters, because we usually have to walk over the ground shown on a map. Each slight climb will take strength away from you and a long hike makes your pack seem to weigh that much more. Go around high spots or swamps and not through them. It is actually faster in the long run and much safer. I may cover map reading and navigation at a later date. It is too complicated to go into here with the space I have.

What about other hunting gear considerations? Well, first consideration should be the type of backpack you want. On short afternoon hikes it doesn't really matter much. I usually just take a fanny pack made of light nylon. But, on the longer trip you want a large, but lightweight, pack that can handle all of your needed supplies. My preference is the military surplus ALICE pack with frame, available at most surplus stores. There are many fine commercial packs on the market, so shop around. I would like to suggest nylon instead of canvas. Nylon is much lighter.

Also, I have found air mattresses to be heavy and not worth the sweat to carry them. I use a rubber/foam pad (once again, military surplus) that can be rolled up and tied to my pack. Cots, stools, camp chairs, and tables, I avoid like the plague. They are heavy, even the light ones, and I am just as comfortable sitting or eating on a log.

Additionally, tents are nice but they do add weight. If you absolutely have to have one get the best quality and lightest one you can afford. *Make sure* you try it in the back yard before you attempt to use it on a real hunt. On a moose hunt once, friend of mine took a newly purchased and highly discounted tent, only to discover it was a play tent for children. It only covered about half of his extended body once erected. And, of course, it rained for three days. I usually just carry a tarp for shelter. But, it is your back that has to carry all of the items you want to take along, not mine.

My cooking gear consists of a small pan, a small pot, and a small coffee pot, all constructed of light weight aluminum. I carry a few sheets of heavy-duty aluminum foil along with my eating utensils (metal spoon, pocket knife, metal plate, and small plastic bowl). That is pretty much it. I don't need a can opener, because I don't take cans. I can peel veggies with my pocketknife and I never need a bottle opener. Of course, like all true hunters, I do have a coffee cup, and yep, it is aluminum.

Hunting trips and camping are constant evaluations for me. I keep what works and what I need. I judge usage against weight. I am willing to do without an item I don't use often or at all. If possible, I try to buy items that serve more than one function. I like to have a good time when I hunt and that is hard to do if you are exhausted after packing a heavy load all day long. I also like to rough it when I camp, so my way may not be for you.

Regardless of your decision, I assure you, you will pay in sweat or pain for anything you carry. So, evaluate, discard, and then retain. It is a constant battle of mind over what matters.

Winter Boating Safety and Survival

Each winter thousands of us head for the water. Just like ducks we splash, swim, and play around in the lakes, streams, rivers and even the ponds of America, regardless of the time of the year. The Coast Guard reports that most fatal injuries occur from the period of October through December, and it is easy to see why. I suspect most of us know very little about how to safely prepare for a boating trip, or what to do in an emergency, especially during the cold months. Oh, and I have done some pretty silly boating things myself.

It was a freezing day in January and we had about three inches of snow covering the Missouri Ozarks. Bill and I decided to go on a float trip down the nearby Little Piney River for a few miles and camp over the weekend. His mother would pick us up on Sunday afternoon. This trip, according to Bill, would challenge us and test our winter camping ability.

Our destination was only about four miles away, and if we took it slowly and cautiously it would be no problem to reach. The first day of the trip we got a late start and put into the water at about dusk. We wanted a mile or two behind us, before we would be forced to camp for the night due to darkness. That was our biggest mistake!

The current was lazy as we meandered down the snake shaped river in all directions. As soon as it *became dark*, we began to look for a place to spend the night. We could not find a suitable camping spot because the river had eroded the banks on both sides of us to the point that ground level was now about five feet above the river. While we were looking for a place to land the boat, we had to use a flashlight to see by.

Suddenly, we entered a stretch of fast water! The river turned sharply to the left as we picked up considerable speed. The boat, without any warning, struck the right bank, drifted sideways, and leaned over enough that we started taking on water. It was only a matter of seconds before I decided to abandon ship and leave the captain of the Titanic to his own doom.

I jumped into the cold water and after the initial shock from the chill, I made my way to the nearest bank. While swimming, I had seen most of our supplies drift pass me headed further downstream. I watched as they floated toward the Mississippi River. As I looked around me, I noticed Bill, a stronger swimmer than I, was already on the same bank. Now, how did that happen? When I was in the boat he was still sitting there cursing.

As I stood in the faint light I looked over at Bill. He gave me a weak smile and said, "Look at yer shoe laces."

I glanced down and watched ice begin to form on the laces and on the outside of the shoe. In a matter of seconds the whole shoe was encrusted with ice. We both knew we had to do something and do it very quickly. To hesitate even a few minutes could mean our deaths.

As I looked around in fear, I noticed lights across the river. I pointed to the lights and said, "Bill, we have to get to that farm house and do it quickly."

My buddy didn't say a word, but nodded his head in agreement. Slowly, Bill and I re-entered the water and swam to the other side. Gradually and drunkenly we made our way to the farmhouse. Strange, but I no longer felt cold; I seemed almost warm and comfortable as I fought the urge to stop and sleep. This lack of concern suddenly triggered an alarm in my pea brain that told me we were close to death. I think both of us were ready to give up when we literally ran into a gate.

The gate latch cut Bill's hand as he forced it up and open. The cold had deadened the feeling to Bill's hand to the point that he was not aware he had been cut by the sharp corners on the latch. We would remain unaware of his injury until we thawed out later. As the gate swung open we could hear the aggressive barking of farm dogs. I was suddenly angry; all this way to have a dog eat me alive.

I remember voicing concern about the barking and growling dogs, but we soon discovered they were locked up, thus not a threat. We sluggishly made our way up to the front door of the farmhouse. We knocked and knocked, but no answer. Then we pounded the door. Still we received no response. We both knew we had to do something and fast. It was then I noticed a light in the barn.

We made our way to the barn and opened the door. We were immediately welcomed by the sour smell of animals and of fresh manure. However, in our condition we hardly noticed it. The barn was full of sheep and two old milk cows wearing bells. Dangling throughout the barn was heating lamps.

With grins we both undressed and used the lamps to warm up and thaw out. The pain we experienced sent tears running down our red cheeks. How had we escaped death? We were both a frozen mess. I believe we resembled frozen T.V. dinners more than we did humans. Bill's big toe had ice crystals under the nail. It was about then his recently cut hand started to bleed. We wrapped his injury in pieces of his tee-shirt and the bleeding soon stopped. All of my life I have always hated to be in a barn (it usually meant work for me), but not on that night.

After a couple of hours warming up in the barn, we decided to attempt to walk to Newburg, which was about a mile away. Our clothes were still slightly damp, but we thought they were dry enough for our purposes. We quickly dressed and made our way to the nearby county road that lead to town. The snowing had quit and a full moon was to be seen. As we walked, I noticed the little white puffs of air as we both exhaled. It was still cold, very cold.

We sang, or I should say Bill sung, I have never been called a golden-throated talent, all the way to town. Once in town, we went to an all night restaurant and Bill called his momma to pick us up. She warned us both to get some hot food and drinks in us quickly and she would pay for it when she got there. Like most healthy young men, eating was never a problem at any time. We ordered eggs, bacon, hash browns, and biscuits and gravy and ate as we waited for his mother. We consumed cup after cup of hot scalding cocoa. We spent the rest of the time discussing just how close we had come to dying

Since that night I like to think I have gotten a little smarter (we were lucky, because we did everything wrong and still survived). I have, nonetheless, learned a few more things about boats, winter weather, and survival. Here are a few rules I would like to suggest:

- Always tell someone where you are going, when you are going, and when you intend to return (it is a good idea to inform this person of your boat Identification Registration number). Also, tell them who is going with you and what you plan on doing, i.e., fishing, duck hunting, etc...

- Check the weather forecast. If the weather will be too rough to safely be out, consider going another time. Remember, winter weather can change very quickly and you could be caught on the open water.

- Have a good quality survival kit with you. Do not use a standard minimum survival kit for your boat. While a standard kit can make up the basis of your kit, you will need to add a few things. I suggest you add at least two casualty blankets (thermal blankets), matches in a water-proof container, a space blanket, a strobe light, flash light, signal flares, and any other items you might want to have with you in an emergency.

- **ALWAYS wear a flotation device** (life jacket or preserver). This is suggested for any time you are in a boat and on the water.

- If you have a cell phone, take it along with you as well. It could speed up your rescue in the event of an emergency.

Also, remember that hypothermia is a killer in the water! Hypothermia is the lowering of *the body's core temperature.* Most of us, let's say, have a body temperature of between 97 and 99 degrees. When our temperature drops internally to below this normal range hypothermia sets in. If the core temperature is not brought back up, death usually occurs. We have all felt the beginning stages of hypothermia when we start to shiver. In the water, this medical emergency can kill within minutes. Here are a few suggestions if your boat overturns in the water.

- Stay dressed! Do not remove any clothing because the air in them will assist in keep you warm (not to mention afloat).

- Most body heat is lost through the top of the head. If you have a cap or hat, keep it on at all times. Additionally, if possible, keep your head out of the water.

- DO NOT attempt to swim to shore, even if it looks to be close. Swimming will allow the air pockets in your clothing to escape and may seriously reduce the odds of your survival.

- Remain as still as you can. The less movement, the more heat you retain and you need to keep that heat next to you! While the cold is painful and you will experience severe shivers, that is a natural reaction by the body to the cold water.

- Keep your head and don't panic! If there is someone with you, you should huddle together to for increased warmth. Assume a Heat Escape Lessening Posture (HELP) to retain heat. Pull your knees up to your chest, and wrap your arms around your legs.

- Never drink alcohol when in a boat. Alcohol is very dangerous on the water and it actually increases the dangers of hypothermia. Alcohol causes vasodilation (increase in surface blood flow), which leads to increased heat loss. Additionally, alcohol will impair your thinking, before, during and following an accident. Keep a clear mind at all times on the water.

Winter is not the best time to be out on the water. However, if you decide to go, follow my simple survival suggestions and your trip will end much better. Survival is never easy, but with the proper equipment, preparation, and attitude, you too can survive.

Experience Counts

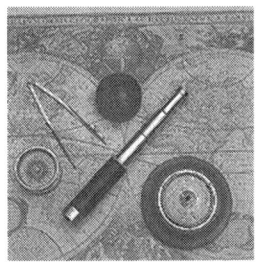

I can remember, a few years back, a very interesting camping trip I went on with two of my friends. We were living in New Mexico and planned to take a few days and head north, into the mountains around Taos. The weather was great, and we had been excited all week about going. As soon as Friday's work was finished, we loaded up the car and headed out.

Of the three of us, John and I were very experienced campers, while Jim was not. He had never spent the night in the woods in his life. All the way to the designated area Jim bombed us with questions about the great outdoors. He wanted to know about bathrooms, sleeping arrangements, and many other things. I could understand his concern and excitement, but for me it was just a hiking and camping trip.

We soon arrived at the spot we were to leave the car. Loading up our backpacks and gear we were soon walking up a meandering mountain trail. I thought our packs were lightly loaded, around forty pounds, and we were making very good time. Then, after about fifteen minutes on the trail Jim called for us to wait. Turning back, I could see he was in no shape to continue walking at that moment.

"What's the matter, Jim?" John asked as he removed his backpack, placing it on the ground. I noticed the John had not even broken into a sweat yet.

"I am tired. This is a rough trail." Jim stated bluntly as he threw himself down on the ground with his pack still on.

I noticed beads of sweat on the man's forehead as he closed his eyes and leaned his head back. I knew right then, our backpacking trip would not go as quickly as I had expected it to. John looked over at me with a slight grin on his face. He knew that Jim was out of shape and our trip would have to be kept at the slowest man's pace. We paced our backpacking to the slowest person for safety reasons. We would never leave a person on the trail because they could not keep up.

John and I both knew that while the trail had a slight upward angle, it was not really that hard. Nonetheless, we both gave a grin and decided to make the best of it. After all, there just wasn't much we could do now except to continue on at a slower pace. After about twenty minutes we were up and moving again.

It took us over three hours to make a hike that would usually only have taken John and I a little over an hour. But, we were there and things, at least in my opinion, were looking better. John and I had camped together so often that most camp chores were not even discussed. We each just did our thing to get organized. As he constructed our shelter, I gathered the firewood, dug a fire pit, and got a small fire going. Jim, I noticed, had fallen asleep. We just let him sleep for a while.

Once the fire had been burning a while, I took out our dinner. Placing a folding grill over the deep red coals, I soon had three nice thick steaks cooking. The smell of the searing meat teased us as John placed a small loaf of French bread near the hot coals. Jim still did not move a muscle. He was obviously exhausted. In less than thirty minutes the meal was done and I jarred Jim awake.

"Oh, dinner is done?" Jim asked as he wiped the sleep from the corners of his eyes. I could still see the redness of fatigue in his eyes.

"Yea, and so is everything else." John replied with a little contempt and sarcasm in his voice.

Jim never noticed that the shelter was up, firing going and dinner done. I honestly suspect it just didn't enter his untrained mind that someone had had to do those tasks, all while he had slept.

"Here, you need to eat something; you've had a hard walk up the trail." I said as I handed the man a nice steak, salad, and a large piece of French bread.

I was a bit surprised as I watched him take a bite of his steak and then quickly spat it out into the fire. Jim put his plate on the ground by his feet and said, "This thing tastes like smoke. I can't eat this."

"Jim, it's a campfire, of course it tastes like smoke. But, that's hickory, a very good barbeque flavoring." John said, obviously attempting to change Jim's mind.

"I don't like it. I won't eat that." Jim quickly responded in a defiant voice. He reminded me of a child when he said it. So, as John and I watched, somewhat surprised, the man rolled over in the dirt and went back to sleep.

Well, this is just dandy, I thought. *Here we are miles from the car with a man who does not, obviously fit in.* He didn't like the hike up to the campsite, he doesn't like the food, and I know soon he will be complaining about the smoke in his eyes. I was not sure what we were going to do. But, one thing I knew, we were not going home that night because he was not a "happy camper."

To make a long story short, it was not a very good weekend. That night Jim complained about how hard the ground was, the lack of a proper toilet, no place to shower and, as I suspected, the smoke in his eyes. He had absolutely nothing good at all to say about the place. He even complained that the temperature dropped when evening came. I had never in my life seen a person just not made for camping. We had actually planned to stay for two nights, but eventually Jim's whines got the better of us and we went home the next day, early.

Once we returned Jim to his house, John and I met for a cup of coffee to determine what had happened, how it had happened, and how we could prevent it in the future. We both quickly realized that some people are just not made for camping. We knew the whole situation was our fault, not Jim's. He would have been best left at home to the comforts he was used to. But, how could we prevent a repeat in the future? How could we know what people to bring and which ones not to bring along?

We both thought it would be very unfair to keep someone from going with us due to a lack of experience. So, we devised a few "trials" for the individual before we would take them on long trips. Of course, we never mentioned these to the unexpected member.

- Start with a short exposure. No serious treks of backpacking, but rather an overnight camping trip in a designated camping spot. You know the places with showers, toilets, and running water.

- Cook with hard woods that are used for campfires, and see if the person can enjoy the meal. Some folks just don't like the taste.

- Take the person on short, but challenging hikes, to see how they hold up with the weight of a pack.

- Measure the person's attitude during the whole situation. Did they view it as a fun challenge, or too much work? Was it fun to them, or was it viewed as punishment?

- Eventually make sure one trip lasts for at least two nights. Many people will tire of the roughness of camping after just one night. But, if they could not take two nights in a designated campground, they for sure would not be able to handle a rough and remote camping trip.

Camping should be no rougher than the weakest individual in your group. If you are with kids, or first time campers, plan accordingly. Don't try to do too much with an inexperienced camper. Take it slowly and expose them to different aspects, one task at a time. Make sure they are gradually exposed to nature and not rushed into it. (As far as I know, Jim never went camping again).

Forcing too much on a beginner will most likely turn them away from the sport of hiking or camping.

Plan your trips, as I have said, to the weakest or least experienced person in your group. I suspect that by teaching as you go you can take a novice and turn them into an experienced outdoors person. But, it takes time, patience, and understanding. Have fun and stay safe in the woods.

How to Survive the Military Way!

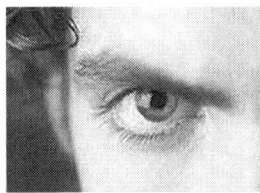

The following information is very general in nature, and designed to get you to *think and then act*. You must gain control of the situation, accept your fate, and plan to survive. **DO NOT** *rush into things*, but rather, sit down and think things out. In a survival situation, rushing can kill you. By reading this you may have already found yourself in a survival situation. Keep in mind, your situation is not hopeless and you are for sure not helpless. Others have survived and so can you.

Your first step is to stop. Find temporary shelter if you can, sit on a log, or just stand there. In hot or cold climates, seek shelter immediately. You can die within minutes in extreme cold or hot weather. Then, stop and look around you. Do you honestly know where you are? Beyond any doubt? You must be totally honest with yourself at this point; believe it or not, your life could depend on it. If the weather is wet and cool, notice I did not say cold, you might even have the beginning symptoms of hypothermia and not be aware of it. (If you are not aware of what hypothermia is, you should not be in the woods. It is the lowering of the body's core temperature and can kill). If the weather is cold, your life may depend on your next step. Stop, take a look around and decide then what needs to be done. If you are honestly lost, relax. All is not hopeless nor may you even be in serious danger. But, plan as if your life depends on it, because it may. As long as you keep your wits about you and have planned in advance you should be all right.

Take a look around and find a place for a shelter. An ideal shelter would be a cave, but those can be few and far between. If a cave is not available you may have to construct a shelter. Now, in a survival situation, a shelter is not hot and cold running water, a heat lamp, or a set of bunk beds. You can sleep under a shelter made with a tarp or rain poncho, if need be. They are easy to construct, are somewhat water resistant, and keep you safe. The key in constructing your shelter is its location. Avoid making it under dead tree limbs, in dry streambeds, or too close to running water. High winds, rain, or other weather conditions could make those types of sites very dangerous. Two trees, eight feet of cord or line, a poncho and you are set for the night. Merely tie the cord to the trees, drape the poncho over the line, and secure the bottom of the poncho so it does not blow around. Tie the end of a piece of line to the poncho grommets and the other end to sharpened wooden stakes you can hammer into the ground. A kind of poor man's tent, but it does work.

In cold snowy weather, you should insulate your shelter. Place pine boughs on top of the tarp or poncho and then add about six to twelve inches of snow on top. This snow will act as insulation and actually keep you warm. Have the opening to the shelter facing your fire. Do not have a fire inside the shelter. Keep the shelter well ventilated to avoid carbon monoxide poisoning. (Shelters of this type are often used in Alaska when the temperature is well below zero.) Of primary concern is to conserve your energy and to keep out of the wind. Wind chill can be a real killer.

In the desert, your first step is to get out of the sun as quickly as you can. Stay under temporary shelter until the sun goes down. Then, try to construct a shelter that has two layers, one layer about 12 inches above the other. This layering will actually keep the shelter cooler in the heat. Also, in the desert limit your movements to the evening and night. This will assist you in retaining body fluids.

Next step, usually for purely psychological reasons is a fire. Keep it small and keep your firewood dry. Wet or green wood is difficult to keep burning. Make sure you have a fire pit and ring your fire with large rocks. Do NOT make the fire too close to your shelter. We suggest your fire be 10 feet from your shelter entrance. Keep a small bit of tinder and kindling in your shelter as well so it stays dry. That makes it easier to start a fire in the mornings. Also, keep your fire small. You will use less wood and a small fire is much easier to cook on, if you have food. A good fire will also assist rescuers in finding you, especially at night. A small fire in front of your shelter and you out of the wind will really make you feel much better.

In deep snow you may have to make your fire on a platform of large logs. If you do not use a platform, the fire will melt the snow and sink. The melting snow will eventually put the fire out. Use green logs for this platform if you can. Also, have some spares nearby because they will eventually have to be replaced as they burn through.

Once you have a shelter and fire the battle is half won. Stop once more and relax a minute and **take inventory of the equipment you have on hand**. Look at what you have, how it is to be used, where it is to be used, and who is to use it. Fishing equipment will not do you much good as fishing equipment if you are land locked. However, the line and the tackle are priceless, no matter where you are. You can make snares with the line or use the pole to catch snakes for dinner, if need be. Look at abnormal uses for all of your gear as well. Let your imagination take over. Keep your mind active. Your desire to survive and your mind are your best tools. Keep them both finely tuned.

Once inventory is completed take a look at a Minimum Survival Kit. This kit is designed to keep you alive until rescued. Your Minimum Survival Kit should have the following items in it.

Minimum Survival Kit Contents

- A quality penknife or jack knife.
- Two Condoms for water storage, un-lubricated.
- Water proof matches, with plastic container
- Flint and steel or a metal match
- Water purification tablets
- A long strip of aluminum foil folded up to cook with
- Fishing kit, i.e., hooks, sinkers, and some line. Nothing fancy.
- Commercial back packing first aid kit (with instructions)
- One small pack of gum and one of hard candy (energy)
- Candle, citronelle
- Safety pens
- A small button compass
- A commando wire saw
- Large, clear garbage bag
- Space Blanket
- Signal mirror
- Whistle

- Survival Guide, small, general purpose
- 550 parachute cord
- Brass wire for snares

Procuring drinking water. This is actually your most important step! However, keep in mind that not all water found in the field is good for drinking. If you camp, hunt, fish, or hike, you should always have some fresh water on you. We suggest you carry a one-quart canteen on a belt on all trips. But, for long term drinking, carry water purification tablets or boil your water. It is funny, when you think of survival most people think of the lack of food, not lack of water. Most of us can do without food for a long time with few ill affects. No, we are not suggesting it is healthy, just that water is more of an immediate need. If you have adequate shelter, fire, and water, you can survive for a surprisingly long time. Food, for most of us anyway, is a habit. We eat too much. Besides, the odds are you will be found within forty-eight hours if others know where you went, so get comfortable and relax.

Signal for Help! Let's take a look at how we attract attention in survival situations. There are means of making sure we are seen and rescued in a timely manner. Most, but not all, of these means of signaling are best done by using the senses of smell, sight, or hearing. Some of the most effective primitive signals are made using the sense of sight.

One method that is not visual is the use of **electronic devices**. If you have an emergency locator beacon (ELT) or a cell phone, you are in good shape. Well, things are great and easy as long as the batteries last. Try to prolong battery life by using the radio or phone at certain times (When I was in the military we briefed our folks to transmit and receive at 15 minutes before and after each hour). Batteries will eventually die and then we have to revert to more primitive methods of attracting attention.

Your vehicle lights can be used to signal with as well. By flashing your lights on and off you will draw attention to your site. Lights work well when you are stranded in a car or truck and awaiting rescue. You can flash an SOS (Save Our Souls or Save Our Ship), international emergency code, by flashing three dots, three dashes, and then three dots. Dots are quick signals whereas dashes are longer (It would look like this, . . . ---. . .).

Signal mirrors, or shiny metal (Heliographs), are about as basic as a person can get. The best part of using something that shines, is the lack of a battery that will eventually die. The drawback is you must have some sunlight for the device to work. Nonetheless, most of the time the United States has sunshine, with the exception of short periods of time when we experience adverse weather conditions.

You should practice using a signal mirror until you can pretty much aim the flash to strike any area you choose. You will be surprised how well you will do with just a little practice. A word of advice here; once you get a person's attention with the flash, *do not* continue flashing in their eyes. It makes rescue more difficult when your rescuers cannot see. Instead, aim the flash at the rear of an aircraft, truck, or group of people. That way, if your rescuers veer off course a bit, you can easily flash them in the face once more, then you should move the flash to the rear again. A piece of smooth metal will work almost as well as a signal mirror.

Another way to attract attention is by **using fires**. At night the light from your campfire will draw attention. In the daytime your fire is a good signal as well. By adding oil, cedar boughs or other things to a burning fire you will change the color of its smoke. Remember, three fires spaced in a triangle shape, is the international signal for help. It means you cannot move on, or, in other words you need assistance. Do not let your fire get out of control. A forest fire is dangerous and greatly reduces your chances to survive.

Placing a large "I" in an open area means you have a very serious injury in your group, while "X" means you are not able to proceed. There is a whole group of ground codes and I will not get into what all of them mean, but the two above are the most important to remember. You can pile wood or rocks to cast shadows, trample the snow, or else clear (or add) brush or grass to make the signal. Use a rough ratio of about six to one. I would suggest your width be 3 feet, minimum, while the length would be 18 feet. Have you ever driven by a handmade sign and discovered you could not read the print? Well, pilots looking for you could have the same problem with your signals! They have to be able to see it! The important thing to remember when making a ground to air signal is to disturb the surroundings enough to draw attention to your area. Think of it as a disturbance between contrast and the human eye.

Three gunshots in quick order are also considered signals. The three shots indicate you need help and cannot proceed alone. The key here, if you have not guessed it by now, is the use of three of anything. It is just understood by rescuers as a signal of distress.

If you are lucky enough to be a survivor and have a vehicle nearby, you have just hit the mother lode. While most cars, trucks, and aircraft make very poor shelters, they are a gold mine of resources for the survivor. We cannot address the various ways vehicles can be put to various survival usage. But, you can burn the fuel and oil to make signals (use extreme caution with the fuel), the insulation and tires generate smoke, and the mirrors, glass, and chrome make good reflectors. Even a headlight can be removed, rewired, and using the vehicles electrical system used to signal passing aircraft. The list is limited only by your imagination.

By day you should **use smoke**, and by night use light, to attract attention to your survival site. Remember you want to make a contrast against the background. If the day is dark and gloomy, you want light colored smoke. If the day is bright, use dark smoke. At night, of course, light is best.

You may not believe this, but one piece of valuable equipment is **a whistle**. Always have a good quality one in your survival kit. A loud whistle can be heard for a long distance (at longer distances than a human voice) and it can be useful when you know rescuers are nearby. Additionally, you can use it to signal between members in your group if one of them strays off the beaten path for some reason. It is a good idea to blow the whistle in three long blasts (once again, a series of three).

If you have a vehicle, keep the snow off of the top and sides as much as you can. Depending on the color of the vehicle it can aid in your rescue. Do not use the vehicle as a permanent shelter because it will either be too hot or too cold, but instead use it as a signaling device. Additionally, have one fire burning all the time, and two others (numbers two and three of your fire signal triangle) ready to light. I would have the numbers two and three piled high with pine or cedar boughs. Be very aware of fire safety at these fires. The last thing you need is to start a forest fire. Also remember if you trampled down snow for a signal and it continues to snow, you will eventually have to redo the signal. The falling snow will fill your tracks quickly.

The key to signals is to draw attention. Look around you and think how you can make the area stand out more. It is helpful if you keep in mind at least three of our five senses, sight, hearing, smelling, can be used to signal with. Disturb the natural surroundings; draw attention to your survival site, and you too will be a survivor!

THE POWER OF THE SUN

How to Cook Using the Sun in an Emergency

In the event of an emergency, such as a terrorist attack, natural disaster, or other type of survival situation, it is important for us to know alternate methods of cooking. Most of us can start a simple fire and cook, but what if you don't have any matches? What if you're unable to get a fire started for one reason or the other? Did you know you can use a casualty blanket, space blanket or car sun shield to cook with? It only takes a few other items and you'll be cooking in no time. While this idea is not new, there are some ways to make the process easier, faster, and more effective. But first, let's look at why some people living normal lives use solar cooking.

People all over the world have been cooking and using the sun for years. In some countries it is an inexpensive way to prepare meals, while in others it is the *only* way to prepare meals, due to a lack of gas or electrical power. Though you may find this hard to believe, wood is even scarce in some countries. The sun, which shines in all lands, doesn't have to be high and bright to cook a meal for you in just about an hour. Of course, it all depends on what you are cooking, how big the meal is, and the amount of sunshine you're getting. I'm sure in desert lands, like the American southwest or some Arab countries the cooking is much faster and easier due to sunlight and heat.

Remember, solar cooking can work in all countries of the world. The concept explained below has been around a long time and it is a proven method of cooking using the sun.

In an emergency you can use a reflective silver reflective car sunshade (1) or a casualty blanket (2), an oven rack (or BBQ grill), 4 ½ inches of male and female Velcro (you can do without the Velcro, but it makes the job easier), a black pot, a bucket or plastic wastebasket, and a plastic baking bag (like we use for cooking 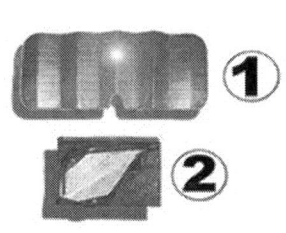 turkeys for Thanksgiving) to cook with. It's easy and most of us will have the needed components in the house. Or, you can carry them with you into the field to insure you always have an alternate method of cooking. This "stove" is easy to make.

To make the funnel shaped solar cooking device:

- The notched side of the sunshade should be toward you (If using a casualty blanket lay it width wise).

- Cut the Velcro into one even piece, each about five inches long. Use the hook and pile on opposite sides so they will "lock" when pressed together.

- Sew by hand (to avoid damage to the soft reflective material) one half of the Velcro ® on edge to the top of the notch (or at the bottom edge of the casualty blanket) sew the matching half of the Velcro ® onto the bottom side (or opposite side of the casualty blanket), so that they "hook and lock" together when attached to make a funnel.

- Push the two pieces of Velcro ® together (1), and place the funnel on top of a bucket, plastic wastebasket (4), box, or any other object capable of holding the funnel.

- Place a black or dark pot (2) with your food on top of an oven rack (3), placed inside a plastic baking bag (2). A normal American oven rack is approximately 10 inches. This is placed inside the funnel; resting the rack on the top of the bucket, wastebasket, box, or other container. Since the sunshade material is extremely flexible, this rack is used to support the pot and to keep the funnel open. By holding the funnel open, the suns rays can reflect on all sides evenly, making the process more effective. If such a rack is not available, a wooden or metal platform could be made or used to work as well.

Simple Survival

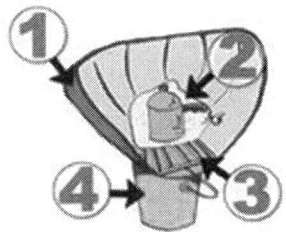

Some hints when cooking with this method. While the technique is simple, here are a few notes to make your cooking easier, faster, and more effective.

1. Tilt the shiny material toward the sun, so the rays strike the surface with full force. This increases the temperature of the funnel and reduces cooking times.
2. Use a stick (1) to keep the material open and it will also keep the "stove" more secure from drooping during use or collapsing when there are winds.
3. Keep in mind, your food will become very hot—near 350 degrees if properly made. Avoid burns when removing the food from the "stove" and oven mittens are recommended.
4. Your reflective material and most of the other supplies, except for the stick and grill, can be placed in the bucket for ease of transportation.

This "stove" can be used to cook any foods that can be prepared with a conventional oven and the temperature will reach around 350 degrees. Total cost to make a solar funnel is less than four dollars if a sunshade is used or space blanket (buy most of your supplies in a dollar store). A casualty blanket will raise the price of your "stove" and can be purchased at an Army Surplus store for around eight dollars. But, the casualty blanket can be used to sleep with once your cooking is done. To make your solar "stove", you'll need,

1. A plastic oven roasting bag (about a dollar each or so).
2. A dark pot; black works the best (from your home).
3. An oven rack or grill rack (from your home).
4. Approximately 5 inches of Velcro ® (less than a dollar).

5. Bucket, wastebasket, or other stable container (from your home)

6. Casualty blanket, space blanket, or car sunshade (from two to eight dollars)

In many African and Arab countries, this method of cooking is often the only one available. And, keep in mind, there are many different designs and ways of using the power of the sun to cook with. I have seen them made with sheet metal, aluminum foil, or just about any shiny and reflective surface. Additionally, there are even commercial "solar cookers" available on the market. For those that lack electrical power, gas, or firewood, this is an excellent way to cook and the cost is absolutely zero per use.

Cooking with the sun is not hard, but it does take a little planning and consideration. Remember to use shiny reflective surfaces for your "stove"; if you have an interior to your "stove" it should be a dark color (black is suggested). If the interior is painted, use a non-toxic paint and one that is heat resistant. Keep in mind, while the pan may not look hot, it can easily reach 350 degrees, so remove the pot with caution to avoid burns. From my research, any foods you can cook in a conventional oven, at 350 degrees can be cooked in a solar "stove" but the cooking times may vary depending on the meal prepared, brightness of the sun, and type of cooker you are using. I also suggest you do a little research on solar cooking to discover the technique you might prefer to use in an emergency.

Solar cooking can be done in most areas of the world, even in the arctic. In the event of a survival situation, it only takes a few minutes to have your stove operational and in use. The key to using the sun to cook with is making sure you have the needed materials on hand *before* you need them. Once the power goes out, the gas quits flowing, the wood is gone, or you're stranded, is not the time to think about solar cooking. Your cooking method should have already been planned. Keep the materials you will need stored in the home or your vehicle for use when needed, and the cost is almost nothing.

If you are interested in learning more about solar cooking, visit Solar Cookers International and *The Solar Cooking Archive* at http://solarcooking.org. They have a large selection of photos and many articles on various ways to cook with the power of the sun.

DOG-GONE TRIPS

When I was in the military, I was ordered north to Alaska. Now, that in itself is enough to scare some folks, but I decided to drive to my new assignment with our dog traveling with us. The whole family considered our dog as part of our family, so there was very little discussion as we talked of the coming trip. As I look back, the trip was hard on all of us, because I  drove from Scott Air Force Base in Illinois to Anchorage, Alaska, but I suspect my dog considered suicide more than once along the way. See, he was sick most of the way, or so it seemed to me, but my kids have said it was only for a few miles.

While our dog was well taken care of on the trip, he still experienced some motion sickness early in the trip. Additionally, later in the trip he developed diarrhea after we were forced to change his dog food because his favorite brand was not available in northern Canada. The trip did, however, teach me a few things about traveling with dogs.

It is getting to be the time of the year when more and more people decide to take Ol' Rover out with them when they hike, fish, camp, or just travel. While I agree it is a good idea at times, depending on the dog's personality, make sure you're allowed a dog or any pets in the area you are visiting. Some campgrounds and other recreational areas may not allow pets at all (some hotels for sure won't allow pets). If Rover is not allowed, or if you suspect he or she might not make a good companion for the trip consider a kennel, a friend to leave your dog with, or maybe consider have someone pet sit for you. Responsible teenagers will usually pet sit for just a few dollars, when compared to a kennel.

I would also start a dog out on short trips first to see how they handle the motion of the vehicle and to determine if they seem to get stressed over the confined space. Some dogs adjust quickly to the limited space of car or truck with no problems, while others appear to never get used to the idea and may get agitated. I can assure you that on long trips you will want a dog that is capable of traveling well, without any serious physical or psychological affects.

Prior to any trip (even in the local area) with your dog make sure your pet has been seen by a veterinarian on a regular basis and is healthy. Keep your pets shots up to date, carry any medications your dogs may need, and if you're crossing a border into another country you might need the animals health record and a rabies shot within 30 days of entry. If you're not sure what is required for your dog to be out in public, or to cross the border, talk to your Vet. If your Veterinarian does not have an immediate answer to your questions about travel requirements, he or she will usually know where to find it.

Keep your dog's identification tag on them at all times and it might be a good idea to use a tattoo or implanted microchip to assist in recovery if Rover gets lost. Some people dislike the idea of their dog receiving a tattoo or having a microchip implanted, but it is a very good idea. If your dog is found and taken to the pound, they will be able to determine who he belongs to quickly with a tattoo or microchip. I also keep a current color photo of my dog, just in case he gets lost and I need help in finding him.

Now, some other considerations I have found to be helpful when traveling with a dog. Keep a good first aid kit just for your dog. Pets get hurt too, and a small first aid kit will do the job of keeping the injury from getting infected. For small cuts, scrapes, or punctures, remember to clean the injury and then cover the wound to avoid an infection. But, with serious injuries your animal should be seen by a veterinarian as soon as possible.

Also, consider comfortable bedding for your pet, especially if you are camping or spending long periods of time outdoors. If your dog has a favorite toy that they play with and it is small enough, bring it along. Your dog will enjoy playing with this toy and perhaps it will be something to assist in keeping the stress level of your pet down. A stressed dog does not make a good traveling mate.

Additionally, remember to keep your dog on any flea and tick medication they are taking when you are traveling. Ticks and fleas can be found in most places in North American, just about any place that has green grass and trees. You'd be surprised where ticks and fleas can turn up later too, and that is one thing you don't need in your vehicle. Besides the obvious medical problems with ticks and fleas, the little pests are a real pain once they invade.

If the weather is warm or hot, do not leave your pet in the vehicle, especially with the windows up. Heat can kill a dog just as it does a person, but many pet owners often forget about a pet. Also, keep a lot of fresh water on hand for your pet and keep them not only out of heat, but also out of direct sunlight. Keep them comfortable and in the shade as much as possible.

Prior to your trip prepare by having enough of your dogs usual food on hand to last *the whole trip.* A sudden change in your dog's diet may cause your pet to become ill (diarrhea). Take more frequent breaks if your dog seems to be affected by motion sickness. Also, carry snacks and treats you know your pet will enjoy and reward him or her after a long period in the car or truck. Depending on the rest location you choose, you might be able to take Rover for a walk and give him a treat as you take a break for everyone's sake.

Traveling with a dog is not that difficult. While long trips, like mine to Alaska are not recommended, they can be done with a little planning. For short spurts out to the park, camping, hiking, or just a fun day in the sun, keep your dogs' physical and psychological health in mind. Make sure your pet is healthy, easy to identify, carry a first aid kit for your dog, and you have their favorite foods along. Also, watch the heat and give them lots of cool fresh water.

I'm looking forward to seeing you this summer as you and Rover travel together.

* Note: This article is not designed to replace your veterinarian's sound professional advice and it has been written to simply suggest some key points to assist you when traveling with a dog. A veterinarian should always be consulted when you have questions pertaining to the health and safety of your animal.

CLOSE ENCOUNTERS OF THE WILD KIND

How to Avoid Wild Animal Attacks

We've all seen the action movie where the hero is spending the night in the woods and he is forced to fight for his life against a pack of wild hungry wolves. At some point in the movie our hero wrestles with the wolves and eventually saves his camp as well as his life. While this makes for a very exciting movie, it's not very realistic from a wildlife point of view. I would suspect you are much safer from a wild animal attack in the field hunting than you are driving down to the corner supermarket. While animal attacks do happen, they are very rare, unless the injured party has in some way allowed the attack to happen in the first place.

Most animal related injuries (bites, cuts, bruises, or other blunt trauma) are often due to the injured person not understanding wild life. I have seen more than one person take an injured, but wild animal home to care for it, only to be injured at some point in the process. Granted most of these animals were small game (raccoons, opossums, squirrels, or rabbits), but wild animals are just that... wild. I suggest if you see an injured or sick animal you contact your government wildlife agency and let them do the rescuing. Most of the time wild animal injuries or attacks are direct results of the human doing something wrong, though there have been cases where a healthy animal has behaved in a way that is not typical. Additionally, there are those other "critters" we share the field with that are known to bite and I'm speaking of snakes. Most of us, if we spend enough time in the woods, will eventually discover a snake along the trail or in our camp.

Snakes is a word spoken when I was young that was right up there with the boogieman. I was especially scared of the name of one local poisonous snake, the Copperhead. Over the years though, I have learned that snakes do not really live up to the terrible reputation they have acquired. I have also discovered that most snakes will avoid you (like most animals), if they have a choice. If you make some noise when you move the snake, if possible, will move away and you'll never see it. Most bites occur when a person places a foot, leg, arm or hand near a snake that may be cornered. However, keep in mind, less than ten percent of the snakes in the world are dangerous to man and so even if you're bitten the odds are it will not be from a poisonous snake. But, if you are bitten most doctors will suggest you:

- *Do not* let the injured person drink any alcohol
- *Do not* cut the wound in any manner (this used to be suggested)
- *Do not* suck the poison out (this used to be done by mouth and is not suggested)
- *Do not use a tourniquet* (also suggested before, but not now)
- *Do not* use ice on the injured area
- *DO wash and clean* the bite with soap and water, immobilize the bite, treat for shock, and immediately seek medical attention. Statistics show that less than one half of one percent of people bitten by a poisonous snake will die from the bite, even if left untreated. But what about other large animal threats in the field?

Bear attacks are in my opinion serious situations to deal with, despite the fact they are rarely experienced by most folks. I lived for over six years in Alaska and only saw one wild grizzly in the field, and that was during a caribou hunt (I backed off and left the area). I am not saying they are not there or a possible threat, but use some common sense in the woods to avoid them. Unless I am hunting I will carry a cowbell and the noise seems to keep bears away from me. Most wild animals will avoid you, if they know you are coming, though there are exceptions to this. I think most bears are a bit like humans in that their behavior (mood) reflects what is going on around them. I suspect that any healthy animal may attack if cornered with no way out, or as psychologist call it, fight or flight. But, keep in mind, bears are short tempered and should be taken as a serious threat when seen in the wild. Always leave a way out for any wild animal, but what if you encounter a bear in the field? *The Canadian Ministry of Environment* suggests:

- Keep your campsite clean, with garbage disposed of and fresh food placed out of reach (I throw a rope over a limb, pull the food up at least ten feet out of reach, and use a solid container). A good place for your food is the trunk of your car, but never in your tent.

- Try to always travel with others. The more folks along the less likely an attack will occur, but it can still happen.

- Make noise, especially if you are alone (unless hunting), and you can do this by using a cowbell, singing, talking, clapping your hands and so on. This is important in thick forests, where you've seen bear sign or fresh tracks.

- Keep your eyes open for bear tracks, freshly killed animals, and if you smell a musky strong odor be very cautious. Additionally, avoid streams during salmon spawning and be extra careful around berry patches and thick brush.

- Never go near a fresh kill, because the bear may be near and want to guard his hard earned meal.

- If you do spot a bear, leave the area very slowly and do not run. Bears may associate your running with game (dinner) and chase you from instinct. Never get between a momma bear and her cubs, *never*.

- *Never* feed the bear food so you can get some good bear photographs or so you can get closer to the animal. This is both dumb and dangerous.

- If you come face to face with a bear, do not make direct eye contact with the beast, they might take that as a threat.

- Remember to make noise, use a bell, clap your hands, scream, sing, or throw rocks.

- Do not approach a bear at any time. Keep in mind not to run or try to climb a tree; the bear can run and climb faster than you can.

- Black bears might back off if challenged, but if you are attacked you should fight, scream, yell, and be aggressive. Once again, it depends on the bear as to whether they will back off or not.

- Kerry Gunther of the *Bear Management Office in Yellowstone Park* suggests you back away and try to make yourself inconspicuous when you encounter any bear. He further adds if you're facing a grizzly bear, "Stand your ground. If the grizzly hits you, fall and play dead."

If you are attacked by a bear,

- Drop to the ground and make yourself as small as you can by rolling into a ball.
- Clasp your hands over the back of your neck and remain still (if you are wearing a backpack keep it on to protect your head and neck.)

Now, we share the woods and fields with other animals besides bears and snakes. Let's look at cougars, moose, other large cats, coyotes and wolves, and see how we can avoid attacks. While some of you may think that each of these animals would need a different approach to avoid an attack and in some situations they may, there are some common sense items that are common.

- Never approach a wild animal.
- Never tease, threaten, or run toward a wild animal.
- Never abuse a wild animal or cause it pain.
- Never attempt to pet any wild animal, but especially large ones (bigger injuries can occur).
- Never feed a wild animal or attempt to "take care" of it if injured.
- Always back off slowly, if you unexpectedly meet an animal on the trail, and move away from the animal allowing it room to run from you if it's cornered.

If you happen to suddenly encounter any large animal on the trail, you should try to stay calm (may be hard to do depending on the animal you discover), stand still at first (may be hard to do as well), do not run (running will most likely be your first thought), talk very softly to the animal, and back away from it slowly. Remember not make any sudden moves. If the animal sees you as either a threat or a source of food it may attack, but most are scared of mankind. So, now we know what to do if we meet a wild animal, what else do we need to know about some of them?

Cougars are very large members of the cat family and while their attacks are rare they do happen. According to the Canadian Ministry of Environment, it seems this animal may be attracted to children due to their high-pitched voices, smaller size (food source size perhaps), and irregular movements. It is suspected that cougars are not able to properly identify children as humans and they may think youngsters are prey. Our neighbors up north suggest:

- Have children play in groups, the more the safer.
- Keep an eye on the kids at all times.
- If you have a dog, keep it near the children. A dog can see, smell, and hear the big cat way before we can do so, and it will act as an early warning system.
- Keep a radio or portable T.V. playing to create noise.
- Keep the kids near during hours of darkness.

Many cougar attacks could be prevented if you follow the same simple guidelines I have used for moving in the field around bears. Make noise, stay in groups, avoid killed prey, and so on. However, never turn your back on a cougar and remain upright at all times. Additionally, do all you can to make yourself look larger and do not try to hide or roll up in a ball, because neither will work effectively. If you are attacked, fight back as hard as you can, with whatever you can pick up to show the animal you are not prey. Most cougar attacks are the result of normal predator (after prey) behaviors by the big cat and thus somewhat predictable, but there are exceptions to all rules.

Most of us who have been up north have seen a moose and they remind me of a cow on stilts. While they may be neat to photograph and watch, I read in the Anchorage Daily News a few years back where a man was killed by a moose on the grounds of a nearby university. Moose are not usually considered to be serious threats of attack by most people, but they have the potential to seriously injure or kill you. While I lived in Alaska, moose were "the biggest attack threat", or so it seemed at least in my neighborhood. So, what about moose?

- Never feed a moose.
- Never threaten or tease a moose.
- Never get between a cow and calf.
- Never allow your dog to chase a moose or harass it.
- Never corner a moose around houses, trees, or fenced in yards; it may attack out of fear.

- If a moose attacks you, ball up and cover your head. Stay as still as you can and make no quick movements.

- Keep in mind if the animals hump is standing up and its ears are back it may be ready to attack you or is at least scared. If that happens, try to make yourself appear to be larger than you are by raising your arms and extending your fingers, but make NO quick movements.

Bobcats are smaller members of the big cat family and they are somewhat inactive during the winter months. Lynx are another member of the cat family and they are a bit larger than a bobcat, even though the bobcat is considered to be the more aggressive of the two. It is possible to encounter either animal up north, but remember most attacks are simply scratches and clawing, but each have been known to go for the throat of a victim during an attack. So, protect your face and throat if you are attacked by one of these cats. The same precautions and preventative action as suggested for other large predators is recommended.

I saved the wolves and coyotes for last, and on purpose, because I started this article with them. Of all the larger animals we share the woods and fields with, the dog family (wolves and coyotes) gets the worse media attention. It is almost impossible to watch a wild western movie or read an outdoor adventure book that does not have a vicious wolf attack at some point. While all of this in a movie or book leads to excitement and action, it is basically untrue. I have never, in over thirty years in the field, known of a wolf attacking a healthy man unless cornered. It is almost unheard of for a healthy wolf or coyote to attack a human, but I'm sure if the animal felt threatened or was starving they would attack. But, unlike the movies or in books, strong healthy wolves and coyotes do not attack a man unless there is no other option, because they fear man. Once again the basic precautions and preventative actions as recommended for any large predators are recommended for wolves and coyotes. Make sure you move slowly, back away, and leave the area. Keep in mind to leave the animal a way out and not to corner it.

If you are attacked by an animal and injured, you should clean the injury with soap and water, and then disinfect it. Keep in mind, often it may be a gouge, cut, crushing of a bone, or scratches that you'll be treating. At times there may be a lot of blood loss, so remember your basic first aid and stop the bleeding first. The results of a bite may be deeper than you suspect and the most serious aspect of the wound may be the risk of infection. Infection is common from animal claws and teeth, which are dirty and may have bits of decayed meat on them. There may also be trauma from being thrown, dragged, pulled, or from impact with an object. If you sustain an animal injury always seek medical attention as soon as possible. Besides the danger from the wound, there is also a possibility of rabies.

Wild animal attacks do happen, but not as often as we'd think. I have spent years hunting, fishing, camping and hiking in the woods, all over the world, and I have yet to be attacked by a large predator. Have I been lucky? I think not, I have always kept my eyes open, made noise (unless hunting), and been prepared for close encounters of the wild kind. Use common sense in the field, stay safe and I'll see you on the trails of North America.

Resources cited in this article are from the U.S. National Parks Service, the Bear Management Office in Yellowstone Park, The Canadian Ministry of Environment, as well as the American Medical Association.

MAKING SAFE JERKY

In 1995 a man killed a cougar in Idaho, during the first part of January, and during the following week he made jerky from some of the meat. Like most of us, he marinated the meat in a brine solution (salt water) and smoked the meat in a commercial smoker. However, he stated later the smoker "never got more than warm." About a week after eating some of his homemade jerky he became ill and was hospitalized with fever, myalgia, arthralia, facial swelling, and extreme fatigue. The medical investigation discovered trichinella larvae in the both the jerked meat and the cougar meat still in his freezer. It was the first case of cougar meat being the cause of an illness that is usually associated with domestic pork, wild bear, or boar.

In another case, the same year in Oregon, there were six confirmed cases of members of a family and friends becoming seriously ill due to exposure to E. Coli in homemade venison jerky. The medical investigation confirmed the presence of E. Coli in the left over jerky, frozen venison in the freezer, on the hacksaw used to process the meat, and on parts of the discarded skin. Further investigation found nine percent of the deer fecal pellets in the nearby woods to contained E. Coli.

Most of us who hunt will eventually get around to making jerky from our wild meats. Commercial jerky is very expensive and it is just natural for many hunters to develop a desire to make their own to avoid paying the high market prices. But during the recent years there have been some big changes in what processes used to make our jerky may be safe and what may not be safe. Traditional methods may no longer be safe to use, so let's take a look at what jerky is, how the process works, how to properly dry the meat, and some considerations on how to make jerky safe to eat.

The process of drying foods (meats and fruits) to preserve them has been around for many years. It is known the ancient Egyptians knew of the process, and it is well documented that Native Americans commonly used the process to preserve large game (elk, moose, buffalo and deer) as well. Native Americans took the process even further by pounding the dried meat into a powder and then mixing it with dried fruit (berries) and suet to make pemmican. Pemmican was an excellent source of energy during the cold winter months or when traveling long distances.

The name jerky comes from the Spanish word *Charque*, which means sun dried meat (you can still order it online from some Spanish sites by that name). In the past, jerky was made by sun drying, a very long and bothersome process. The meat had to be protected from insects, protected from rain or snow, and had to be gathered up and placed inside a shelter at night to keep the dew or other moisture from making the meat damp or wet. The sun method is a time consuming process at best, but with the development of electricity all of that changed (though you can still sundry or use a smoker).

Jerky is simply meat with most, about three quarters, of the water removed by drying. So, if you want a pound of jerked meat when you finish the process you'll need to start with four pounds of meat. When we jerk meat, most of the moisture is removed, thereby denying the enzymes in the meat the ability to react. So, in a nut shell that means there is no biological action in the meat once processed (decay or bacterial growth).

There are many different ways to remove the water from the meat. It can be dried, as I stated earlier, in the sun, by using a smoker or making a tee-pee to trap the smoke, in the oven, or by using a commercial food dehydrator. The key to which method you use is to keep in mind that the meat must dry before it starts to spoil. Now that you know how the process works and how it can be done, let's consider how to safely make jerky.

As stated above, the traditional methods of making jerky are no longer supported by the USDA or the AMA due to E. Coli dangers. In the days of old, meat was simply cut into thin strips and allowed to dry, but it has only been within recent years that some changes for safety's sake have been suggested.

The biggest change in safely making jerky is *at some point* the meat should be heated to 160 degrees F to kill any bacteria in the meat, especially with wild game, and keep in mind most commercial dehydrators do not address this step in the jerking process at all. I have discovered three ways to heat the meat to the required temperature that work, though each one is a bit different.

In the first method, the meat can be placed in a roasting pan, with about an inch of water added, and then cooked with the lid on, rotating frequently to avoid dry spots (though I am sure some of the steam from the cooking is absorbed by the meat as well). The problem I found using this method is the meat texture changes and it will, no matter how frequently you rotate the meat, develop some dry spots (the finished product resembles a roast). This texture change of the meat also makes it more difficult to slice the meat with a meat slicer (some of the meat I sliced using this method with a slicer was so dry it flaked and fell apart) and it would be very difficult to do by hand. Additionally, the idea behind dehydrating is to remove water, not add more. I sliced the meat and then marinated it, because thinly sliced meat will absorb the jerky spice mix more thoroughly.

Or, using the second method, the meat can be boiled in a large pot filled with water until the proper core temperature of 160 degrees is reached. While this method allows the temperature to be reached without drying the meat, the meat took about an hour longer to dehydrate. I used this method only once and didn't like the results in drying time, so I don't recommend it. Remember, we want to remove moisture from the meat, not add more.

Finally, meat can be sliced, fully dehydrated, and then brought to the temperature of 160 degrees to kill the bacteria. I have found this to be the easiest and fastest method of both dehydrating and killing any bacteria in the meat. It also has the advantage of being less of a "mess-maker", there is no increase or additional water in the meat and it slices easily (when compared to the other two methods). But, like most things in life it's an individual choice, so use the method that works the best for you.

Regardless of the method you use, it is crucial that at some point prior to consuming the meat it be heated to 160 degrees. This step is crucial in making safe jerky especially if you're using wild game. Some other safety considerations apply as well:

- Prior to processing keep your meat stored at 40 degrees or lower.
- Frozen meat should be thawed in the fridge and not on the kitchen counter. It is important to remember that bacteria grow rapidly at room temperatures.
- While you marinate your meat prior to making your jerky (most folks will slice the meat first and then marinate) do so in the

fridge and discard used marinate when the meat is removed for dehydrating. It could be dangerous to reuse marinate that has been used for your meat.

- I usually use a commercial jerky spice mix to make my jerky, but a key ingredient in the process is salt. Salt speeds up the drying time and will improve the flavor of your end product. Make sure you follow the directions on the mix package.

- Trim *all* of the fat, gristle, and white tissue from the meat. You want a very lean piece of meat to work with.

- Use a meat thermometer when you heat the meat to insure the 160 degrees F is reached internally (if you decide to heat the meat before you slice it) by roasting or boiling.

- Allow the meat to cool to the touch before you start cutting it and keep in mind it will take some time to cool down.

- Make sure your hands and all surfaces the meat may come in contact with are cleaned with soap and water. And, while you're at it, don't forget to do the same with your knives, cutting board, or commercial meat slicer (if you use one).

- Since most of us will have difficulty keeping a nice uniform thickness using a butcher knife, I suggest the meat be sliced using a commercial meat slicer or have your butcher slice the meat if he processes your wild game. Cut the meat no thicker than a quarter of an inch and cut it across the grain on the meat.

- The meat can then be placed on commercial dehydrator drying racks, hanging bacon racks for the oven, or cookie sheets. Make sure the racks and the cookie sheets have all been cleaned with soap and water. You do not want the meat to overlap but it can touch.

- Turn the dehydrator on (following the manufacturer's directions for making jerky) or set the oven temperature between 130 and 140 degrees F, keeping the door open slightly to allow moisture to escape as the meat dries.

- The time needed for the meat to dry will depend on the method you are using to dry it. Your commercial dehydrator's instructions will give you a pretty accurate idea of the time needed, and with an oven (at 130-140 degrees F) it will take between 10 and 12 hours.

The key, no matter what method you use to dehydrate, is for the temperature to stay between 130 and 140 degrees F during the whole process. This temperature will keep the organisms in the meat from being able to grow, due to water removal. Also, the heat will assist in killing bacteria at the same time.

When your jerky is finished, it should be dark in color and when bent it will crack but not break.

There are some folks who will want to use hamburger or ground-up wild game to make jerky. Personally, I don't recommend that any ground meats be used to make jerky because research (USDA) has shown that E. Coli can survive in ground meats at temperatures up to 145 degrees F and for periods up to 10 hours. Additionally, the use of commercial beef jerky spice mixtures is recommended because studies conducted by the USDA have shown it has a higher destructive rate for bacteria than traditional processes.

Another aspect that has a big influence on the safety of the meat you use to make jerky is how your wild game was procured. Depending on the type of weapon used to down your game (force of impact and internal trauma), where on the body the animal was hit, and what organs were damaged are all concerns. Obviously a deer struck by a rifle in the gut will have ruptured internal organs which may contaminate some of the meat. While those are considerations, I feel most of the contamination of meat occurs during the field dressing process.

When field dressing any game, avoid rupturing the bladder or causing any internal organs to leak. Also, when gutting your game, make sure no fecal matter from an intestine comes in contact with your meat (this can be hard when removing the anus, but you can always tie it off with cotton cord). Additionally, keep your meat in game bags; keep it clean and away from insects. Another consideration is how long your downed game remains in the field. The longer the meat is at ambient temperature (during warm weather) the higher the rate of bacterial growth, unless it is very cool or cold at the time. I am not talking about a cool temperature used for aging, but rather warm temperatures.

The process of drying meat and fruits has been around almost since the beginning of time. It is simple to do and can be done at home with very little expense or effort. But, keep in mind traditional methods may no longer be safe to use and some new safety considerations are very important if you want to make your jerky safe to eat. Remember to store (or thaw) your meat properly in the fridge before you use it, keep your tools clean with soap and water, watch your personal hygiene, maintain a temperature between 130 and 140 degrees during the entire drying process, and remember to heat the meat to 160 degrees F at some stage of your process. Bon appetite!

Note - According to research conducted by the American Medical Association "E. Coli can survive drying times of up to 10 hours and with temperatures up to 145 degrees F. Venison, or other wild game, should be preheated to an internal temperature of at least 160 degrees. Wild game should be handled and cooked with the same considerations given other meats."

SURVIVING A NATURAL DISASTER

The wind picked up tremendously and I noticed a sudden drop in air pressure as the windows in my house popped loudly. I quickly ran into each room and lifted one window about a quarter of an inch to allow the pressure inside the house to remain equal to the pressure outside the house. The sky suddenly darkened and it was  curling violently up and around overhead. The light rain I had been watching just a few minutes before suddenly turned into a thick wall of water. As I looked outside my front door, I could see paper, lids to trash cans, and empty cardboard boxes being blown down the street. The loud boom of thunder followed a long finger of lightning across the black sky.

"Daddy, the weather station says we're having a tornado!" My eight year old daughter, Lisa, yelled out as she moved toward me with deep fear reflecting in her young eyes.

"Lisa, we'll be fine; we're ready for bad weather, remember?" I spoke with confidence to my daughter, as I thought, *time to move the kids down into the basement and get ready for this, but am I really ready?*

When natural disasters happen (or acts of God), they usually happen when we expect them the least. This surprise comes from the fact that as Americans we have lived pretty safe lives overall in the past and though we do have tornadoes and hurricanes each year, they usually happen to someone else and not us. See, the less people suspect a natural disaster, the more damaging the results. This is especially true of the psychological affects. Remember the terrible feelings all of us experienced when we first heard of the damage done and loss of life in New Orleans? Some of us felt deep shock, confusion, and a very profound fear, because it could have been us. Those feelings are exactly the type of psychological responses we should feel, because lives were lost and the damage sustained was devastating to the whole country. After all, this is America and we rarely have disasters to that level, right? Well, we have had a few, but keep in mind being Americans does not grant us any special protection from natural disasters, so I suggest we all prepare for future events. Well, you may be asking, what exactly is a natural disaster?

- Flood
- Tornado
- Earthquake
- Extreme heat
- Extreme cold — ice and snow storms
- Forest and woodland fires
- House and building fires
- Thunder storms/lightning

Even though natural disaster strikes without warning, there are certain preparatory actions we can take that can reduce stress and reassure our families that we have some measure of control over events. The following checklist will take us through the following steps (Source: *American Red Cross*):

Preparation

What can possibly happen in your area?
Determine what can happen and where. Discuss it with your family/spouse.

Create an emergency communications plan.
Choose a person out of the area that you and each member will call or e-mail if a disaster occurs. Make sure they know they are your chosen contact person. Give each family member the contact's e-mail address and phone numbers (home, work, pager and cell phone). Leave these numbers at home, work and school. Advise your family to try e-mail if the phone lines are busy or down.

Setup a family meeting place.
If your area is evacuated, you and your family should meet at a predetermined place away from your home. Since shelters or hotels don't usually accept pets, a friend or relative's home that will accept your pets will avoid unexpected problems. If you are responsible for school-age children, check on the school's emergency plan and required pickup authorizations.

Assemble a disaster supplies kit.
To prepare for an evacuation, assemble a disaster supplies kit in a bag or small plastic trash can. Include the following items:

- Special needs equipment for disabled family members, prescription medicines, change of clothing, sleeping bag or bedroll, battery-powered radio or TV with extra batteries, food, bottled water and tools.
- Cash.
- Copies of important family documents, e.g. birth and marriage certificates, passports, licenses, military discharge papers, advance health care directives and a copy of your will.
- First-aid kit.

Execution
When disaster strikes, take the following actions:

- Remain calm and patient (easier said than done).
- Listen to the radio/TV for news and emergency instructions.
- If your building is involved in the damage, check for injuries and get help for the seriously injured.
- Do not light matches, candles or turn on electrical switches. Check for fires and damage using a flashlight.
- Sniff for gas leaks at a gas water heater. If you smell gas, turn off the main gas valve, open windows and get outside immediately.
- Shut off any other damaged utilities.
- Confine your pets.
- Call your family contact. Do not use the phone again or call 911 unless it is an emergency.
- Check on your neighbors, especially the elderly or disabled.

Evacuation
When the evacuation order comes, heed the order immediately (this is important to avoid a bad situation if possible).

- Listen to radio or TV broadcasts for information on blocked evacuation routes.
- Wear long-sleeved shirts, long pants and sturdy shoes for protection. Bring gloves with you.
- Take your disaster supplies (I suggest you also take your first aid and survival kit).
- Take your pets with you to either your preplanned meeting place or a pet-friendly motel.
- Lock your home.
- Use approved evacuation routes instead of shortcuts which may be impassable.
- Stay away from downed power lines.
- If no gas leak is present, leave natural gas service **ON**. Upon return, you will need gas for heating and cooking, and only a professional can restore gas service. This could take weeks.

What if you can't evacuate?

I also recommend that all of us, to various degrees, organize our homes in the event things go bad quickly because we might not be able to leave. I believe most professionals who deal with the weather, well tell us that it is only a matter of time before we are subjected to more bad weather of some sort. A natural disaster could affect our water supply, our fresh foods, shelter, heating, and even the air we breathe (a volcano eruption creates ash). A natural disaster could consist of any conceivable "act of God" listed above (or others) at any location. So, just what can we do to prepare our homes and loved ones if something should happen? What if we were stuck in our homes for a week? Could you survive with what you have on hand right now?

Start getting ready now, not tomorrow. Remember what I said above; a natural disaster will most likely happen when you least expect it. Take a look around your house. If you live like most people, you have many things you can use for emergencies on hand. But, do you have special clothing, canned foods, first aid items, battery or self powered radio, or other things that could be placed in storage for emergency use? Don't get paranoid and put all you own in the closet for emergency use, just those items you seriously don't use much. Limit it to items you may need later. Also, remember, most of the things I am listing here you already have in use in your household.

What types of things should you consider storing or having on hand? I have broken it down to some very simple items. Keep in mind, each household has different supply requirements and the purpose of this article is to get you thinking about an emergency. One of the things you need to consider is the needs of yourself and your family. If you have a handicapped member, or a person with special needs (i.e. medication or special care), you may have to evaluate your situation much closer than most people. But, for most of us we will need the same things we need to survive in the bush.

Food is always on the top of most people's desires during survival. I know most of it is psychological, but regardless, the desire is very deep in all of us. Food leads us to feeling content and that all is well around us. I prefer to keep Meals Ready to Eat, MRE's, on hand. I ate them by the hundreds in the military and they are actually quite good. I keep the complete meals on hand, because I eat them a little at a time to get the maximum enjoyment out of one pouch (the meal lasts longer that way).

Freeze dried foods are pretty good too, in my humble opinion. The only drawback to them is the water needed in preparation. If your water source is limited, freeze-dried foods are not a wise choice. Never eat dehydrated foods without lots of water on hand; your body will take water from your system to process waste. You can find all different kinds of menu items offered commercially.

Regardless of the type of foods you prefer, remember to maintain a healthy diet. Make sure you get as close to the daily minimums as you can (keep vitamins stored, too). Actually, if you can afford to do so and have the storage space, go beyond the daily minimums. If you can store the foodstuffs, why go hungry? Plus, remember, in a survival situation we tend to burn more calories just attempting to stay alive.

Once our food problem is behind us, we can start considering what I feel is our primary concern, water. The first step here is to procure several large water storage containers. Depending on the number of people you are responsible for you will need to evaluate your water needs carefully. Most survival professionals will recommend a bare minimum of a gallon a day. You will need much more if you plan on cooking and washing in it, or if the temperature goes way up. Make sure your water containers are designed to store water in and are not discarded chemical containers. Mark each container in large letters, WATER ONLY, and store only water in these containers.

Another tool you will want to have on hand is a water filtering system. A natural disaster that impacts your primary water source may prevent you from being able to use it (the line may burst or the water may become polluted), so you may have to use water from clean ponds, lakes, or streams. If you believe there are human or animal remains in any open water source, *do not use* the water, use only pre-stored or packaged (canned, bottled or in bags) water, or find another source. A good temporary source of drinking water is your hot water heater and they all have a spigot on the bottom.

Prepackaged water is sold in different quantities. I have seen water sold in pouches, plastic two liter bottles, and in cans. The size of the container may vary, but most survival pouches or cans are around ten to twelve ounces. I recommend everyone have some prepackaged water placed in storage as a precaution. It is relatively inexpensive and it could become your only source of clean, safe water. Once again, you need to evaluate the number of people who live with you and consider their water needs.

Finally, my old favorites are water purification tablets. I keep a bottle in my survival vest, in my tackle box, in my truck, and in the house. They are easy to use, just drop two tablets in the water container, usually a canteen, but check on the label to see how much water the tablets treat. An old vet trick here, add a little flavored drink powder (Kool-aid) to your treated water to mask the chemical smell and taste.

Let's see, we have food and we have water...I think our next concern is clothing. If a disaster happens with no warning, you may have to react very quickly. You may have set aside a portion of your basement, garage, or other area for emergency storage, so you need to store special clothing items there. Aren't your day-to-day clothes good enough? Nope, not at all.

I feel that survival wear (and the time following a natural disaster is a survival situation) should be tough and comfortable. That is why during most of my outdoor trips I wear military surplus or heavy jeans. I have discovered that cheap imitations of military gear fall short in the long run. I wear some of my old Battle Dress Uniforms (BDU's) and they are perfect. Remember, BDU's have been proven tough, even in combat. I don't plan to fight any wars anymore, but that makes them strong enough for most survival situations. Jeans are good too, but usually are too tight and restrictive, compared to BDU's. Also, with jeans you don't get all the pockets to put survival items in. Another added incentive for me to buy BDU's is the low cost when compared to jeans.

Other clothing requirements will depend on where you live. If you need rain gear often, then have it available. If your area gets little rain, then decide on what you do need. Consider socks, underwear (perhaps long and insulated), parkas, gloves, good quality boots, and the list goes on. In all situations have a cap, a wide brimmed hat, and at the very least, a nylon windbreaker. Even the desert can get cold at night.

What about cooking? Yep, we are back to food once more. You have the stored foods, but how can you prepare them? Well, hopefully your electric or gas stove will still work. Determine in advance if you have a separate tank of propane for your gas stove. You should know that by the gas bills from the company that periodically fills the tank. If you have a tank, the odds are it may still work. However, depending on the type of natural disaster, you may be without electrical power or a source of gas for cooking. If this is all that happens then you don't have much of a real problem, except one of comfort (and perhaps the loss of some refrigerated foods).

Make sure before using ANY gas appliance you check for gas leaks. If you smell gas or suspect a leak, do NOT us any open flames. Using electrical power or gas when the lines are broken could lead to injury or death. Do not use a charcoal grill or other open flames in the house or in a closed space; ventilation is required to avoid carbon monoxide poisoning. Additionally, check your power lines and if you see they are down, mark the area as a danger. *If you know the power and gas are down, turn them off* (at the gas line or the breaker box).

I recommend that you use the perishable food from the fridge first. Save your canned or stored foods for later use if need be. Use the meats, veggies, and other stuff before you hit your survival items. Also, if you have ice, place foods in an ice chest before they thaw completely out. Previously frozen foods will stay at a higher quality longer if they are stored in a good quality ice chest before they are thawed out.

If you are without a stove, you may have to cook outside, if it is safe to do so. I would never cook indoors with an open flame due to the dangers of carbon monoxide poisoning. I just don't feel it is worth the risk. The first aspect of making a fire, besides the ignition source, is tinder, kindling, and fuel. Let's look at tinder first.

Tinder should be small, shredded, or finely shaven pieces of material. You can use birch bark (it contains a resinous material that will burn hot), dried grass, wood shavings, pine pitch (has a resinous material in it, too), down from birds, charred cotton material, or lint. You want low ignition heat so keep the material you use fluffed up to allow lots of oxygen flow as you ignite it. You can also coat some parts of your tinder with Vaseline, Chap Stick, or insect repellent to make it burn hotter once lighted. Once the tinder has been ignited, you slowly add the kindling and once blazing well, add your fuel.

Kindling is small pieces of material you have decided to use for your fire. I suggest squaw wood, which are the small dead pieces of wood (limbs if you will) found on most trees at the lower levels. This wood is often found on live trees as well. It is usually dry if found on the lower levels of a large tree. The upper limbs keep the rain or snow off of it. But, you can use small twigs and branches found on the ground. Just make sure any woods you select are dead and dry. This is important for your kindling. Also, remember you want small pieces not large ones. You want kindling in a variety of sizes and thickness. This is so you can gradually increase the size of the wood to increase the size of your fire. If you place a piece of kindling on your tinder that is too big, the fire may go out. Slowly increase the wood size. Try to use soft woods for your kindling, if possible. Soft woods burn fast and give off sparks. This unique trait of softwoods will assist your kindling in burning better and hotter.

Fuel is just about anything you can burn. Animal dung, from plant eaters, can be burned, fuels, oils, animal fats, and even most woods. Wet wood should be placed near the fire to at least partially dry out before being added to the fire. In wet weather, stumps, logs, or limbs may be broken open and the inner pieces of wood removed to add to your fire. This inner wood will be at least partially dry. Keep in mind, soft woods will burn fast, give off sparks, and may be an excellent source to start with. Some soft woods are spruce, pine, cedar, or willow.

Make sure you use good fire safety sense and control your fire. Keep a bucket of water or sand near your fire at all times.

Okay, let's look at sanitation and waste methods. All of us will need to use the toilet at times, but you may use it less often in survival situations. For some medical reason the production of human waste is slowed down when the diet is reduced and stress is increased. I could go into why this happens, but all you need to know is that it is normal for most of us. Nonetheless, you have to prepare for human waste disposal. If your water is working (and your toilet), all is great. If your water source is not there, you may have a slight problem.

I suggest you store a portable toilet with your survival items. You can buy a toilet commercially, or go back in history and make a honey bucket. A honey bucket is a large bucket used to collect human waste. It can be a mop bucket, or a large empty coffee can, and I suggest you use a plastic trash bag to line it with. But regardless of which choice you make, sooner or later, someone will be forced to empty the thing (wait until the container is at least half full).

Make sure human waste is not discarded along rivers, streams, lakes, or other potential sources of drinking water. Select a spot that is a good distance from your living area and not uphill from you. In the old days in Europe, before gunpowder was popular, the flight of an arrow was considered a good distance for toilets. And, that was only popular and followed by a select few. But, I'd suggest a couple hundred feet at least to avoid the smell.

You can buy biodegradable toilet tissue, sanitizing chemicals, and other accessories if you feel the need. Remember, a magazine or newspaper can do the same job as tissue. Yes, I am as concerned about nature as the next person, perhaps more so, but we are talking about survival here. If you centralize your dumping spot, it will be easier for you to clean up your waste site once the emergency is over.

One last item and I will get off of my soapbox. A list of additional miscellaneous items I think would be helpful for an individual family survival kit:

- A portable radio with extra batteries or a Solar or wind-up powered one.
- Condoms for water storage, un-lubricated.
- Good quality blankets and sleeping bags (make sure they are adequate for your temperature zone).
- Any prescription medications your family may need. Make sure you check the expiration dates. Talk to your doctor about special needs you may have.
- A good professional type first aid kit, with booklet or manual. You may be the only medical help available in an emergency. A good survival manual or book (I recommend, of course, my new book, "*Simple Survival, A Family Outdoors Guide*"). Videos are great, too, but they are of no use if you are without power.
- A magnesium fire starter, along with some type of tinder (cotton lint from the dryer is excellent).
- Several boxes of waterproof matches and a lighter.

- A small waterproof match container that can be carried in a pocket (this could come in handy if you have to leave the survival area looking for food or water).

- Any special needs items you or your family may have in an emergency (medication or diet concerns).

The lists of items I have suggested in this article are just that, suggestions. In no way am I suggesting this list is complete for any and all emergency survival situations. I want you to think about what you need. While each individual is different and unique, so is each family. Keep in mind; you may have to improvise to survive. Additionally, many of my suggestions here are in the event you are "confined" to your home immediately following a disaster for a period of time.

Our choice is simple, we can live in fear and cringe each time the power goes off, or we can be prepared. We can prepare by storing what we will need and preparing our minds on how we will survive. Once the emergency hits, while others are attempting to buy what they need in crowded stores, if they can find one open, we will be comforted in knowing we have what it takes to survive. Be a survivor; *"Knowledge Means Survival."*

Food (and Water) for Thought

How to safely store food and water for emergencies

One aspect of an emergency a lot of folks rarely consider is the storage of food and water, or even how long they can be safely stored. If an emergency were to occur right this minute, how safe are the canned goods you have in the cupboard? Or, how long could you drink the bottled water you have in the basement? How safe is your food and water supply, or do you even have one? With today's uncertain political world, it might be to all of our advantages to have at least a two week supply of food and water on hand. For most of us, we could live for two weeks on what is in the freezer, cupboard, or the fridge, but in some homes it might result in a more limited food intake.

In the event of a natural disaster or a terrorist attack, you may have to survive on what is available in your home when it occurs. If an emergency does happen and you still have electrical power, turn on the television to see what local authorities suggest you do—stay *or* evacuate the area. Additionally you should have a battery or alternate power radio available in case the power goes out, so you can listen to local radio stations to keep informed of suggestions and events. Knowing what to do and when to do it is very important in an emergency situation. If you are instructed to stay you might have to change your lifestyle a bit, but a lot will depend on if you have utilities and the extent the emergency situation limits your movements.

If you stay and have no utilities at all, your first priority in most situations (in extremely cold weather you can stay warm under your blankets, but in hot weather you'll need to increase your water intake and stay out of direct sunlight if you can) is water. Most folks would think of food as the number one concern, but without water people can die in as little as three days during moderate temperatures (faster in hot weather) and yet a healthy person can go as long as two weeks without food. Water is your first concern, because it is a life sustaining consideration, and remember it can be stored prior to emergencies, you have emergency water sources, and most suspected unsafe water can be treated to make it safe to drink.

According to the American Red Cross, water can be stored safely in clean plastic containers, in glass, in fiberglass, or enamel lined metal containers. Make sure any container you use has never been used to store harmful chemicals or materials in it. I would suggest using empty two liter pop bottles for water storage; they even come with a cap to seal the container. You can also purchase commercial water storage containers, plastic drums, or buckets. I prefer those containers with tight lids to keep the water from being spilled and to keep it clean. If you use a sealed container (pop bottle, drum, or other container) label it on the outside with a permanent maker "Drinking Water" and add the date. Keep your water stored in a cool, dry and dark place, rotating it every six months (that is the reason for the date on the container).

In an emergency you can find water in ponds, lakes, rivers, and streams but keep in mind this water is not safe to drink until it has been purified. In your home you can use the water stored in your pipes as well as your hot water heater; just make sure the gas or electrical power is turned off before you drain the water heater. It is important for you to determine where your water comes from too, so you can determine in advance if your water might be safe or not in some emergencies. If your water at home comes from a private well it may still be safe to use (if you live in the country), but in some emergencies (terrorist acts, floods, or tornadoes) public water sources might not be safe (streams, ponds and rivers may not be safe then either) and may even be the target of some terrorist acts. In most cases, unless I knew for sure my water source was clean I would shut my water off and use what remains in the pipes and hot water heater. Most hot water heaters are around the forty gallon size and that's enough for two people to survive for around twenty days at a moderate temperature (most survival experts suggest a gallon a day in mild temperatures, though you can survive on less if you do not eat).

If you are forced to use emergency drinking water from an unknown source at any time, (streams, ponds or lakes) you will have to purify it before drinking. Try to get water from a fast moving source, river or stream, and avoid water that has a bad smell, has scum on it, or is obviously polluted in some way. There are four ways most folks purify water and though they all work to various degrees, there are only two suggested by the Canadian Red Cross.

Water can be boiled for 3 to 5 minutes and then allowed to cool before drinking. This boiled water will have a very flat taste and this is because the process removes most of the air from the water as it boils. To improve the taste, take two containers and pour the water between them to mix air with the treated water.

Another highly suggested method is to add 16 drops of household bleach to a gallon of water, but do not use color safe bleach, scented bleach, or bleach with any additional cleaners in it. Once you have added the drops of bleach stir the water very well and then let it sit for thirty minutes. When you smell the treated water it should have a slight bleach smell and if it does not, repeat the process and let the water sit for an additional fifteen minutes.

There are two other methods that old timers might use and neither is recommended by the American or Canadian Red Cross. Those that camp or backpack a great deal may decide to use a drinking straw (filter) or water purification tablets and while both work to a degree, neither are one hundred percent safe to use. This, according to the Red Cross, is because *the only safe way* to treat water is by boiling or using bleach. Neither the drinking straw nor water purification tablets contain a 5.25 percent of sodium hypochlorite, which kills all the micro critters in our emergency drinking water. I suggest we be safe and use the bleach.

After the water problem has been taken care of we should give our food situation some serious thought. First, if you do not have sufficient water (a gallon a day) cut back on your food intake and if you have no water at all do not eat. This is because if you do eat and are dehydrated, your body will use what fluids it has stored to process waste, so water is very important. Second, with a limited water intake avoid salty foods, foods high in fats and proteins, and foods that require water to prepare. Remember that most of us can survive for up to two weeks without any food at all, if we are in good physical condition. But, even if you have plenty of water, there are still some things you must consider.

Your goal, if you can achieve it, is to find foods that are high in calories, because in a survival situation you'll burn calories much faster than normal. You also want foods that require no refrigeration, little or no preparation, and no cooking. Keep in mind that almost all canned foods require no cooking or water to prepare, so after you eat all the perishables in the fridge and freezer, go for the canned foods.

If you are unsure about how long your various food stuffs are good for, here are some basic guidelines for rotating common emergency foods from the Red Cross.

Use within six months:
- Powdered milk (boxed)
- Dried fruit (in metal container)
- Dry, crisp crackers (in metal container)
- Potatoes

Use within one year:
- Canned condensed meat and vegetable soups
- Canned fruits, fruit juices and vegetables
- Ready-to-eat cereals and uncooked instant cereals (in metal containers)
- Peanut butter
- Jelly
- Hard candy and canned nuts
- Vitamin C

May be stored indefinitely (in proper containers and conditions):
- Wheat
- Vegetable oils
- Dried corn
- Baking powder
- Soybeans
- Instant coffee, tea and cocoa
- Salt
- Non-carbonated soft drinks
- White rice
- Bouillon products
- Dry pasta

- Powdered milk (in nitrogen-packed cans)

If you have doubts on the safety of a canned product, check to see if it has a "use by" or "best by" date printed or stamped on it. If there is no date, the product should be discarded after six months. I keep dry beans on hand, because they are an excellent source of protein (if you have the water to cook them) and they can be stored indefinitely if sealed containers are used and they are kept in a cool and dry place.

Recommended foods (by the Red Cross) include:

- Ready-to-eat canned meats, fruits and vegetables. (Be sure to include a manual can opener)
- Canned juices, milk and soup (if powdered, store extra water).
- High energy foods, such as peanut butter, jelly, crackers, granola bars and trail mix.
- Comfort foods, such as hard candy, sweetened cereals, candy bars and cookies.
- Instant coffee, tea bags.
- Foods for infants, elderly persons or persons on special diets, if necessary.
- Compressed food bars. They store well, are lightweight, taste good and are nutritious.
- Trail mix. It is available as a prepackaged product or you can assemble it on your own.
- Dried foods. They can be nutritious and satisfying, but have some have a lot of salt content, which promotes thirst. Read the label.
- Freeze-dried foods. They are tasty and lightweight, but will need water for reconstitution.
- Instant Meals. Cups of noodles or cups of soup are a good addition, although they need water for reconstitution.
- Snack-sized canned goods. Good because they generally have pull-top lids or twist-open keys.
- Prepackaged beverages. Those in foil packets and foil-lined boxes are suitable because they are tightly sealed and will keep for a long time.

Food Options to Avoid:

- Commercially dehydrated foods. They can require a great deal of water for reconstitution and extra effort in preparation.
- Bottled foods. They are generally too heavy and bulky, and break easily.
- Meal-sized canned foods. They are usually bulky and heavy.
- Whole grains, beans, pasta. Preparation could be complicated under the circumstances of a disaster.

In a natural disaster or emergency situation most rescues will occur within a few days or things will simply get back to normal, unless the situation is widespread or there has been a heavy loss of life. Keep in mind that most of us have sufficient food in our cupboards, refrigerator or freezer to survive for a week or two, so concentrate your efforts on water procurement. Rotate your water supplies every six months and remember the alternate places to find water, as well as the various treatment methods to insure it's safe to drink. Also keep a close eye on how long you've have your food stuffs in storage and rotate your foods so you always use the oldest foods first.

Water and Ocean Survival

How to survive in a life raft on large bodies of water

Surviving after a mishap on a large body of water is tough business, and one mistake can cost you your life. When I attended the United States Air Force Water Survival School, at Homestead Air Force Base, they stressed that water survival was difficult, challenging, and often fatal for the unprepared. While most of us may never intend to buy a yacht and head out to sea, there are a number of different ways we could end up on a large body of water fighting for our lives. If we fish on the Great Lakes or one of the oceans, fly in private or commercial aircraft, or take a cruise, we could find ourselves in the water as a result of bad weather, a collision, mechanical failure, or other emergency.

A lot depends on the type of vessel you are on when the situation becomes an emergency. On a large boat, you'll have a better chance of survival than if you're in a ditched aircraft (aircraft landing in water may cause some serious injuries). Then again, you're somewhere in the middle if you're on a private fishing boat of average size. Commercial aircraft carry life rafts and they are often huge twenty person rubberized rafts (or larger) that work fairly well, if you have the time to deploy them before you go into the water and most of the time you will. The only complaint I have, and I've been in one in the ocean, is the fact they ride rough in even mild weather. But, let's assume you have a raft or small boat because you most likely will; how can you survive long enough to get rescued?

My first consideration would be both the water temperature and the ambient air temperature, because both will affect your survival odds. If the weather is hot, you'll need to keep as much of your body covered with clothing as you can (to avoid sunburn and sweating), as well as a shelter of some kind if you can make one. Most commercial life rafts come with a canopy made of a light weight rubberized material that is bright in color on one side (orange or magenta usually) and dark on the other, so a type of shelter (the canopy) is packed in the survival kit.

The bright color should be placed toward the sky in hot weather, because it will reflect sunlight and help keep you cooler. During cold weather, the dark color (black is the most common) should be toward the sky to absorb the heat from the sun. Once again, keep your body covered to retain body heat and consider huddling with other survivors to help keep each other warm. The canopy is held in place (on some rafts) by aluminum rods (others may have an inflatable canopy and they are very warm) and once in place, the canopy will actually have sides that can be lowered and tied closed to give you additional protection from the elements.

Next, consider your water supply. If you are floating on fresh water, you don't have much of a problem, just purify the water and enjoy. On an ocean or large body of salt water, you may have a dilemma. Many of the commercial survival kits will come with water, though they may be packaged in cans (about the size of a pop can), pouches, or bottles. Do not ration your water, because it does your body no good if it is not used as needed. It is important for you to drink enough water to keep functioning and that means a minimum drink of a quart a day, if possible. Keep in mind at a moderate temperature most people can live for around three days without water and the majority of rescues occur within forty-eight hours, so there is no need to ration your water supply. Additionally, dehydration is a very dangerous situation for a survivor in any emergency, not just at sea. But, how can you find additional sources of safe drinking water?

I would suggest you use your imagination as well as some common sense to procure drinking water. Have empty containers (most survival kits will have empty canteens, water bottles/bags, collapsible bailout buckets, or other containers in them) available and ready to use immediately to store rainwater or to collect ice (need a container with a wide mouth perhaps). *Do not drink sea water*, because it will increase dehydration and may cause salt water poisoning. However, it you are in a cold environment, you can collect sea water and then let the water freeze. Since fresh water will freeze before salt water, you will see a lump of ice (fresh water) in the container; remove it to use for drinking and discard the salt water.

There are two other methods to collect drinking water and both are found in most survival kits. In the survival supplies you may find chemicals that look like small bricks, only they are used to treat salt water to make it drinkable. These bricks remove the salt and alkaline from the water making it safe to drink. Usually these chemical bricks are a very dark, almost black, color. Additionally, you will most likely find a distillation kit in the survival gear. The kits I have seen require you to inflate a balloon looking container that sits in the water and through the process of evaporation safe water is collected for drinking. I know from experience you will need to inflate this, using a small hand pump, as soon as you can because it takes a lot of energy. Don't wait until you're very weak to start to inflate it, or you may never get the job done. Water from both the chemical bricks and distillation kit does not require purification.

If you have over a quart of water a day to drink, you can now consider food. The survival kit in most rafts will have some foods in it and the kind of food will vary depending on who packed the survival kit. Many of the survival foods will be high in calories; over 2,000 calories per meal is about the average, and there will be some hard candies (energy) in the kit as well. Food in the ocean or large body of water is all around you, but you'll have to find it and it may be hard to catch. Personally, I'd never worry too much about food because we can go weeks without eating, if we're healthy. Mostly food is a psychological factor in survival, or a full stomach is a happy stomach if you will. If you have to procure food, keep the following in mind;

- Fish are always a source of protein in the ocean and saltwater fish can be eaten raw. All commercial aircraft will have a fishing kit in the survival gear, so do a little fishing; however *avoid eating any fish that does not look like a fish* should. Some saltwater fish have sharp teeth, spines, and can be poisonous or cause damage to your raft.

- Pull seaweed from the ocean and go through it closely, looking for small edible crabs, shrimp, or fish. You'll find some, so don't waste them, eat them or use them for bait.

- All birds can be eaten, though some (sea gulls) may have a very fishy taste when eaten raw. I've always had a hard time getting raw bird of any kind down, but if need be I'd eat it. Birds can be caught with shiny lures, baited hooks, or by using brightly colored cloth. At the odd time, they can be caught by hand, but you will have to be very quick.

Food procurement must be done using a lot of caution, due to hooks and sharp points you might use. I suggest you pack all sharp items not actually being used in the survival kit bag to avoid an accidental puncture of the life raft material. Keep in mind your raft is nothing more rubberized material filled with air and though it has various compartments you don't want to puncture it. I have inflated the partial compartments of large life rafts by hand and it is a tremendous amount of hard work using a hand pump. All life raft survival kits will contain both a pump and repair plugs. To use a pump, simply screw the nozzle attachment to the pump and then lock the end of the nozzle to the manual inflation valve. But, what if you get a serious hole in the raft? Always repair an air leak quickly, because it takes less energy to do a repair than it does to keep bailing a raft free of water.

All raft survival kits will have a repair kit, which includes patches, glue and other tools. If the hole is too big you may have to float with that particular chamber deflated, but if the hole is small you can use a life raft repair plug. It is a three pieced device that is very easy to use (inner part, outer part, and wing nut on an extension wire).  You should cut the fabric on the raft no wider than the narrowest part of the plug face, insert the plug and then rotate ninety degrees. Both the inner and outer part of the plug are coated with rubber to assure an airtight seal once secured. After the inner and outer parts of the plug are lined up properly, screw the wing nut down tightly and bend the extension wire downward and around the wing nut. You will then have to inflate the chamber by hand using the pump.

As you drift along you can set out a sea anchor, which is part of your life raft, and it is often packed in a small pocket at some point on the outside of your raft. It looks very much like a miniature parachute and its job is to keep your raft from drifting too fast, thus keeping you near the mishap location. Search aircraft will first key in on the spot the boat sank, the aircraft went down or your last known location, and then gradually they will begin to work out from that spot looking for you. So, set the sea anchor properly and that means when you are at the crest of a wave (the top), the sea anchor should be in the trough of the wave (very bottom). This anchor will retard your drift and keep you in the general area for a while longer than if it was not used at all.

There may come a time when you might be near land, but will you be able to tell when it happens? Use the following as a guide:

- Clouds that seem to be alone or hanging over something (land?)

- You hear the sounds of birds, animals, boats, vehicles, or of people (then blow your whistle or pop a flare from the survival kit).

- Suddenly you notice more flying insects, birds other than gulls, and an increase in the amount of seaweed floating around you.

- You smell trees, jungle rot, smoke or other smells associated with people.

- You see more driftwood or debris in the water, along with more vegetation.

- As you float, keep your mental and physical health in mind at all times. You can expect to feel isolated and perhaps deeply depressed at times, but remember all efforts will be made to find you. People will be searching and looking, so stay alive until you are found. Some physical health concerns that may come up are:

- Dehydration, which you'll notice by dark urine, so drink more water if you can.

- Sunburn or hypothermia; keep all clothing on and the sleeves down on your shirt and your pant legs down as well. For sunburn protection use the sun screen in the survival kit and for hypothermia you'll need to try to stay dry and increase your body heat. A fire will be out of question, so huddle with other survivors and eat hard candies for the energy.

- Immersion foot is caused by your feet being constantly wet. Try to keep your feet as dry as you can and a couple of times a day place your feet on an air chamber to dry out by the sun.

- Salt water boils are normal and painful, but do not pick or squeeze them because it will usually result in an agonizing infection. Use the first aid cream in the survival kit.

- Sea sickness, *keep drinking water*. There is not much you can do about this illness, except hang tough and avoid dehydration due to vomiting up your fluids.

- Sun blindness, keep your eyes covered with sunglasses or smear some dark substance (if you can find something) under your eyes to reduce glare. You can also make a pair of goggles from cloth, wood, or plastic. This injury is very painful and can cause severe headaches and eye pain.

If you suspect you are near land (noises or you see people) and people you can blow a whistle, pop a flare (avoid burning the raft with hot cinders falling from the flare) or wave a piece of material. Keep a lookout on duty twenty-four hours a day and their job is to keep the raft pumped up with air, bail out water, keep an eye out for leaks, as well as watch for rescue aircraft or land.

If a rescue aircraft is near, use a signal mirror to flash into the cockpit of the aircraft, but then move the flash back to the tail of the aircraft, so you do not blind the pilot. If it is overcast and no sun, use a flare from the survival kit or an emergency radio (most kits will have one or two radios with spare batteries) to get the aircraft's attention. If an aircraft sees you it will rock its wings up and down to indicate you have been sighted, or communicate with you over the radio. Due to its limitations, (fuel or rescue capability) the aircraft might fly away, but don't worry because your position will be sent and another aircraft will soon come for you. A lot of times a large aircraft will fly low over you, rock its wings to communicate your sighting, and then fly away. You can expect a quick rescue following a wing rocking from a search aircraft.

Survival on a large body of water is not all that much different than survival on land, in the jungle or the arctic, believe it or not. The key considerations remain the same; water, shelter, warmth, food, first aid, signals, and rescue. Remember that all life rafts and boats should have a survival kit, first aid kit, and signaling devices. The key difference with open water survival is the lack of a fire, water procurement, and the simple fact you are stuck in the raft/boat until you make land or are rescued.

Take care, stay safe, and remember that survival is never easy, but it can be done with the proper gear and the right attitude—in any environment.

Hooked on Fishing

It has been my observation that there are only three kinds of fishermen in the world, those who have never had a fishhook injury, those that have, and those that don't answer honestly. I have also discovered that those who have never been hurt by a hook will eventually experience the injury, if they fish long enough. I have seen hooks in legs, arms, fingers, heads, and even rear-ends. While some of these injuries may sound funny, they are painful to the victim. For the average fisherman, the most common area to get a hook is in a finger (or hand) followed by the head. With fly fishermen the reverse is true, but not hard to believe the way the line and hook are often seen flying around.

While all hook injuries cannot be avoided, I have found most were experienced by the novice fisherman or children. The beginner is often attempting new casting methods or learning to use their new equipment. As a result, a poor cast or a split-second loss of concentration can often cause a hook to go where it is not wanted. Additionally, most beginners aren't as cautious as old timers when it comes to just picking up a hook from the tackle box. Children, on the other hand, are often uncoordinated in casting and at times will be joking around (both of which can result in hook injuries). This is not to say that experienced fishermen don't receive hook injuries, because they do.

If you have a fish hook injury, do you know how to administer first aid, remove the fishhook, or when to seek medical treatment? The situation can be appear to much more complex when first viewed because of the type and size of hook (single hook, treble hook, barbed hook, etc.) that may be involved. If the hook is embedded in or near an eye or if the injury is to the face, do not attempt to remove the hook and immediately seek medical attention. A fishhook in the eye is a very dangerous situation and most medical authorities will recommend you shield the hook from further movement. Additionally, avoid moving the eye as much as possible so additional injury does not occur. A fishhook in the eyes is considered a serious medical emergency!

There are many different procedures used to remove fishhooks, but I have decided to discuss the top three used by most medical professionals and survival instructors. I will explain the push through and cut off method, the string yank or pull method, and the multi-barbed hook removal method. Not all of your fishhook injuries will require any of these techniques and in some cases the hook can simply be backed out of the injury with little pain or effort. It depends on how deeply the hook is impaled in the skin.

While somewhat painful for the victim, these hook removal procedures do work very well in most cases. Nonetheless, to give you an idea of the pain level usually experienced by the victim, in emergency rooms a local anesthetic is usually administered. Then again, some of my "hooked" friends said the fishhook removal process was almost painless. In a survival situation you may not have a choice but to remove the hook without the aid of an anesthetic. Regardless of the method you plan to use to remove the fishhook, your first task is to clean the wound area and your hands well with soap and water. Remember to check to see if the hook is near an artery, joint, tendon, or to the head. All head injuries should be seen by a doctor. One aspect of hook removal often forgotten is to reassure your patient. While most hook injuries are very minor, the victim is often scared of the removal process (this is especially true of children). Explain the removal procedure to the person and tell them why you are using it. Once the person has a basic understanding of what is going on they should calm down for you. Wait until the injured person is ready (with some adults and children this may never happen) before you start the removal procedure.

When using the push through and cut method, there are some things you need to consider. This procedure will cause additional tissue damage when the hook is pushed through and the pain level is higher for the victim. Additionally, there is the increased risk of contaminating newly damaged tissue from the hook itself, increasing the risk of infection. Of course, one big advantage is this procedure is almost always successful regardless of the location of the injury or the size of the hook.

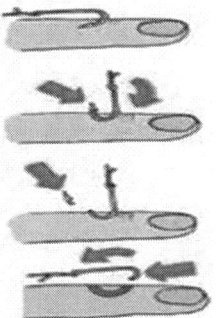

Push the hook forward and force the barb through the skin until it is clearly showing on the outside. You may have to use pliers or needle nose pliers to push the shank forward.

Simple Survival

- Cut the barb off, using a pair of wire cutters. Most of us carry a pair in our tackle boxes (or use any tool you have on hand capable of doing the job).

- Then, push the shank of the hook back through the original hole in the tissue.

- Clean the injury well with soap and water and apply an antibiotic ointment if you have it available.

I suggest a simple band-aid be applied to protect the wound from foreign matter and the injury be kept dry and clean.

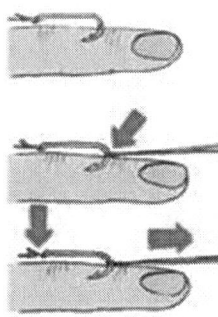

When using the string yank or pull method I believe you will find it is much less painful for the injured party. Also, this technique keeps the wound size down and decreases the risk for additional infection when compared to push through and cut method. It is a good procedure to use when you may not have a pair of wire cutters along as well. Once again, as in all cases where you are removing a hook, clean the wound and your hands well with soap and water prior to starting.

Tie a long length of fishing line or strong string to the bend in the hook. At the other end of the line, I usually tie it to a small piece of green wood or a pocket knife handle (closed) to give me additional leverage (handle) when I pull the line.

- Push the hook shank down parallel to the injured tissue to disengage the barb on the hook (on the inside).

- While the hook shank is down, give the line a hard and sharp jerk in the direction the hook entered the tissue. The hook will usually come right out of the entry hole with very little pain.

- Clean the injury well with soap and water and apply an antibiotic ointment if you have it available, just like the push through method.

- Use a band-aid to protect the wound from foreign matter and remember the injury should be kept dry and clean.

The last method of removing hooks I want to explain is multi-barb hook removal. This type of hook has barbs on the shank that may prevent the use of the string yank or pull method. Additionally, some of these barbed hooks can be large and they cannot normally be backed out the entry point very easily. This method has the same negative aspects as the push through and cut off method (tissue damage, painful, contaminates additional tissue and raises the risk of infection).

- Push the hook forward using pliers or needle nose pliers and force the barb through the skin until it is clearly showing on the outside.

- Cut the eye of the hook off, using a pair of wire cutters. Most of us carry these in our tackle boxes (or as I said above, use any tool you have on hand capable of doing the job).

- Then, push the shank of the hook forward and through the new hole in the tissue that was formed when you pushed the barb out of the skin.

- Once again, clean the injury well with soap and water and apply an antibiotic ointment if you have it available.

- A band-aid should be applied to protect the wound from foreign matter and the injury should be kept dry and clean.

Regardless of the technique you decide to use to remove the fishhook, it is very important to clean the area both before and after you remove the hook. While infection is a rare occurrence for healthy individuals who sustain hook injuries they do happen (but most often from fresh water fishing hook mishaps). Also, if you have not had a tetanus booster shot within the last five years you should seriously consider discussing your injury with a medical professional or your doctor. At any time after removing the hook the injury develops redness, swelling, discharges pus, or increased pain, consult a doctor immediately because you may have an infection.

Those of us who fish with our friends and family should know how to remove a fishhook, administer basic first aid, and when to seek medical attention. We should all remember that hooks in the head require medical attention and if the injury is to an eye to use extra caution. We should also avoid trying to removing hooks from injuries near joints, bones, tendons, ligaments, or arteries.

The odds are, some of you reading this article will have to remove a fishhook sooner or later. Perhaps it will be a simple removal or it may be a more difficult process, but at least now you have the knowledge to do it successfully. Take care, stay safe, and don't get "hooked on fishing."

About the Author

Gary L. Benton has previously authored over fifty books, fiction, non-fiction and Southern Humor. Such notable authors as, Matt Braun, Stephen Lodge, Don Bendell, actor James Drury (*The Virginian*), and many others have endorsed his historical fiction work. His western writing is published under the pen name, "W.R. Benton." His survival book, "*Simple Survival, a Family Outdoors Guide*," is a Silver Award Winner from the Military Writers Society of American. Additionally, this book was recently added to the prestigious Estes Park Library in Colorado.

His hobbies include hunting, camping, fishing, hiking, cartooning, web design, and reading. Mister Benton has an Associate's Degree in Search and Rescue, Survival Operations, a Bachelors Degree in Occupational Safety and Health, and a Masters Degree in Psychology completed except for his thesis. Sergeant Benton retired from the military in 1997 with over twenty-six years of active duty.
Mister Benton and his wife, Melanie, live in Jackson, Mississippi.

Visit Gary online at http://www.wrbenton.net
or
http://www.simplesurvival.net

Other Books by Gary 'W.R.' Benton

My Child is Missing: Based on the True Story of Jared Ropelato
Alive and Alone (a Young Adult Survival novel)
The Fall of America series

Non-Fiction
Simple Survival, a Family Outdoors Guide
Impending Disasters

To explore more than 50 other books, ebooks and audio books by W.R. Benton, visit:

http://www.amazon.com/author/wrbenton/

Alive and Alone
Available in paperback & for the Kindle at Amazon.com

A Story of Survival and faith...

On a trip to the Lake Clark area of the Alaskan bush, a sudden arctic weather system forces down the small plane of Dr. Jim Wade, and his son David. Both have survived the crash, but not unscathed. Food, fire and shelter are all a priority. Following the death of his father, now it is up to David to figure out what to do next, and how to survive, on a remote Alaskan mountain - in winter!

This is a fictional story of survival, resilience and of the spirit to live. It is both authentic and accurate, having been written by a former Air Force life support survival instructor.

Young adult: For ages 12 and up

SIMPLE SURVIVAL

Available in paperback & for the Kindle at Amazon.com, Nook, Kobo and iBooks versions.

Read Gary's guide and you'll be ready for nearly anything...

"Retired USAF Senior Master Sergeant and survivor expert Gary Benton has written the best outdoor guide for families - bar none, that I have read! "Simple Survival - A Family Outdoors Guide" is more than a book - it is an outdoor resource bible that every family should have a copy of. This is one of those books that you should have in your camping bag along with the tent and other equipment.

There is one chapter that deals with the greatest fears that all parents have - having your child get lost in the woods. This is a must read for parents. This information needs to be shared with all their children so they know what to do in the event of getting lost or separated from their parents or the campsite. This is the kind of information that you hope you never need to put into use.

— Bill McDonald - MWSA President

IMPENDING DISASTERS

Available for the Kindle at Amazon.com, Nook, Kobo and iBooks versions.

"**How you and your family can survive America's deadly changing weather**"

Detailed information and advice for most major disasters; how to stay safe if you decide to evacuate or stay. This book helps you to evaluate and prepare, mental and equipment-wise for nearly any type of emergency. It has a section on prolonged survival, which will assist keeping you alive after the natural disaster has done its damage. Many people die following natural disasters, from one mishap or another, but you can learn to survive.

A top-notch guide with info that could save you and your families lives.

Audiobooks by W.R. Benton
Available now at Audible.com and iTunes

Made in United States
Orlando, FL
24 June 2024